THE BOOK IN THE JEWISH WORLD
1700–1900

THE LITTMAN LIBRARY OF JEWISH CIVILIZATION

Dedicated to the memory of
LOUIS THOMAS SIDNEY LITTMAN
who founded the Littman Library for the love of God
and as an act of charity in memory of his father
JOSEPH AARON LITTMAN
and to the memory of
ROBERT JOSEPH LITTMAN
who continued what his father Louis had begun

יהא זכרם ברוך

'*Get wisdom, get understanding:*
Forsake her not and she shall preserve thee'

PROV. 4:5

The Littman Library of Jewish Civilization is a registered UK charity
Registered charity no. 1000784

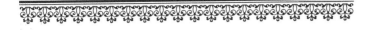

THE
BOOK IN THE
JEWISH WORLD
1700–1900

ZEEV GRIES

London
The Littman Library of Jewish Civilization
in association with Liverpool University Press

The Littman Library of Jewish Civilization
Registered office: 4th floor, 7–10 Chandos Street, London WIG 9DQ

in association with Liverpool University Press
4 Cambridge Street, Liverpool L69 7ZU, UK
www.liverpooluniversitypress.co.uk/littman

Managing Editor: Connie Webber

Distributed in North America by
Oxford University Press Inc., 198 Madison Avenue,
New York, NY 10016, USA

First published in Hebrew © Hakibbutz-Hameuchad 2002
English translation © The Littman Library of Jewish Civilization 2007
First published in paperback 2010

Catalogue records for this book are available from the
British Library and the Library of Congress

ISBN 978–1–906764–05–0

Publishing Co-ordinator: Janet Moth
Copy-editing: Anthony Goldberg, Janet Moth, Connie Webber
Proof-reading: Kate Clements
Indexing: Sarah Ereira and Zeev Gries
Designed and typeset by Pete Russell, Faringdon, Oxon.

Printed and bound in Great Britain by
CPI Group (UK) Ltd., Croydon, CR0 4YY

For the elevation of the soul of

MEIR AYALI

who initiated and accompanied
the writing of this book, and who strove to be a man
where none was to be found

This publication has been supported by a donation
in memory of

SIMON WILSACK

(1911–2004)

whose shop at 41b Manor Park Crescent, Edgware, opened in 1954,
pioneered the sale of Jewish books in that part of London

and in memory of

ESTHER WILSACK

(1913–1967)

who dedicated her life to teaching children
to read and enjoy Jewish books

✸

A gesture of respect and affection
from their daughter Connie
whom they inspired to publish Jewish books

Preface to the English Edition

OVER THE PAST THIRTY OR SO YEARS I have written extensively on various aspects of the history of books in the Jewish world but have long felt the need for a more comprehensive account of that history. In 2002 I published a slim volume on the subject in Hebrew, entitled *The Book as an Agent of Culture, 1700–1900*, in an attempt to provide an introduction to the subject for the general reader. It incorporated revised versions of material previously published in a number of articles as well as new material deriving from my continuing research. The volume was published by Hakibbutz Hameuchad in its Heillal Ben-Hayyim Judaica Library at the suggestion of the founding editor of that series, Meir Ayali, who had long encouraged me in my research and writing. The present volume draws heavily on that work but is not a direct translation, though I must straight away thank Jeffrey Green of Jerusalem for diligently translating the Hebrew text as the basis for this present book.

The questions I raised in the Hebrew edition concerning the role of books in shaping and defining Jewish national identity have still not been conclusively answered; new questions have arisen in my mind, and new thoughts have taken shape. I have incorporated much of this new material in this volume, but would like to draw attention here to a matter I consider of particular relevance.

In the second, revised edition of his book *Imagined Communities*, Benedict Anderson noted the development of printing, especially in vernacular languages, as the key stimulus for the creation of a sense of national identities among European peoples.[1] But the Jewish case is rather unusual; with the Jewish diaspora extending over all continents, there were several vernacular Jewish languages—for example, Judeo-German (Yiddish), Judeo-Spanish (Ladino), and Judeo-Arabic. The linguistic factor uniting the Jewish people was not their vernacular language, as Anderson would have it, but rather their ancient sacred language, Hebrew, which lay at the heart of Jewish religious life

---

[1] Anderson, *Imagined Communities*, ch. 3.

and education wherever Jews lived and throughout the centuries, till today. Thus, a discussion of the history of Hebrew books forms the core of my work here.

While the printing of Hebrew books was obviously a major factor in cultural transmission, the library of printed books grew relatively slowly in the early centuries of printing. Although the first Hebrew book was printed in 1475, by the end of the sixteenth century the number of editions printed did not exceed 2,600, and a significant proportion of these were in fact multiple editions of important texts rather than new works. By the end of the seventeenth century this number had increased by around 1,000, giving a total of some 3,600 editions; by the end of the eighteenth century the total was closer to 9,000. During all this time, printing in vernacular languages lagged far behind. The publication of books in Yiddish, the major Jewish vernacular language of the period, began only in the late sixteenth century, around a hundred years after the beginning of printing in Hebrew, and only really took off in the eighteenth century.

A further factor of relevance to the role of the Hebrew book in the Jewish world is that despite the advent of print, the most important factor in maintaining Jewish national identity continued to be Jewish religious ritual and the annual and daily cycle of Jewish customs—rituals and customs that were completely different from those of the non-Jews living on the same lands, and which until the twentieth century were everywhere performed exclusively in Hebrew. Prior to modern times, Jewish life meant Jewish religious life; the chief factor in transmitting that life was the mimetic tendency that caused children to imitate their parents and adopt their way of life. This mimetic tendency was far more potent that the written word, whether in Hebrew, Yiddish, or other Jewish vernaculars,[2] at least until the period of the Enlightenment and the concomitant changes in Jewish civil rights that started to take root from the end of the eighteenth century. But the more that Jews adopted the language and manners of the peoples among whom they lived (which was particularly true in this period in the German-speaking lands), the less they were exposed to the traditional Jewish way of life; in other words, as exposure to the Enlightenment increased, the power of mimesis served to reinforce the spread of gentile culture rather than of Jewish culture.

---

[2] See Soloveitchik, 'Rupture and Reconstruction', 66–74.

In other words, I strongly believe that Anderson's model is inapplicable to the Jewish case because Jewish identity was forged long before the development of printing in the High Middle Ages. Because the ancient Jewish sages had drawn up a body of Jewish law, known as *halakhah*, which was transmitted to successive generations, and established communal institutions that were set up in each and every Jewish community, Jews shared a vigorous sense of a living community long before the other peoples living in Europe did, and did not need an imagined one. Spread over continents and separated by vast distances, Jewish communities succeeded in maintaining physical and intellectual contact both before and after the advent of printing, but the magic of the printed word seems to have rendered invisible to academic scholars a series of factors that were far more important in forging a sense of Jewish peoplehood. These included the old oral traditions that were preached in public and supported the above-mentioned mimetic tendency; the Jewish involvement in international Jewish trade, which facilitated the communication of ideas as people and written traditions were transported along with other merchandise between Jewish communities in different locations; and the international character of the world of Torah, with students and teachers wandering far from their homes to study Torah and carrying books and manuscripts from one end of the Jewish world to the other as they did so, while also bringing living traditions and customs from one community to the other. These agents of communication between the Jewish communities all continued to be of relevance even with the development of printing.

But our concern here is with the role of books. The first Hebrew books to be printed were those that had been in demand during the age when books were handwritten, whether for liturgical use, education, or moral instruction. Somewhat later, around the mid-sixteenth century, works of Jewish mysticism begin to appear, though until the eighteenth century their study was restricted to certain close circles of Jewish mystics. The present book is dedicated to the age of great changes in the function and place of print in the Jewish world: the eighteenth and nineteenth centuries.

It is a great honour for me to publish the English version with the Littman Library of Jewish Civilization, which has itself done so much to promote the book as an agent of culture in the Jewish world. A number of individuals were responsible for facilitating this, and it is my pleasant duty to thank them all.

First, however, I must acknowledge the tremendous debt I owe to those involved in the publication of the original Hebrew edition, and particularly, as I have said, to Meir Ayali. Meir was my intellectual patron over a long period, and he constantly encouraged me to produce the original Hebrew book from which this volume derives. For years I would send him everything that I produced, whether or not it was intended for publication, to solicit his opinion and comments. Long telephone calls ensued, following which I would try to apply Meir's advice so as to present my scholarship and ideas as gracefully as I could. Meir's spirit therefore permeates this entire work, both in what is written and what is between the lines. My debt to him is incalculable. He was not only an unstinting source of wide-ranging intellectual and cultural support but was also a wonderful role-model in the restraint and self-control that a scholar needs. I was deeply sorry that he did not live to celebrate the finished product with me, neither the original Hebrew edition nor this English version. At the same time, however, I must also mention the assistance I received from his colleagues Avraham Shapira and Yehuda Friedlander, both of whom also helped to shape the present work and to soothe the birth-pangs I experienced in producing it.

The idea of publishing an English version originated with Dr Ada Rapoport-Albert of University College London, an old friend who has long been interested in my research, and it was she who proposed it to Connie Webber, the managing editor of the Littman Library. Many others have since worked on the project, but without the support and close supervision of these two initial sponsors, and the generosity of the Littman Library itself in translating the original text, this publication would not have been possible. It has been a complicated project because of the need to make the English version book more accessible to a broader readership less familiar with the world of Jewish books than the Hebrew version was. Anthony Goldberg in Jerusalem, and later Janet Moth and Connie Webber in Oxford, all played their part in doing this, teaching me in the process that it was possible for my Hebrew to make sense even in its transformation into English. I should also like to thank Ludo Craddock, Littman's chief executive officer, for efficiently facilitating every aspect of the process.

The greater part of my work on the initial revision of the English text took place while I was a visiting scholar at the Center for Jewish Studies at Harvard University during the spring of 2003. The freedom to work in a stimulating academic atmosphere was made possible by the generosity of the Chair of the

Center, Jay M. Harris, and its administrator, Mrs Rachel Rockenmacher. However my prime academic home since 1995 has been at Ben-Gurion University of the Negev; had I not found that home, the book's gestation period would, without doubt, have been far longer. I must therefore thank Ya'akov Gerald Blidstein and Haim Howard Kreisel, Chairs of the Goldstein-Goren Department of Jewish Thought at Ben-Gurion University of the Negev, for the warm and supportive academic environment they have created.

Z.G.

Goldstein-Goren Department of Jewish Thought
Ben-Gurion University of the Negev, 2006

Contents

List of Illustrations

Figures 1–6 are from A. M. Haberman, *Title Pages of Hebrew Books*
[Sha'arei sefarim ivriyim] (Safed, 1969), published by the Museum of Printing (an
institution which has since closed). Figures 7–9 are from
Isaac Yudlov, *Printers' Marks* [Diglei madpisim] (Jerusalem, 2002),
and are reproduced with permission.

Note on Bibliographical
Conventions and Transliteration

THE bibliographical conventions and transliteration in this book reflect consideration of the type of book it is, in terms of its content, purpose, and readership.

On the assumption that the majority of people reading this book are not fluent in Hebrew, the titles of all works mentioned are given in English translation. Primary works are cited by their Hebrew or Yiddish titles, with the translation in parentheses at first mention. The titles of scholarly works are cited in English, followed by '(Heb.)' to indicate that this title is a translation, but that the original Hebrew title is to be found in transliteration in the bibliography.

The transliteration system adopted likewise reflects a broad approach, rather than the narrower approaches found in the *Encyclopaedia Judaica* or other systems developed for text-based or linguistic studies. The aim has been to reflect the pronunciation prescribed for modern Hebrew, rather than the spelling or Hebrew word structure, and to do so using conventions that are generally familiar to the English-speaking reader.

In accordance with this approach, no attempt is made to indicate the distinctions between *alef* and *ayin*, *tet* and *taf*, *kaf* and *kuf*, *sin* and *samekh*, since these are not relevant to pronunciation; likewise, the *dagesh* is not indicated except where it affects pronunciation. Following the principle of using conventions familiar to the majority of readers, however, transcriptions that are well established have been retained even when they are not fully consistent with the transliteration system adopted. On similar grounds, the *tsadi* is rendered by 'tz' in such familiar words as barmitzvah, matzah, and so on. Likewise, the distinction between *ḥet* and *khaf* has been retained, using *ḥ* for the former and *kh* for the latter; the associated forms are generally familiar to readers, even if the distinction is not actually borne out in pronunciation, and for the same reason the final *heh* is indicated too. As in Hebrew, no capital letters are used, except that an initial capital has been retained in transliterating titles of published works (for example, *Shulḥan arukh*).

Since no distinction is made between *alef* and *ayin*, they are indicated by an apostrophe only in intervocalic positions where a failure to do so could lead an English-speaking reader to pronounce the vowel-cluster as a diphthong—as, for example, in *ha'ir*—or otherwise mispronounce the word.

The *sheva na* is indicated by an *e*—*perikat ol*, *reshut*—except, again, when established convention dictates otherwise

The *yod* is represented by *i* when it occurs as a vowel (*bereshit*), by *y* when it occurs as a consonant (*yesodot*), and by *yi* when it occurs as both (*yisra'el*).

Names have generally been left in their familiar forms, even when this is inconsistent with the overall system.

Thanks are due to Jonathan Webber of Birmingham University for his help in elucidating the principles to be adopted.

Introduction

THE BURGEONING INTEREST in cultural history, in Europe and elsewhere, in the last part of the twentieth century has prompted an increasing number of scholars to turn their attention from detailed discussions of beliefs and opinions to consider the history of the manuscripts and books that shaped ideas in times gone by and to examine their dissemination and readership. Their research has covered an impressive array of topics, from the makers of books—the typesetters, proof-readers, printers, and type-casters, and those who illustrated them with woodcuts, copper prints, and lithographs—to those involved in their publication and circulation: those who financed the printing, the booksellers and pedlars who distributed them, and the libraries that made them available to a broader public. Related studies have examined the development of printing techniques and materials as a reflection of shifting cultural patterns.

Scholars of Jewish history and culture have also begun in recent years to engage in this type of research (which in the past was regarded as suitable only for librarians and bibliographers), but it is true to say that the study of the book in the Jewish world is still in its infancy, and much work remains to be done. To this day there is still no comprehensive list of all of the cities in which Hebrew books were printed, nor do we know the names of the printers, editors, and others who worked on the books. Not even the National and University Library in Jerusalem has compiled such a list, even though more than half a century has passed since the Hebrew Bibliography Project was initiated in 1950 to register all the Hebrew books in its collection (which is the largest in the world). This situation is due to the fact that from the beginnings of the Wissenschaft des Judentums movement in the 1810s and 1820s until quite recently, the history of the transition from manuscript to print was considered a rather tedious field of Jewish history, best left to bibliographers; proper historians dealt with the larger issues of Jewish history that were perceived as more appropriate to the modern era. The history of the book in the Jewish world was not perceived as a pressing issue. Moritz Steinschneider (1816–1907), the Moravian-born father of modern Jewish bibliography, left many dossiers filled with fragments of information and hints for succeeding generations, in addition to a large number of publications. This impressive legacy did not appeal to a new generation, however. Much of Steinschneider's work (for example, his catalogue of the Bodleian collection in Oxford), was written in the spirit of his time, and in what had been the language of culture for generations—Latin. Intimidated by such factors, younger scholars fled from the subject and devoted themselves instead to the history of belief and opinion, without which the study of Jewish history and culture would perhaps have a body, but no soul.[1]

The contribution of the Ukrainian-born literary historian Israel Zinberg (1873–1939) to this field is worthy of note: there is still no rival to his monumental *History of Jewish Literature*. In the course of his peregrinations among authors and books he collected a great deal of information on obscure agents of culture—the typesetters, printers, and others who produced the books, and particularly the *magihim*, the editor-proofreaders who prepared them for the press.[2] Zinberg's writings are a source of inspiration that has not faded with the years. One must also mention the German-born scholar Abraham Berliner (1833–1915), who also applied himself to the study of books and printing in the Jewish world,[3] though opinions about him are more divided. In my view he was not as talented as Zinberg, but I would not go so far in my criticism as Eugen Teubler, who once told Ben-Zion Dinur, when the latter was a young and enthusiastic student in Germany, that all of Berliner's writing were *Kugelgeschichte*.[4]

We are also fortunate that among Israel's librarians—Abraham Ya'ari, Abraham Meir Haberman, and others—there have been many bibliophiles who collected information on the makers of books. Though they did not necessarily do so from an understanding that the history of books and their makers was a significant chapter in the cultural and social history of the

[1] In fact Steinschneider dreamed of writing a comprehensive history of Jewish literature which would also include its cultural aspects, and he left several indications of this aspiration in print. An extensive discussion of this is to be found in Marx, 'Moritz Steinschneider', 112–84.

[2] See Zinberg, *A History of Jewish Literature*, iv, pt. 5, pp. 50–2, and Haberman, *History of Jewish Literature* (Heb.), ii. 426.   [3] See Berliner, *Selected Writings* (Heb.), iii–43.

[4] Lit. 'pudding stories' (i.e. twaddle). See Dinur, *Historical Writings* (Heb.), iv. 265–6.

Jewish nation, we are nevertheless indebted to them for their efforts in this direction.

Despite the varied input of all these scholars and men of books over the years, we still lack a systematic analysis of the great contribution to, and transformation of, the Jewish world which resulted from the transition from manuscript to print. My purpose here is to point the way at the treasures that such a study could reveal and encourage others to take up the challenge of developing this field.

Within the limited scope of this introduction I cannot present a detailed discussion of either the huge impact printing had on the communication of ideas or its far-reaching consequences for those strata of society first exposed to the printed word.[5] It is self-evident that expansion of the circle of readers, including for the first time women as well as men in significant numbers, created a new class of nascent intellectuals—a thin segment of the population that now began to possess an awareness of the possibility of new ideas and knowledge. This led in turn to social and cultural advancement and to an increase in the intellectual power of the community to which the new readers belonged—a power that also engendered many changes in practical aspects of daily life. Among the practical consequences of this growing sense of self-worth among the newly literate was an increasing demand for a new and fairer distribution of wealth, but that is not the topic with which we will be concerned here. I mention it merely as an illustration of why the history of the book is so important.

Those who opposed the growth in printing and advocated the continued copying of manuscripts by hand fought a rearguard battle. They did not see books in the same way as other goods that should be freely available to all, but rather as precious items whose availability should be limited to those few who knew how to use them correctly. They therefore favoured the continued reliance on a cadre of expert scribes, masters of calligraphy, such as were found in religious circles and among the learned professions. If scribes might

---

[5] As far as I know, the first person who tried to describe, in vivid colours, the communications revolution brought to the world by printing was not a historian but a professor of English, Marshall McLuhan, in *The Gutenberg Galaxy*. See criticism of this book in Eisenstein, *The Printing Press as an Agent of Change*, pp. x–xi, xviii, 16–17, and also the critique in Yates, 'Print Culture', 185–92. On Hebrew manuscripts and printing, see the important article by Beit-Arié, 'The Relationship Between Early Hebrew Printing and Handwritten Books', 1–26, and the additional bibliography there.

stumble and err here and there while copying, the very need for each scribe to examine every single word of his predecessors would lead him to discover errors and to correct them. Printing, however, would perpetuate the errors of typesetters and proof-readers and circulate them through hundreds of copies. In this way, error would be permanently fixed in the collective consciousness of the readership.[6]

The first known printed Hebrew book was actually published in Reggio Calabria, Italy, in 1475 (this was Rashi's commentary on the Torah), but there were no Hebrew printing presses in a Muslim country until 1504, when Jewish exiles from Spain and Portugal came to Constantinople. This was in fact the first printing house of any kind in the Ottoman empire:[7] the first Turkish

[6] The abbot of a German monastery, Johannes Trithemius, wrote a fervent defence of scribes and manuscripts in which the arguments presented above may be found: see the bilingual Latin–English edition of *In Praise of Scribes / De Laude Scriptorum*. On this book and its sources see Eisenstein, *The Printing Press as an Agent of Change*, 14–15. On the importance of the history of the work of copying classical manuscripts, see Reynolds and Wilson, *Scribes and Scholars*. In Jewish studies there is no worthy successor to the pioneering work of the father of modern Hebrew bibliography, Moritz Steinschneider; see his *Lectures on Hebrew Manuscripts* (Heb.).

Riegler's doctoral dissertation 'The Colophon of Medieval Hebrew Manuscripts as a Historical Source' (Heb.) analyses the information to be gleaned from colophons. Such manuscripts are known to be a valuable source of information about the world of the Jewish book, and it is unfortunate that this valuable study has never been published.

The colophon was replaced by the title page after the introduction of printing. To this day there is no comprehensive study of the title pages of Jewish books in general or of Hebrew books in particular. On errors in copying manuscripts and setting type, see Rabinovits, 'The Role of Initials in the Hebrew Language' (Heb.), 90–4, and Haberman, 'Unintentional and Intentional Typographical Errors' (Heb.). Haberman showed that even a bibliographer as meticulous as Steinschneider could make an error in transcribing from the index cards he used to prepare his great book on the collection of the Bodleian Library, and that he perpetuated that error in print. Other scholars then copied it from him and thus the error was preserved for generations. See Haberman, 'An Error that Led to Errors' (Heb.), 528; see also Katz, 'The Logic of Typographical Errors' (Heb.), 20–1. Haym Soloveitchik's *Responsa as a Historical Source* (Heb.) offers edifying examples of the need to examine the traditions of manuscripts and printed editions of rabbinic responsa which have been corrupted, and how it is possible to use them as a historical source. Special attention should also be given to the satire by Ephraim Kishon on the subject of typographical errors in newspapers, 'The Memory of a Righteous Man is a Blessing' (Heb.), 134–8. See also S. Y. Agnon's poem on the proof-reader, 'The Praise of Noah', reproduced by Haberman in *Hed hadefus*, 12 (Tevet 1959), 33.

[7] See Ya'ari, *Hebrew Printing in Constantinople* (Heb.), 11–12; Hacker, 'Intellectual Activity Among the Jews of the Ottoman Empire' (Heb.), 576–80.

printing house to print books in Arabic was established only in 1728, because of the restrictions in Islam with regard to the printing of religious texts. As a result of this, the first books to be printed in Arabic were printed in Italy rather than in a Muslim country.[8] The Islamic countries paid a heavy price for rejecting printing as a cultural tool for three hundred years after its introduction in Germany. In point of fact, the entire world is still suffering, because for all those years millions of people failed to benefit from the development, and the spread of knowledge, characteristic of those countries where printing took root.

It was not only Muslims who took this view. The desire to limit knowledge to initiates—of necessity a select few—likewise impelled the Lurianic kabbalists of the sixteenth and seventeenth century, for example, to copy their esoteric texts and kabbalistic doctrines by hand rather than having them printed. Then, with the rise of Shabateanism, the expectation of redemption that filtered into Lurianic kabbalah from the 1670s led to a popular circulation of kabbalistic rituals (rather than doctrines) in pocket-book form.[9] It was not, however, in general, the diffusion of Lurianic teachings that attracted the masses to Shabateanism. They were drawn to that messianic movement mainly because of the cataclysmic events of the late sixteenth and early seventeenth centuries; these were consciousness-changing developments, and they also had an impact on the printing and circulation of popular books in Hebrew and in Yiddish.[10]

Another important topic that deserves more serious attention, despite pioneering work by Raphael Nathan Neta Rabinovits, Abraham Berliner, and Isaac Zeev Kahana,[11] is the reaction of the halakhic authorities to the phenomenon of printing and the connection between printing, printers, and the study and diffusion of halakhah. Since Judaism, like Islam, is a religion of law

---

[8] On the late development of printing among Muslims, see Pedersen, *The Arabic Book*, 131–42. Pedersen attributes this delay to the fact that most Arabic literature had been written in manuscript before the advent of printing and claims that, by the time printing developed, Islam had already passed its peak so there was no one to encourage its use. It is difficult to accept this argument, for printing developed and expanded until it reached its apogee in the eighteenth century, while the Ottoman empire was still gaining strength.

[9] For more extensive discussion, see my *Literature of Customs* (Heb.), pp. xv–xvii, 42–5, 56–7, 81–6, 91, and the additional bibliography on these pages. [10] See ibid. 41–102.

[11] See Rabinovits, *On the Printing of the Talmud* (Heb.); Berliner, *Selected Writings* (Heb.), 118–26; Kahana, 'Printing in the Halakhah' (Heb.), 49–61, 139–59.

and therefore permeates every aspect of life, we must applaud our teachers of religious law who permitted the widespread use of printing, leaving to traditional scribes only the copying of Torah scrolls on parchment for liturgical use, and the writing of parchments for *tefilin* and *mezuzot*. Much work still remains to be done in this field, however; topics requiring detailed analysis include the types of books and literature that attracted readers, the history of their public reception, and the lessons that can be learned from these matters regarding the intellectual and social history of the Jewish people.[12]

Let us return to the subject with which I began: the revolution in the communication among Jews that occurred as a direct result of the spread of printing. Different genres of literature in Hebrew and in Yiddish were increasingly popularized as publishers sought to expand the demand for books, and as learned men came to regard publication as an opportunity to communicate their ideas more widely. Some scholars credit the Protestant Reformation with the huge change in the status of those sectors of the Christian population whose intellectual demands and expectations had previously been ignored;[13] among the Jews, this development is closely linked to the spread of printing, and to the significance of the book becoming a commodity widely available and not restricted to a scholarly elite.[14]

It may be argued that a small group of producers and consumers of books had come into existence as early as the sixteenth century. People involved in the world of books often moved from place to place, because of the growing demand for their products and their skills; new ideas and concepts travelled with them, serving to reinforce and extend a nascent intellectual network. The growing demand for books gave rise to a circle of itinerant booksellers, some

[12] Scholars of Jewish literature and history have not yet written a comprehensive study of the various genres of literature—apart from halakhic literature—that led to the expansion of the circle of readers. Thus the history of the rise of these genres, from homiletics to hagiography, seeks an author, someone who will trace the transition from manuscript to print, including all the agents who served as intermediaries in the process, including those who recorded oral traditions. For a description of one not particularly colourful literary genre, its evolution, and the history of its public reception, see Gries, *The Literature of Customs* (Heb.).

[13] See ibid., pp. xii–xiv, 43–51, and additional bibliography there. Recently historians have challenged the generalization that the Catholic establishment opposed printing. See Walsham, '"Domme Preachers"?', and the bibliography there. See also Ch. 1 n. 11 below, and the associated text.

[14] Gries, *The Literature of Customs* (Heb.), ch. 2, demonstrates the process of the popularization of books in a single literary genre, the prescription of proper behaviour.

of whom were authors peddling their own wares. Their activities promoted the circulation of information on customs and law, on remedies and cures. There was also interest in literature with practical applications: guides to proper conduct, advice, and even prayers and penitential services. A literature of etiquette and customs emerged, fixing in print rituals which had long been practised among Jews in specific communities. The expansion of readership and of commerce in books showed the potential inherent in strata of society that had been ignored prior to the spread of printing.

Printing also brought the literature of Midrash, aggadah, and ethics into public consciousness. This literature had previously been marginalized in comparison with works of more immediate usefulness, such as daily and festival prayer books and those tractates of the Talmud that were regularly studied.

The printing of books for the Jewish market, whether by Jewish printers or by Christian printers who published Hebraica and Judaica for commercial reasons and employed Jews to assist then in this, was concentrated in specialist centres. From the fifteenth to the seventeenth centuries the centres of printing were principally in Italy and Constantinople, but in the eighteenth century the centre shifted to central Europe and Amsterdam, and from there in the nineteenth century to eastern Europe and particularly Vilna, Lvov (then Lemberg), and Warsaw. But although the printing may have been localized, the books themselves circulated throughout the entire Jewish diaspora. For a wandering people like the Jews, books became a portable homeland, and to a great extent they formed the ground upon which the Jews felt they could temporarily encamp.

In Europe generally, the first peak in the mass circulation of books took place during the seventeenth century. Among the Jews, the first major peak was during the eighteenth century.[15] I decided to concentrate my studies on the eighteenth and nineteenth centuries since during that period great changes took place in the world in general, and in the Jewish world in particular. I wanted to investigate how the general changes occurring in society at that time and the associated displacement of religion and its institutions had affected the Jews, and how this was reflected in books circulating in the Jewish world. I likewise wanted to investigate the extent to which secularization had spread among the Jews and how much, if at all, it affected the traditional Jewish conception of time, for the Jewish people are said to have lived for

---

[15] See ibid., pp. xi–xxi, and the additional bibliography there.

hundreds of years with an immutable conception of time, in which they perceived themselves as living in the context of sacred history. Further, I wished to see whether their books, more or less canonical, demonstrated an awareness of chronological considerations, since traditionally they are thought to derive from the revelation Moses received on Mount Sinai. As the early rabbis put it, 'There is no "earlier" or "later" in the Torah.' Ideas that such rabbis introduced, therefore, were thought of as simply having been brought to light at that point, since their origins dated from time immemorial. The giving of the Torah transmitted teachings to subsequent generations, who were destined from the start to discover them—each a revelation in its own time— according to the calculations of the Holy One, blessed be He, whom we can never comprehend.

Another topic that interested me was the degree to which Hebrew and Yiddish books furthered Jewish nationalist sentiment, and in what way, if at all, they helped concepts of nationhood to take root. The revival of Hebrew as a secular literary language after the end of the eighteenth century unquestionably contributed to the renewal of national consciousness and the search for identity among those who participated in this revival, but their number was not large. It also cannot be denied that this linguistic revival contributed significantly to the establishment of the foundations of the national revival movement in the last years of the nineteenth century and especially in the twentieth century, even though it was insignificant in the overall context of Jewish literary activity in this period. Nonetheless, I shall demonstrate that this ostensibly secular literature was in fact deeply connected to and influenced by the world of the sacred, and moreover was totally alienated from that great revolution in the lives of the Jews of its time—migration to America; rather, it was constantly concerned to fan the embers of the national fire, which at that time was barely alight.

My main focus in this book is works that could be understood by a general readership rather than the more specialized works of halakhic scholarship, although I have made reference to such higher literature as appropriate. I am primarily concerned with books published in Hebrew, as well as books published in Yiddish—Yiddish being the main vernacular language of the Jews of eastern Europe in the period we are considering, which is where the great majority of Jews then lived. In Part I, I choose various indicators and case studies, moving from a discussion of reading and the readers of books, through ethical literature in Hebrew and Yiddish and the literature of folk stories, mainly in Yiddish, to an examination of the place occupied by literature dealing with metaphysical and supernal elements: the literature of kabbalah. The popularization of this literature through the religious customs it inspired determined its relationship with halakhah, which has only now begun to be clarified satisfactorily.[16] At the same time, I assess and re-evaluate the changes prompted by the introduction of the Hebrew and Yiddish book to a population consisting primarily of women, but which also included children, young people, and men who were unable to study Torah to a high level, or who were prevented from doing so by the necessities of life, in particular the need to earn a livelihood. I attempt to demonstrate that exposure to independent reading in Hebrew, and especially in Yiddish, awoke the consciousness of a nascent intelligentsia. Members of this intelligentsia, which represented a far greater proportion of the population than the elite of Torah scholars, experienced in consequence an expansion of its vocabulary, an increase in conceptual ability, and an awareness of the world and of their place within it.

In Part II, I re-examine the place of Hebrew literature in the life of the Jewish people, looking particularly at the genres popular in the eighteenth, and more particularly the nineteenth, centuries and their readership. I try to describe the extent to which it was a continuation of the traditional Jewish literature of the world from which its authors came, and I ask to what degree it may be considered revolutionary. I consider the role of Hebrew-language periodicals in promoting books through the announcement of new publications and through book reviews, and by examining the demand for books also consider the extent to which readers were influenced by book reviews.

Last, but far from least, has been my effort to describe the activity of the bibliographer and librarian as an agent of culture by focusing on Abraham Ya'ari's work on Jewish printing in eastern Europe in the eighteenth and nineteenth centuries. I undertook this to demonstrate to myself and to my readers that, even if Ya'ari frequently failed to gather the pearls of detail and fashion them into the cultural necklace they deserved, the treasure he scattered among the pages of seemingly boring bibliographical journals eagerly awaits someone willing to make use of it. Moreover, we need to remember that Ya'ari

---

[16] For an expanded discussion of this topic and additional bibliography, see Gries, 'Kabbalah and Halakhah' (Heb.), 187–97. See also Ch. 1 n. 4 below.

was just one of a group of bibliographers and librarians—Abraham Meir Haberman, Hayim Lieberman, Dov Wachstein, Yeshayahu Sonne, and many, many others—whose work lies almost untouched in such journals, particularly *Kiryat sefer*.

Those who wish to delve more deeply into these and related topics on the history of the Jewish book should turn to my earlier and more specialist works, all of which are in Hebrew. These include an initial description of some of the agents of printing—those who prepared books for printing[17] and itinerant printers[18]—and a discourse on literary questions such as handbooks of proper behaviour and hagiography, their design in print, and their circulation and reception among their audience.[19] I have discussed the relationship between literature and history in two earlier works: one examines homiletic exegesis,[20] while the other deals with the first hasidic hagiography, *Shivḥei habesht* (Praises of the Besht).[21] In a detailed critical review of Moshe Rosman's *Founder of Hasidism: A Quest for the Historical Ba'al Shem Tov*,[22] I sought to demonstrate the vital importance of the history of the book, and of the text, in any attempt to write a spiritual biography of the great founder of a movement that has continued to exist to this day. This present book, however, is designed to provide a short and more accessible introduction to the topic as a whole.

[17] See Gries, 'On the Figure of the Jewish Managing Editor in the Late Middle Ages' (Heb.), 7–11, and *Book, Scribe, and Story in Early Hasidism* (Heb.), 47–67, 127–34, where I discuss the hasidic managing editor as an agent of culture.

[18] See id., 'Printing as a Means of Communication' (Heb.), 5–17.

[19] See id., *The Literature of Customs* (Heb.); id., 'Is It True That the Best Part of a Story Is Its Falsehood?' (Heb.), 85–94; id., 'Definition of Shabatean Hagiographical Literature' (Heb.), 353–64.   [20] See id., 'Between History and Literature' (Heb.), 113–22.

[21] See id., 'Between Literature and History: Introductory Remarks for the Examination and Discussion of *Shivḥei habesht*' (Heb.), 153–81.

[22] See id., 'The Historical Figure of the Besht' (Heb.), 411–46. The article refers to the English edition of Rosman's book, which appeared first, and which is identical to the Hebrew edition.

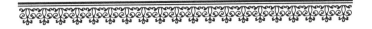

PART I

THE AWAKENING OF THE NASCENT INTELLIGENTSIA

ONE

Expanding Horizons

IN OCTOBER 1960 David Ben-Gurion made the following entry in his journal:

Yigael [Yadin] told me that he had received a letter from an Englishman (or an American), saying that he could obtain all the hidden scrolls that have been discovered and are in the hands of Bedouin, so long as the matter remained secret and he was paid one million dollars for each scroll. There are ten such scrolls. I told him the story about the rich Chinese man who drowned in a river. A poor fisherman recovered the body. The drowned man's sons came and demanded the body, and the fisherman asked for a large sum of money. The sons went to a lawyer and asked his advice. The lawyer said: the fisherman doesn't need the body, and no one else will come to take it from him. Therefore it is better for you to wait. They accepted his advice and did not go to the fisherman. The fisherman saw that days were passing, and the corpse was still in his house. He went to the same lawyer and asked his advice. What should he do? The lawyer told the fisherman: the sons can only recover the body from you, and not from anywhere else—therefore, wait. The story does not tell us how the matter ended, but you, Yigael, can wait, because in the end the scrolls will be published, and we will know their contents, and that is the main point. Wait.[1]

Yadin waited.

Those of us who are involved in cultural history, or, if you prefer, intellectual history, are apt to forget that books, the mirrors that reflect life for us, are not life itself. Ordinary life requires the investment of many resources for routine maintenance, and in the above case, the requirements of daily life prevented Israel's first prime minister from agreeing to the request of one of the leading spokesmen for scholars of Jewish history and culture. Furthermore, it is only in recent years that scholars have begun to pay any attention to

[1] See *Yoman d. ben-gurion* (Journal of D. Ben-Gurion), IDF Archive, entry dated 12 Oct. 1960.

the history of books in the Jewish world and their public reception over the generations, or to examine their influence on people's daily lives. From this anecdote, and from what I have said so far, it may be concluded that, in parallel with efforts to collect and preserve Jewish writings over the generations, we also need to consider how they have been received. We need to examine the extent to which books have shaped people's views and way of life, or, in this case, how much they were responsible for their intellectual development and education.

Education relies on many agents, institutions, and people, with an important role being played by the formal institutions and those who work for them. In traditional Jewish society these were the *ḥeder*, for young boys; the *talmud torah*, for older boys; the *yeshivah* for young men, whether studying Talmud for its own sake or to attain rabbinical ordination; and the *beit midrash* (*beismedresh*, or house of study), generally attached to a synagogue, where men, both married and unmarried, studied traditional texts, principally the Talmud, in a less structured way. These were the foundations and the cornerstones of Jewish education until the emancipation introduced by the Haskalah movement, when, especially from the nineteenth century onwards, far-reaching changes took place.

Modern Jewish historiography has neglected another key factor in the spread of education, and that is the history of printing and its part in the process. As the availability of books increased from the eighteenth century onwards, so a Jewish intelligentsia emerged that went far beyond the relatively small scholarly elite that had had access to manuscripts. In this sense, printing paved the way for the transition to the new concepts and skills that were prerequisites for enlightenment and emancipation. Jewish historiographers have barely dealt with this subject; librarians and bibliographers have diligently recorded a substantial amount of information on Jewish printing and books, and particularly in relation to the publication of the traditional religious texts, but have not touched on the cultural implications of the appearance of new types of books aimed at a wider readership. Even such pioneering historical studies such as those of Jacob Katz[2] and Azriel Shohet,[3] which deal with the

---

[2] See Katz, *Tradition and Crisis*; id., *Out of the Ghetto*.

[3] See Shohet, *With the Change of Epochs* (Heb.). Two critiques of this book were published: one was by Getzel Kressel, 'The Beginning of Haskalah in German Jewry' (Heb.), who opposed Shohet's 'teaching' on the tendency of German Jewry in the 18th century to adopt the

eighteenth century and the changes that took place in the Jewish world at that time, did not discuss the impact of printing on the education of the Jewish nation. Similarly, Gershom Scholem—though an indefatigable bibliographer (as we can see from the comments in the margins of the books in his marvellous library, which is open to the general public)—neglected to consider, in his studies of kabbalah and the dissemination of kabbalistic doctrines and customs, that by studying the history of the books on the subject he could evaluate its importance to the reading public.[4]

There are, in fact, hardly any proponents of the history of the book in the Jewish world. The scholarly community still needs convincing that it should pay attention to the history of the writing, printing, and circulation of books beyond those required for the formal system of Jewish education, the way in which these works were received by their readers, and how they influenced them.[5] Research into Hebrew-language publishing is of paramount importance in fostering an understanding of the place such works occupied in the

ways and language of the local non-Jewish community. The second was by Barukh Mevorakh in *Kiryat sefer*. He acknowledged the importance of the book, although he disagreed with some of its claims. For an assessment of Shohet's work see Ch. 2 at nn. 24–6, and Ch. 6 n. 40. It should be added here that in the important collection by Simcha Assaf, *Sources for the History of Jewish Education* (Heb.), the subject of printing and education was not included. Dinur, *The Jews in Exile* (Heb.), vol. ii, bk. 6, includes important material, but from periods far earlier than the 18th century.

[4] See the remarks in Gries, 'The Copying and Printing of Books of Kabbalah' (Heb.), reworked as Ch. 5 below. In recent years a radical change has taken place in research regarding the relationship between halakhah, custom, and kabbalah. Jacob Katz, Meir Benayahu, Moshe Halamish, and Israel Ta-Shma have made special contributions to this development. See the up-to-date, perceptive, and illuminating survey of the field in Ta-Shma, *The Revealed Within the Hidden* (Heb.), 13–23 (introduction), 88–104 (appendix III), and the notes and bibliography, all of which give details of the most important works in this field. However, there has so far not been a general study of how kabbalistic customs were disseminated and adopted. I have attempted to examine the history and uses of one literary genre which was very common among kabbalists in my *Literature of Customs* (Heb.); see also the comprehensive collection of articles, revised and updated, in Halamish, *Kabbalah in Prayer, Halakhah, and Custom* (Heb.), and my review of this book, 'Kabbalah and Halakhah' (Heb.), 187–97, where the reader will find (p. 187 n. 2) a list of recent articles by Ta-Shma and of reviews of his book.

[5] In my *Book, Scribe, and Story* (Heb.) I sought to present, through the example of hasidic literature, a methodological introduction to the use of the history of the book as a research tool in Jewish studies. Another fascinating field, entirely neglected in the study of Jewish history and culture, is the role of technology and its development as an educational agent among the

lives of biblical exegetes, the authors of religious and ethical books, of works of kabbalah, or of books of philosophy, which hover between the sacred and the profane, as do folk stories and poetry. To these must be added works written in Yiddish or translated into Yiddish and other vernacular languages.[6]

The eighteenth century occupies a special place in Jewish publishing history, since the number of titles printed during that period almost quadrupled, as, apparently, did the number of books printed. This fact alone, which is well known to every bibliophile, should long since have stimulated intellectual historians and scholars of Jewish literature and thought to study this increase in printing—as expressed in surviving catalogues, bibliographical lists, and other sources—and consider its implications. Thanks to the expansion of printing, in Hebrew and in Yiddish, the circle of Jewish readers similarly expanded in the eighteenth century, as we have seen, to include people whose connection with the scholarly elite was, at best, tenuous. What books did they read? How did their reading shape their world-view and further their intellectual development? What, moreover, can be learned from this about Jewish society in the eighteenth century in general, and that of eastern Europe in particular?

The publication of large amounts of popular and middle-brow literature in Hebrew and Yiddish in the eighteenth century served to awaken the consciousness of a broad Jewish public. It allowed them to acquire both expressive and conceptual abilities, expanding their horizons and giving them the tools

Jews. This is surprising, because one of the first scholars of the 'science of Judaism' in Germany, Leopold Zunz, noted the need for such research in his master plan for the study of Jewish literature and its history, 'Something About Rabbinical Literature' (Heb.), 87–8, esp. p. 88. For the past seventy years, historians of culture have done fascinating work on the application of achievements in technology and on the influence of technological change on the development of culture. See the survey in White, *Medieval Religion and Technology*, pp. xi–xxiv, and the review of this book by J. R. Strayer in *Technology and Culture* (21 (1980), 82–5).

[6] See at length in Gries, 'Between Literature and History' (Heb.), 154–60, and also my critical essay 'Between History and Literature' (Heb.), 113–22. There has still not been a proper assessment of the relative importance of Hebrew and vernacular languages in Jewish daily and spiritual life. In this connection it is especially appropriate to mention the 'heretical' words of one of the greatest scholars of Jewish history in recent generations, Shlomo D. Goitein: see his 'The *Makamah* and the *Maḥberet*' (Heb.), 32–7, and compare his earlier 'Jewish History and Arab History' (Heb.), 107–10. It would be worth while to investigate the difference of opinion regarding the place and function of Hebrew in Jewish history between Goitein, who had the soul of a poet, and the great Hebrew poet Hayim Nahman Bialik, who had the soul of a scholar. See the remarks in Bialik, 'On Nation and Language' (Heb.), 15–20.

to develop the talents needed in a rapidly changing world. Arousal of a nascent intelligentsia in this way marked a highly significant expansion in the general intellectual ability of Jewish society. This fact should certainly stimulate a re-evaluation of Jewish intellectual history with a focus on the changes in the world of the populations hitherto regarded as marginal because they did not belong to the rabbinic elite.[7]

For several decades now, various groups of scholars, initially anthropologists,[8] followed by intellectual historians, and finally by religious thinkers and theologians,[9] have been examining the transition from oral to written culture in detail. These scholars have expanded our view of the human ability to manipulate thought beyond the acquisition of reading and writing by demonstrating that cultural literacy may be acquired in ways other than through books: for example, through voice and sound, movement, and images, whether in a private setting or a public performance, with or without musical accompaniment and dance. In other words, individuals have access, over the course of their lives, to traditions, beliefs, and customs through media other than the written word, thereby adding to the richness of human culture.[10]

I have written elsewhere at length about how the Reformation led to the extensive use of vernacular languages in print,[11] and thus to the expansion of the circle of readers in Europe generally, and similarly about the effect of this development on both the language used in books for Jews and on their

[7] Here I wish to counterbalance the implications of the important article by Elhanan Reiner, 'Capital, Social Class, and the Study of Torah' (Heb.), 287–328, who correctly notes the changes in the organization of institutionalized study and the support of wealthy men for groups of scholars, but does not refer to the far-reaching changes in the reading habits of the new intelligentsia, whose members were not necessarily scholars.

[8] I refer mainly to the many important studies by Jack Goody, including *The Logic of Writing and the Organization of Society* and *The Interface Between the Written and the Oral*, where the reader will find references to additional works by him and others.

[9] Primarily Ong, *Orality and Literacy*.

[10] Much scholarship has been published on this in recent years. Some of this work emphasizes the many aspects of literacy, which I have mentioned briefly, and the fertile and continuous contact in every society and period between orality and literacy: see Harris, *Ancient Literacy*, and McKitterick (ed.), *The Uses of Literacy*. For a discussion, including extensive bibliographical references, see Graff, *The Legacies of Literacy*.

[11] See Gries, *The Literature of Customs* (Heb.), pp. xi–xiv, 41–102. It should be noted that Weber, in *The Protestant Ethic and the Spirit of Capitalism*, does not discuss printing or the book as advancing the social and cultural revolution. In addition to the bibliography presented in *Literature of Customs* (Heb.), detailed scholarly attention has been given in recent years to

readership, particularly from the sixteenth century onwards. For those among whom intellectual reasoning had blossomed even in the absence of the specific influence of literacy, printed texts in a language in which they could read and write permitted them, in an intellectual sense, to spread their wings and take flight. Carlo Ginzburg has revealed the fascinating world of a sixteenth-century Italian miller who was arrested by officers of the Italian inquisition on suspicion of heresy and interrogated about his literary diet. Through his testimony concerning the books he read and how they influenced him, we are able to enter the rich and complex world of someone who belonged to a stratum of society whose intellectual life was otherwise hidden.[12] It is regrettable, however, that we have no similar studies of the identity and nature of the Jewish reader at various periods, or of how the influence of different literary genres on him or her can be assessed.[13]

In intellectual history it is very unusual to find growth *ex nihilo*. It may thus be stated with certainty that the tree that bore fruit in the eighteenth century in the books published for Jews had its roots in the sixteenth century, as did similar developments in the wider world. Thus, meticulous analysis by French scholars of the development of reading habits in France has highlighted the decline of classical Latin and its literature from the sixteenth century on, and a concomitant rise in the status of the vernacular novel, an interest in the charms of the immediate natural world, and a fascination with descriptions of distant, exotic countries.[14] From these works we see how, with gradual change in the institutions of formal education controlled by the Church and a reduction in

Strasbourg, centre of the printing battle between Lutherans and Catholics. These studies have shown that the Lutheran Protestants used printing as a means of propaganda with more success than did their Catholic rivals; it has also been proved that Luther and his supporters did not always control the way in which their printed propaganda in the vernacular was received. See Chrisman, *Lay Culture, Learned Culture*, and its separate bibliographical volume, *Bibliography of Strasbourg Imprints*, which gives a detailed analytical list of the types of literature printed in Strasbourg during this period. A valuable book which expands the discussion from Chrisman's data and conclusions is Edwards, *Printing, Propaganda and Martin Luther*: see the preface, n. 13.

[12] See Carlo Ginzburg, *The Cheese and the Worms*.

[13] See Chartier, *The Order of Books*, 1–23, 93–8, which notes the reflection in print of the changing consciousness of readers and their self-image, as well as of changes in the internal and external design of the books produced for them.

[14] For extensive treatment of this subject, see Darnton, 'History of Reading', 143; see also Grafton, Shelford, and Siraisi, *New Worlds, Ancient Texts*.

the emphasis on the learning by rote of the catechism and devout literature,[15] a true revolution took place in the reading audience and in reading habits beyond the school-room walls.[16] In western and central Europe the printed book became popular as early as the mid-seventeenth century, and within a hundred years this popularity had reached unprecedented levels. The circulation of 'penny books' and pocket books, initially restricted to the large cities, expanded in the eighteenth century to towns and villages. The implications of similar developments in the Jewish world are considered more fully in the next chapter.

[15] See Darnton, 'History of Reading', 154–5.

[16] Darnton (ibid. 144) draws attention to the great literary ferment produced by the masses of German books which appeared during the *Sturm und Drang* period of the late 18th century. On that period and the influence of events in Germany on European culture, see Garland, *Storm and Stress*, and Reed, *The Classical Centre*. For a French perspective, see Chartier, 'The Bibliothèque Bleue and Popular Reading', 240–63.

T W O

On Reading and Readers

Ｉ N RECENT YEARS there has been increasing interest in the culture of reading and in the reading habits of various populations. However, even what is perhaps the major work on the history of reading in the West has only one chapter, by Robert Bonfil at the Hebrew University of Jerusalem, which discusses the reading of books among the Jews in the Middle Ages.[1] The period with which we are concerned, the eighteenth and nineteenth centuries, receives no attention at all.

Scholars of non-Jewish European culture are fortunate in having access to catalogues of book fairs for the eighteenth century,[2] and to the inventories of booksellers,[3] although these alone are not enough to determine reading habits and the way in which reading influenced people's lives. To supplement information gleaned from the catalogues, historians make use of the memoirs of

[1] See Bonfil, 'Reading in the Jewish Communities of Western Europe in the Middle Ages'. An important study preceded Bonfil's: Baruchson, *Books and Readers* (Heb.). Two other important books in this field are Manguel, *A History of Reading*, and Sharpe, *Reading Revolutions*. Particularly interesting is Johns, *The Nature of the Book*, esp. pp. 380–443; see also references in its index to readers and reading. A more recent work is Parush, *Reading Women* (Heb.), which I discuss further below.

[2] Darnton, 'History of Reading', 143–4, discusses the statistics that can be elicited from the detailed catalogues of the Frankfurt and Leipzig book fairs and notes the vagueness of some of the data, where the definitions of the types of literature are general and don't identify specific literary phenomena, and records the lack of comparative research across national borders.

[3] Chartier made impressive use of these in his article 'The Bibliothèque Bleue and Popular Reading'. See also Spufford, *Small Books and Pleasant Histories*. There have been virtually no organized catalogues of Jewish books since the time of Menasseh ben Israel, the Amsterdam rabbi and printer, who circulated a list of the contents of his warehouse in the 17th century. See Ya'ari, 'The Original Catalogue of the Printing House of Menasseh Ben-Israel in Amsterdam' (Heb.), 192–201. See also Cecil Roth's remarks on the catalogue published by Ya'ari, in *Kiryat sefer*, 24 (1947–8), 85–6, Ya'ari's response (ibid. 86–8), and Roth's additional remarks in 'List of

those who wrote about their reading experience.[4] But what of the Jews in the eighteenth and nineteenth centuries? Our main sources are the contents of large libraries and private collections as recorded by bibliographers. These provide information on the numbers of titles and new editions, and permit classification by genre. They do not, however, tell us anything about the number of books printed. It is well known that books required for traditional religious and educational purposes in a formal setting were printed in large quantities—for example, the tractates of the Talmud, the Pentateuch, and the daily and festival prayer books—but little is known about other books. There is somewhat greater knowledge of books in the nineteenth century thanks to the spread of the Haskalah movement, which promoted books in its periodicals through announcements and book reviews, and the printers, publishers, and booksellers associated with the movement put out catalogues of their wares.

In the eighteenth century books were purveyed to the Jewish community by itinerant salesmen, some of whom were penniless writers, some virtually beggars, and others pedlars who sold their books alongside haberdashery and the like. These people played a key role in the distribution of popular literature, and continued to do so into the nineteenth century. This explains why one of the greatest Jewish writers, Shalom Jacob Abramowitsch (1835–1917) took the pen-name of Mendele Mokher Seforim ('Mendele the book salesman'). S. Y. Agnon, writing of his late nineteenth-century childhood, mentions the pedlar's role in distributing books and pamphlets, especially those in Yiddish, in contrast to the respectable booksellers who sold their wares to the formal institutions of Jewish learning.

Mention must be made here of the contribution of Russian-born Menahem Mendel Slatkine (1875–1965), who studied in the Volozhin yeshiva with Hayim Nahman Bialik and became a book dealer in Switzerland as well as a prolific writer on the history of books. Slatkine wrote what purported to be the memoirs of a Lithuanian rabbi (which he had supposedly found in a late eighteenth-century manuscript). This work devoted extensive space to the description of a learned book salesman, Reb Grunem. The rabbi explains

Books from the Commercial House of Rabbi Menasseh ben Israel' (Heb.), 413–14. See the more detailed comments on Menasseh ben Israel's work as a printer in Dorman, *Menasseh ben Israel* (Heb.), 17–22 and nn. 22–32 and 103–4, where there is additional bibliography.

[4] See Chartier, 'The Bibliothèque Bleue and Popular Reading', 257–63.

that—in contrast to other members of his profession, who were ignoramuses and dealt in daily and festival prayer books and books for women such as *tekhines* (as petitionary prayers were known in Yiddish) and *Tsena urena* (a popular Bible commentary in Yiddish)—Grunem sold books of Torah discourses and halakhic rulings. He also attempted to convey knowledge to his customers about the outside world, and particularly about the disputes between hasidim and mitnagedim. In this way Grunem served as spokesman for what were in effect Slatkine's thoughts on the scale of the opposition between the two camps.[5]

By the second half of the nineteenth century, maskilim began to feel that interest in secular knowledge had grown to the extent that it was possible to make a proper living as a bookseller. In an initiative in this direction in the late 1870s, the bookseller Abraham Zuckerman of Warsaw, together with his partner Kalman Shapira of Bialystok, published a list of their wares. Their list, which contains 220 titles in Hebrew, 35 in German, 12 in Russian, and another 13 in bilingual Hebrew–Russian editions, affords us a glimpse of the demand among the maskilim of the period for non-fiction, fiction, and poetry.[6]

It is not possible to deal at length here with the lists of books of booksellers and collectors which were published in the eighteenth century. This period also saw the beginnings of publication through subscriptions—*prenumeranten*—so there are lists of subscribers available too. Although these enterprises have to some extent been documented, primarily by Berl Cohen,

[5] See Agnon, *From Me To Myself* (Heb.), 365. On Mendele Mokher Seforim see the stimulating discussion in Bakon, *Mendele Sholem Aleikhem* (Heb.), 16–31, and my comments on travelling book salesmen in general in *The Literature of Customs* (Heb.), pp. xiii–xiv. See also Slatkine, *From the Memoirs of a Lithuanian Rabbi* (Heb.), 60–85: these memoirs were supposedly written during the month of Elul 5548 (September 1788). Slatkine wrote one of the most important studies of the history of the Hebrew book, *Titles of Hebrew Books According to their Type, Nature and Objectives* (Heb.), and a study of the pioneer of Hebrew bibliography, R. Shabetai Bas, author of *Siftei yeshenim* (The Lips of the Sleeper), entitled *The Beginnings of Bibliography in Hebrew Literature* (Heb.). The past twenty years have seen an increase in research on the place of women in Jewish culture and literature, and on women's spiritual aspirations. Prominent among recent studies is Weissler, *Voices of the Matriarchs*.

[6] This list appears in the introductory pages of *Hashahar*, 8/5 (1877). On another bookshop, that of Eliezer Isaac Shapira in Warsaw, as a cultural institution see Rappel, 'The Bookstore as an Educational Institution for the Jewish Maskil' (Heb.), 336–44, and, on Jewish booksellers in 19th-century eastern Europe, Cohen, 'In the Bookseller's Shop' (Heb.), which discusses Zuckerman and his shop on pp. 99–101, and which gives additional information on Shapira's influence on pp. 69–82.

figures for the eighteenth century are few and far between, and most of the information we have derives from the nineteenth century. One major eighteenth-century publishing initiative worthy of note, however, was that of Moses Frankfurt, a *dayan* (religious judge) and writer from Amsterdam (and the son of Simon Frankfurt, the author of *Sefer haḥayim* (The Book of Life), the most important book in modern times to deal with Ashkenazi customs concerning the sick and the dead). Moses Frankfurt's idea was to sell subscriptions for the publication of a magnificent large-format edition of *Mikraot gedolot*, a compendium of traditional commentaries on the Bible. Published under the title *Kehilot mosheh* in Amsterdam in 1724, this was (and still is) the largest edition ever published.

Valuable information about the world of Jewish books has been provided by some eighteenth-century bibliophiles and book collectors. Foremost among these is the rabbinical scholar, writer, bibliographer, and traveller known as the Hida (Hayim Joseph David Azulai). In the course of his journeys collecting funds among the Jewish communities in North Africa and Europe for the poor of the Land of Israel, he collected information on books and recorded it in detail in his travel journal *Ma'agal tov hashalem* (The Complete Cycle of Good); he used this information extensively in his bibliographical work *Shem hagedolim* (The Name of the Great). We learn from the Hida's writings, for example, that many Jews in North Africa and Europe still studied from manuscripts and regarded them as valuable possessions.[7] We also read of his differences with David Meldola, a Torah scholar who had become a travelling bookseller in order to augment his income and who attached himself to him; concerned that remaining with Meldola would detract from his ability to raise money for the Land of Israel (for he himself carried books for sale, in order to finance his charitable endeavours there), the Hida distanced himself from him.[8] The Hida's record of his visit to Tunis in 1774 also reveals the limited nature of people's knowledge of Lurianic kabbalah, which says something about the limited availability there of books on the subject.[9]

[7] See *Ma'agal tov hashalem*, 7–9, 12–13, 15, 26–7, 40–4. On p. 57 Azulai reports on the development of the talmudic curriculum in Tunis, stating that only in the last generation did the rabbis of Tunis change from studying the Talmud with Rashi's commentary to studying it with the commentary of Tosafot, to which they added the comments of Solomon Eliezer ben Jacob Luria (Maharshal) and Samuel Edeles (Maharsha). Azulai adds that the rabbis of Tunis were not well versed in responsa and halakhic rulings.   [8] *Ma'agal tov hashalem*, 28–9.

[9] Ibid. 58–9. Azulai's words support my own remarks and those of Moshe Idel on this sub-

Another thing we learn from the Hida is that, just as at the time of the expulsion from Spain and Portugal in 1492, Jews moving from place to place within eighteenth-century Europe often purchased valuable religious books as a way of converting their wealth into property that was eminently portable but that the authorities could not easily put a value on.[10] Thus, the Hida tells how in 1754 he travelled from Padua to Verona in the month of Iyar:

Midway, I looked for the case for my *tefilin* and it was missing, and I was very sorry, *because apart from its being full of valuable books*, it also had *tefilin* of Rashi of blessed memory, written by the finger of the great rabbi and disciple of the Ari of blessed memory, our master Rabbi Suleiman of blessed memory. And our master Rabbi Hayim Alfandari, in his book *Magid mireshit* [The Narrator from the Beginning], used to list their praises. But blessed be the Name of His Honour, who does not abandon his mercy and his spirit invested the *vetturino* [Italian: coachman]. And he rode on a horse [one of those that was pulling the carriage in which Azulai was riding] and raced back more than a mile and questioned every passer-by. And there it was said that they had seen a hunter, who, when he raised his hand, was holding a large pouch. And he went on his way and searched him and found it and he recognized it and said it was charity from me, and no one would save it from the hand of the cheating hunter, and he brought it all, thank the Blessed Lord.[11]

Another prolific writer whose testimony has survived is Jacob ben Zvi Emden (1697–1776), many of whose polemical works were printed at his private printing press in Altona. Rather than informing us about the spirit of his generation and the world of the book in general, Emden's testimony reflects the endless battles he waged against all those who did not understand how easy it was to provoke him, and whom he saw as libidinous Shabateans, or simply men of ill will—moneychangers, merchants, booksellers, and the like—whose sole intention was to infuriate him.[12] Since his curiosity and thirst for knowledge were no less acute than his irascibility and desire to record his life and works, Emden has supplied us with a good account of how a well-bred young Jewish man taught himself European languages. He studied them partly in order to be able to read medical books and discover cures for his illnesses;

---

ject: see Gries, *The Literature of Customs* (Heb.), pp. xv–xvi, xvii–xviii, 82–3, 92, and 101, and Idel, 'One from a Town, Two from a Clan', 79–104.

[10] See Hacker, 'Intellectual Activity Among the Jews of the Ottoman Empire' (Heb.), 579. Naturally, the view of books as property does not mean that those who took books on their wanderings were not learned, or lovers of books.

[11] See *Ma'agal tov hashalem*, 10.   [12] See Emden, *Megilat sefer*, 211–12, 215–25.

he also wanted to learn about the wonders of the wider world, which are not documented in Jewish literature:

During my first long period of exile [in Amsterdam], in the days when I dwelt in the house of the eminent R.B.K. [the reference is not clear—z.g.], until the autumn season had passed, I wanted to be able to read and understand the German script which my late master and teacher [his father, the Hakham Zvi] had not taught me; I did not learn this writing from a teacher, but had to study it by myself. I knew nothing of the books of gentiles or their writings, But I was constantly drawn to worldly matters involving the nations, their beliefs, their ways, opinions, history, and knowledge, none of which can be found in our holy books. My soul yearned to know all of these things from the books themselves, but I could not find a way to do it as I did not want to hire someone to teach me to read books in the vernacular for fear of the great waste [of time that should have been devoted to Torah]. It also seemed despicable to me to spend money in this way, and I was ashamed to do it because of what others might think.

Eventually I became acquainted with a boy from among the servants who was learning writing and reading in the vernacular. I took him aside secretly and asked him to show me the form of the letters of the alphabet of the vernacular in print—which he had begun to learn from a gentile scribe. He still barely knew the appearance of the letters separately, and did not know how to read them when joined together in words or understand what the words meant. The boy showed me just once or twice, saying: this is 'A', this is 'C', and nothing more, and with the help of the Almighty, who endows man with knowledge, I was immediately able to recognize the form of the letters. Afterwards, I made the effort by myself to combine words, and I managed to understand things without any help from a teacher or instructor. In a short time I was able to read books in the German vernacular as well as if I had been learning with a teacher for several years. I only managed to learn to read their printed books, and so also with Latin script, but writing in the vernacular, which is done with a sweep and flow, I still do not know owing to my complete lack of study, and even in printed Latin there are some forms and signs, or changes in the shape of the letters, that I do not know to this day. For how can such things be achieved in a rush? Even the boy who showed me it had not learned it all. Afterwards, I was ashamed to ask anyone when I did not know something. Nonetheless, I hastened to read all their printed books by myself immediately, until I even became skilled in reading the Dutch language and gazettes and understood much of the Latin language. I read many of their books on different areas of knowledge in Europe, to familiarize myself with the opinions of the people of the world in beliefs, religion, and customs, and to reveal their thoughts about us and about our holy faith.

My soul also yearned to know and understand the position of the globe of the earth, as explained in their books on the movement of the heavenly bodies, which is explained only very briefly in our books. I also wanted to know and understand natural things—the nature of minerals and the properties of plants and herbs, and especially medicine, and the government of states, and wars, and their history, and other stories; and the chronicles of generations and the innovations in geography: seas and rivers and deserts and the accounts of their situation, handicrafts and arts and machinations and deceits and fraud; and stories of vanity and fiction—all of these things I saw in their writing. I am learned in them and in their deeds, and all of their thoughts, their forgeries and their good actions; I know it all, and it was visible before me, so that I should not to be naked in the wisdom of men of the world. But I remembered not to read them or to look at them except in a place where it is forbidden to think about words of Torah [then a common way, among Orthodox Jews, of refering to the toilet]—nowhere else at all. Indeed, several times, when I took sweetness from bitterness and found honey in it [an allusion to Judg. 14:14—z.G.], I forced my hand to use it for holy work in various recondite and hermetic matters. And above all I managed in that way to know how to answer them and not to be regarded as a fool by them; especially in the wisdom of medicine and knowledge of preserving health, which is lifegiving. I researched their books in my spare time, as I have described, and I studied the natural sciences, to enable me to keep myself in good health.[13]

Emden's words are corroborated by the autobiography of Polish-born Solomon Maimon who was several years his junior. Maimon describes his early education in the Hebrew wisdom literature in his father's home,[14] unwittingly testifying that the apple did not fall far from the tree. His father had also been interested in science and knowledge, and he satisfied some of his son's curiosity with books he bought for himself. Maimon describes the importance of books in his life:

To satisfy my lust for the sciences there was no other way than to learn foreign languages. But how could I achieve this? It was impossible to study the Polish or Latin languages with a Catholic, because of the prejudices of the members of my nation on the one hand, according to whom it was forbidden to learn any language except Hebrew, or other knowledge and sciences, except the Talmud and its innumerable commentaries, and because of the prejudices of the Catholics on the other hand, who forbade the teaching of these subjects to a Jew.

Apart from this, I was in a very difficult financial position. I was forced to support a family by teaching, correcting Torah scrolls, and the like, and in the midst of all this I yearned in vain for many days to give satisfaction to this natural desire of mine.

---

[13] Emden, *Megilat sefer*, 125–6; cf. the words of Shohet in *With the Change of Epochs* (Heb.), 220–35.   [14] See Maimon, *My Life* (Heb.), 69–72.

In the end, happy chance came to my assistance, and this is what happened: in several Hebrew books which were very thick, I noticed that there were other alphabets. Since it was impossible to mark the numbers of the folios with Hebrew letters alone, it was necessary to use the letters of a second or third alphabet—mainly Latin or German.

I had no idea whatsoever about printing houses. I imagined that books were printed the way that cloth is printed, and that every page was printed separately. However, I surmised that the written symbols next to each other indicated the same letter. Since I had already heard something about the alphabetical order in these languages, I guessed, for example, that the letter 'a', which stood next to the letter *alef*, was also an *alef*. In that manner I gradually learned the Latin and German alphabets. By means of a system of deciphering, I began to combine the various German letters into words. I still had my doubts, however, in case all my efforts should prove to be in vain, for it was possible that the written symbols next to the Hebrew letters might indicate something else. Then, to my delight, a few pages of an old German book fell into my hands and I began to read. How great was my joy and astonishment, upon seeing that, by combining them, the words were completely consistent with those I had already learned. Outside my Yiddish vocabulary, there were still many words, whose meaning I did not know, but from the phrases in which they were used I was able to discern the general content, even without those words.

The method of study by decipherment serves me to this day as my own special method of grasping the ideas of others in order to discuss them. Here I can state categorically that, as long as a person sees himself as constrained to present an author's arguments in their set order, joining them with expressions that the author uses, that is only a matter of memory, and he still cannot claim that he understands the author's book. A person cannot boast that he understands the opinions of an author until that author's ideas, which at first he perceives only vaguely, stimulate him to think about the same subject and to produce those ideas by himself, although prompted by another. This difference between one level of understanding and another cannot evade a sharp eye. For that very reason, I cannot understand a book until the ideas that are stored in it fit together after all the gaps between them have been filled in.[15]

Maimon goes on to recount his successful acquaintance with a rabbi whose interest in science, and knowledge of German from having lived in Germany, led him to import books in German to his library in Poland. When the young Maimon, who had acquired a knowledge of German, asked if he could use the

[15] Ibid. 107–8. Regrettably, I cannot enter into a discussion here of the methods employed in learning to read and understand texts that emerge from the writings of Emden and his predecessors or from Maimon's works. These memoirs will prove to be an important source for future research on informal methods of education in Jewish society.

books, the rabbi was astonished, for no one had asked to do this in the thirty-one years since his return from Germany![16]

In contrast, when Pinhas Elijah Horowitz (1765–1821), the author of *Sefer haberit* (The Book of the Covenant) needed to master scientific literature in foreign languages, he did not trouble to learn them. Rather, he relied on the assistance of someone who knew

how to read every book and language, and he would read things to me from the books of the nations as written, and in their language, and first I would copy everything he read from all the languages of the gentiles on paper in the language of my people [Yiddish], and from there into a book in the Holy Tongue, and it was very hard to copy.[17]

He went on to explain that the difficulty lay in the limitations of biblical and rabbinic Hebrew in the precise transmission of scientific concepts.

The great majority of Jews, even those who could read, did not know how to read non-Jewish languages. Small wonder, therefore, that there was great curiosity and a desire for knowledge among this potential Jewish readership, who would have been amazed to know that future scholars would write about their absolute isolation from the world. From travellers, merchants, and wanderers, and from rumours and news from wayfarers, they would most certainly have heard about the written literature available to the wider, non-Jewish society, with its tales of the new world that had been revealed with the discovery of America, chivalric romances, and other genres that were not available in Hebrew but which fired their imagination. When printers responded to the yearnings of the masses by making such books available in Hebrew and especially in Yiddish, it was like opening a window on to a new world, to intellectual adventures and new ways of thinking.

In eastern Europe particularly, the window thus opened allowed wisdom of a new sort to enter the Jewish home. The Jews of eastern Europe had until then had little or nothing to do with the humanities, with literary and historical scholarship, with the natural sciences, mathematics, engineering, chemistry, or technology.[18] This even applied to medicine, a field in which Jews had

---

[16] Maimon, *My Life*. 117–20.

[17] See Horowitz, *Sefer haberit*, pp. xii–xiii, and Ch. 9 at nn. 40–3 below.

[18] See my comments in *Book, Scribe, and Story* (Heb.), 13. Scientific literature in Hebrew or Yiddish in the 18th century, including medical works, books of remedies, and also philosophy, was of a low standard, and I shall not discuss it here; for this type of literature see my *Literature of*

led for generations but from which they were virtually absent by the turn of the seventeenth century.[19] In this context it is appropriate to quote Tobias Cohn (1652–1729), the famed physician (also known as Tuviah Katz) and key figure in the history of Jews and medicine, explaining how he came to write his encyclopaedic work on medicine:

My thoughts made me bold enough to go to the land of Italy to study the science of medicine in the academies of wisdom in the city of Padua, may God protect it. And behold, the Lord made me chance to meet a wise and intelligent man, the perfect sage, who became my friend, Rabbi Gabriel Rofe, may he rest in peace. And there was

Customs (Heb.), 93–9, and the additional bibliography there. See also Matras, 'Books of Remedies and Cures in Hebrew' (Heb.), and my critique of this dissertation in 'The Historical Figure of the Besht' (Heb.), 416 n. 17. There has been an upsurge of research into 'Masters of the Name': Gedaliyah Nigal has devoted almost an entire book to the topic, *Magic, Mysticism, and Hasidism* (Heb.); see also the long article by Immanuel Etkes, 'The Place of Magic and "Masters of the Name" in Ashkenazi Society' (Heb.), 69–104. In comparison to the kinds of literature discussed in the present volume, the number of 18th-century titles on remedies and cures is small, and as a literary phenomenon the importance of the genre is marginal. I have already discussed the success of one of the Masters of the Name in circulating his books— Benjamin Benish Hacohen of Krotoschin, who, in order to ensure their circulation, included in them a considerable number of *tikunim* (penitential prayer services). However, I doubt whether their appearance in print was, as Etkes suggests ('The Place of Magic', 102–4), a sign of the professionalization of Masters of the Name and public acknowledgement of this; indeed, the late 17th and early 18th centuries also saw the awakening of east European Jews to the medical profession. Rather, as I suggest below, the publication of the methods of the Masters of the Name presaged the decline of their profession and its status.

[19] Little is known about the renewal of interest in the medical profession among Jews. On Jewish doctors in Poland in the 18th century, see Gelber, 'On the History of Jewish Doctors' (Heb.), 61–9. On the doctor Moses Marcuse and his book, *Ezer yisra'el* (Help of Israel), see Shmeruk, *Yiddish Literature* (Heb.), 187–97. The father of Hebrew bibliography in the modern period, Moritz Steinschneider, the breadth of whose knowledge of Jewish literature over the generations has so far not been equalled, noted that 'during the eighteenth century Jews also wrote scientific dissertations to earn the degree of doctor. The number of these steadily increased over the years of that century, hence, so did the number of doctors': see his *Jewish Literature* (Heb.), 432, and also his comments there about Tuviah Katz. On the number of Jewish students in German universities (both overall and those studying medicine) from the late 17th to the mid-19th centuries, including the number who came from Poland, see Richarz, *Der Eintritt in die akademischen Berufe*. A digest of the data from Richarz's book and its cultural meaning for Jewish history can be found in Eisenbach, *The Emancipation of the Jews of Poland*, 43–4. For further data on the opening of German universities to Jews for the study of medicine, from the late 17th century onwards in Frankfurt an der Oder, and during the 18th century in Giessen, Halle, Göttingen, Heidelberg, Königsberg, and elsewhere, see Mahler, *A History of*

a holy oath between us, and we were like loyal brothers all of our lives, and the Lord made our path prosper. And he favoured both of us wherever our feet trod, and especially in the eyes of the Grand Duke of Frankfurt an der Oder, who received us with a favourable countenance, to study science in their houses of study, even though it was against their laws and customs, for *never did any Jew study in that house of study*. In addition, that same duke gave us our meals every year, so that we could satisfy our desires. And in truth, the sages of that house of study showed us great honour, and every day they would dispute with us regarding faith, with wit and at great length as is their custom, *and sometimes they reviled us*, saying, 'Where is your wisdom and intelligence, for it has already been taken from you, for there is no one who knows anything among you? And there is no knowledge or wisdom among you, acknowledge that, and know well that there is no God among you, and therefore your wisdom is lost and degenerate . . .'. And were it not for the grace of God and his help, we would not have been able to raise our heads and answer them anything, for we had no experience of disputes of that kind although we were, thank God, learned in biblical verses, and passages from the Gemara, and *midrashim*. In any event, *in disputes with them we were weak*. Then I was possessed by a spirit of zeal, zeal for the Lord of Hosts, and I swore to the Mighty One of Jacob that I would not rest, or lie on a bed, or give sleep to my eyes, or slumber to my eyelids, until I had written, with God's help, a general work containing much wisdom and knowledge, to answer my revilers and to show them that wisdom was not given to them alone.[20]

This is not a case of dramatic cultural change, where the majority of Jews suddenly abandoned traditions which, in Haym Soloveitchik's phrase, they had learned 'in mimetic fashion'[21]—but rather a slow transition from oral to literary culture. The Hebrew and Yiddish poet Abraham Ber Gottlober (1810–99), for example, records in his memoirs that many Jewish women in the second half of the nineteenth century would still gather around one woman who could read Yiddish, and she would preach to them from a book she was holding, giving them moral lessons and telling tales that were common in popular literature.[22] According to the autobiographical account of S. Y. Agnon in *Mi'atsmi el atsmi* (From Me to Myself), the same custom existed in his childhood in Buczacz in Poland at the end of the nineteenth

---

Modern Jewry 1700–1815, 150. See also the letter of Moses Mendelssohn, the father of the Haskalah movement in Germany in the 18th century, to Naphtali Herz Homberg, according to which three callings are open to Jews: the study of medicine, engaging in commerce, or begging for charity. See Bernfeld, *Generation of Upheavals* (Heb.), ii. 12.

[20] *Ma'aseh tuviyah*, introduction.   [21] Soloveitchik, 'Rupture and Reconstruction', 65–7.
[22] Gottlober, *Zikhronot umasa'ot*, i. 165.

century.[23] The scholar Shmuel Werses has published an important article with further evidence on the subject from maskilim such as Samuel Fuenn and the author Mendele Mokher Seforim; he also discusses changing attitudes to women's right to education and knowledge, and women writers. Elsewhere he comments in detail on the ambivalent attitude of Haskalah writers to Yiddish.[24]

Not enough attention has been paid to the important material gathered by Azriel Shohet on methods of education in eighteenth-century Ashkenazi society, including information on the extent and depth of knowledge of reading among women, and men from the middle class and from the masses. Shohet was the first to make extensive use of the critical remarks of an important rabbi of that generation, Yehiel Mikhel Epstein. Epstein was aware of the spiritual needs of a growing number of people who could read Yiddish but did not understand Hebrew well, so he wrote books in Yiddish that would give them the information they sought on religious customs and prayer.[25] Shohet was also the first to make use of the diary of the merchant Isaac Wetzler, the *Libes briv*, which was written in Yiddish and which contains important information on education and literacy among his contemporaries.[26] Although

[23] See Agnon, *From Me To Myself* (Heb.), 364–5; this point was made to me by Shmuel Werses.

[24] Werses, 'The Voice of Women in the Yiddish Weekly *Kol hamevaser*' (Heb.), 55–7; id., 'The Right Hand Pushes Away, the Left Hand Brings Close', 9–49. In the second half of the 19th and in the early 20th centuries a change took place in the cultural life of Jews, especially in the larger cities. On events in Warsaw and, among other things, the reading of books, see Shatzky, *History of the Jews of Warsaw* (Yid.), ii. 123–35, and esp. p. 134, on the reading habits of the masses who read Yiddish translations of the famous Arabic stories of *A Thousand and One Nights*, and more; Shatzky also provides information on around 100 to 150 subscribers to Haskalah books (p. 130), a topic mentioned below. See also the extensive discussion in Parush, *Reading Women* (Heb.) esp. pp. 136–73, and see Ch. 11 below at nn. 33–4. On Parush's book see also Ch. 9 n. 18 below. Among the articles in Werses, *Awaken, My People!* (Heb.), which had not previously been published there is an important contribution: 'The Jewish Maskil as a Young Man' (Heb.), in which he devotes much space to 'the reading of Haskalah books openly and in secret' and to 'methods of learning a foreign language': see pp. 88–101 and the additional bibliography there.

[25] On Yehiel Mikhel Epstein, author of the well-known *Kitsur shenei luḥot haberit* (The Two Tablets of the Covenant Abbreviated) and his activities, see Gries, *The Literature of Customs* (Heb.), 58–61, and the additional bibliography there.

[26] See Shohet, *With the Change of Epochs* (Heb.), 123–38, esp. pp. 124–6. A good edition of this, with an English translation and commentary, is *The Libes Briv of Isaac Wetzler*, ed. and trans. M. M. Faierstein (Atlanta, Ga., 1996).

Shohet does not mention it, Wetzler complains about women who have learned to read Yiddish and now eagerly read *Tsena urena*. One of them, opinionated and sure of herself, told him categorically that, according to *Tsena urena*, the prophet Jeremiah was descended from Rahab the prostitute.[27] Wetzler does not say that she discovered this because the author of *Tsena urena* based his remarks on Rashi's commentary on Jeremiah 1: 1, which in turn was based on an aggadah in chapter 18 of *Seder olam* (Order of the World) attributed to the second-century rabbi Yosei ben Halafta. He does say, however, that had that arrogant woman read a good Yiddish translation of the Bible such as that of Yekutiel Blitz (published in Amsterdam in 1679), her mind would not have been 'clouded with vain words'.[28]

Evidently, book readings were an important step in the transition to independent reading. This phenomenon had significant consequences: as the custom of reading aloud in public gained popularity, the vocabulary of the more intelligent listeners expanded; and as reading, especially in Yiddish, spread among the Jews, they acquired or consolidated cognitive skills. While I cannot deal in detail here with the process of learning to read and write, I should at least mention that the ability to read often preceded the ability to write and was not necessarily concomitant with it.[29]

These skills were of great importance to those who found themselves displaced during the migratory movements that, as can be deduced from the registers of the Council of the Four Lands and the Council of Lithuania, increased in Europe from the seventeenth century onwards on account of the economic and political instability affecting the area at that time.[30] Moreover, if we review the data on the origin of the Jews in German-speaking lands, which Azriel Shohet presents in his important book *With the Change of Epochs*, we find that most of the forerunners of emancipation there came from eastern Europe. The majority of these migrants, men and women alike,

[27]   See *Libes Briv*, Yiddish version, 49–50, and in English, 95–6.

[28]   On the translation of Yekutiel Blitz and another effort at translation by Alexander Vitzenhoyzn, see Erik, *History of Yiddish Literature* (Yid.), 230–9. For more on these and on translations of the Bible into Yiddish, see Turniansky, 'The History of the "Yiddish Translation of the Pentateuch"' (Heb.), 21–58, and esp. pp. 23–30.

[29]   See Stampfer, 'Knowledge of Reading and Writing Among the Jews of Eastern Europe in the Modern Period' (Heb.), 459–83. More generally, see Darnton, *The Kiss of Lamourette*, 154–87, and the bibliography there. See also n. 1 above.

[30]   Shulvass, *From East to West*, and see my comment in 'Between History and Literature', 117. See also Slutsky, 'Migration as a Factor in the History of the Jews' (Heb.), 67–79.

brought with them a certain level of popular cultural knowledge and experience. They succeeded, in the blink of an eye, historically speaking, in assimilating themselves to German culture, such that within less than a century they were making a major contribution to it.[31] It would seem that the huge burst of creativity among the Jews of the United States is to be explained in the same way. Their parents too had emigrated from eastern Europe but were quick to adapt to the new culture. The conclusion that can be drawn from this is that the idea that it was only the members of the rabbinical intelligentsia who were able to think analytically and creatively needs to be reappraised: it was these very abilities, heightened by exposure to books written in the vernacular, that permitted increasing numbers of ordinary Jews to integrate into the modern world.

As regards the circulation of printed literature aimed at the Jewish reading public there is no doubt that books in both Hebrew and Yiddish crossed national borders. The history of the book in the Jewish world must therefore be considered not in the context of those places where books were *printed*, but rather in relation to where they were *circulated*. Even so, the facts of their printing cannot be ignored. By my reckoning, more than half of the books printed for a Jewish market during the eighteenth century—5,870 out of a

[31] *With the Change of Epochs* (Heb.), 15–21. Shohet's data do not offer incontrovertible proof that the Jews had mastered the languages and literature of their surroundings; see ibid. 58–63.

[32] See Benayahu, 'The Transfer of the Centre of Printing from Venice to Amsterdam' (Heb.), 41–67. My estimate is about 5% lower than Vinograd's in *The Treasure of the Hebrew Book* (Heb.), vol. i, table 1, introd. 24–36, because I did not include second editions. The classification according to genre in Vinograd's index (i.e. vol. i), based on Darnton's definition ('History of Reading', 143–4), is too general to be adequate. For example, 'ethical literature' is given as a single category, with no reference to the many subgenres that can be identified, e.g. ethical wills; hagiography; sermons; ethical epistles; customs and etiquette; commentaries on biblical wisdom books (Job, Proverbs, Psalms and Ecclesiastes); commentaries on Tractate *Avot* (The Ethics of the Fathers); moral epigrams; comprehensive ethical works; ethical anthologies, etc. It is also unhelpful in that because under the heading for each type of literature, the reader is given only the names of the cities where books in that category were published and the number of books published there, rather than the actual titles; for these the reader must consult the entries for each city, as listed in Vinograd's vol. ii. Thus for example Vinograd has many entries for 'stories adapted from the Zohar' at i. 415, but examination of vol. ii shows that in the 18th century these were all editions of the same Yiddish work, *Ma'aseh adonai* (The Deeds of God), which includes, in some of its editions, also additional (i.e. non-Zoharic) sources. See Zfatman-Biler, *Narrative in Yiddish: Annotated Bibliography* (Heb.), 188. Similarly, with regard to travel books, an examination of the inventory of 18th-century print-

total of 9,060 titles—were printed in German-speaking areas: Germany, Moravia, and Holland.[32] The main centre for the printing of Jewish books during the eighteenth century was Amsterdam, where 1,597 titles were printed; most of these were intended for sale abroad, and especially in eastern Europe: demand here was great as Jewish printing had been in decline in Poland since the middle of the seventeenth century because the printers of Prague and Amsterdam were able to produce more attractive books more cheaply.[33] Thus, whereas the development of printing in Poland and Russia during the eighteenth century was a factor of importance for general cultural history, this development was of little relevance for the spread of knowledge in the Jewish world.[34]

ings reveals that there were only two such books, which were repeatedly reprinted: *Masa'ot binyamin mitudelah* (The Journeys of Benjamin of Tudela) and *Sibuvo shel r. petahyah miregensh-burg* (The Round Trip of Rabbi Petahyah of Regensburg). On the latter, see David, 'The Round Trip of Rabbi Petahyah of Regensburg in a New Version' (Heb.), 235–69. I have no wish to disparage Vinograd's pioneering work, but his indexes are not user-friendly. One must work hard, paging through the two volumes and the additional bibliographies, in order to find most of the titles of a given literary genre in a certain period. Moreover neither Vinograd nor Friedberg, author of an earlier major catalogue of Hebrew books, had ever actually seen many of the books to which they referred, but merely copied the data from existing sources. See Reiner's remarks in 'The Adventure in Bibliography' (Heb.), 9, who prematurely pinned his hopes on the 'processing of information' which this work would supposedly offer to scholars of culture in general and those of the history of the book in particular.

[33] See Shmeruk, *Yiddish Literature* (Heb.), 176–80. Below I discuss at greater length the cultural significance, and especially the circulation and reception, of Yiddish literature.

[34] See e.g. Marker, *Publishing, Printing and the Origins of Intellectual Life in Russia.* Moreover, Russia only began to give Jews permission to settle in the last quarter of the 18th century, when parts of Poland were annexed, a process completed with the annexation of the kingdom of Warsaw in 1815. There is thus little or nothing to look for of a Jewish nature in the cultural and social life of Russia during the 18th century and, *a fortiori*, no significant connection between printing in Russia and Jewish printing in Poland.

THREE

Elite Literature: Halakhic Works and Textual Commentaries

HALAKHIC AND TALMUDIC LITERATURE

This book is concerned primarily with literature other than the key works of halakhic and talmudic literature that form the main corpus of study in traditional Jewish education. I cannot, however, completely neglect the great changes that took place from the end of the seventeenth century through the eighteenth century in the methods of study and in the approach to the talmudic and halakhic texts that had moulded earlier generations.

Until the nineteenth century the Talmud was not sold as a single unit containing a complete set of tractates; the standard practice was to print it tractate by tractate, as required for study. The condition of the tractates that have come down to us from the late seventeenth and the eighteenth centuries, particularly from eastern Europe, is poor; this suggests that they were in short supply, with each copy being used by many students. This was because the Jewish printing houses in eastern Europe could not compete with those elsewhere during this period, and as books had to be imported they were in relatively short supply. Even so, this did not prevent the study of the traditional texts, and the development of new techniques for studying them. Since the sixteenth century the influence of the technique of meticulous examination of the text inspired by the writings of Solomon Luria (the Maharshal) had been spreading. As it spread, it developed into the logical method of disputation known as *pilpul* or *ḥilukim*—a degeneration, in the opinion of some rabbis.[1]

---

[1] See Rabinovits, *On the Printing of the Talmud* (Heb.); see also Heller, *Printing the Talmud*; Breuer, 'The Rise of *Pilpul*' (Heb.), 341–55; Ta-Shma, '*Tosefot gornish*', 153–61; Dimitrovsky, 'On

1. Title page for *Shulḥan arukh* (Mantua, 1721)

However, *pilpul* did not prevent the development of textual correction and emendation, editing, and close reading which are the basis of all critical study dating from the time of the yeshiva of the Maharshal.[2]

Examination of data published by Yeshayahu Vinograd confirms, despite the inevitable errors and omissions, that the spread of printing made it possible for many writers to make their work known. Books by the most important authors were reprinted frequently, enabling their expert knowledge on such subjects as the laws of ritual slaughter to be disseminated to a whole new generation.[3] The number of editions printed in some relevant categories is as follows:

	Pre-18th century	18th century
General halakhic works	319	303
Laws of *sheḥitah* (ritual slaughter)	105	97

There were also more new editions of commentaries on the *Shulḥan arukh* in the eighteenth century than in the entire period since it was first published in the sixteenth century:

	Pre-18th century	18th century
Commentaries on *Tur oraḥ ḥayim*	3	22
Commentaries on *Tur ḥoshen mishpat*	1	8
Commentaries on *Tur yoreh de'ah*	2	16
Commentaries on *Tur even ha'ezer*	2	6

A similar increase in the printing of commentaries on Maimonides' *Mishneh torah* in the eighteenth century, as well as of new editions of the work—a total of 34 in both categories combined, as against 6 in all the previous centuries—is evidence of increasing interest in this work at that time.

the Method of Pilpul' (Heb.), 111–81; Rappel, *The Dispute About Pilpul* (Heb.); and Reiner, 'Changes in the Yeshivas of Poland and Germany' (Heb.), 9–81, esp. p. 11 n. 3, where there is additional bibliography.

[2] On this see Kaufmann, *Die Familie Gomperz*. I am grateful to Professor Ya'akov Sussmann for bringing this important work to my attention.

[3] My discussion here is based on data in the first volume of Vinograd, *The Treasure of the Hebrew Book* (Heb.), i. 400–5, as reconciled with Friedberg, *The Library* (Heb.), and information compiled by the Hebrew Bibliography Project of the National and University Library in Jerusalem.

2. Title page for *Midrash rabot* (Sulzbach, 1755)

The growth in interest in commentaries on the Talmud is particularly striking, with 464 commentaries published in the eighteenth century as compared with 75 in the previous centuries. These figures underscore the most important change to take place in the world of rabbinic literature in the eighteenth century: the return to commentary on the talmudic text. This was a development comparable to the return, in the fifteenth century, of scholars of the Academy in Florence to commentary on classical Greek texts. It reflected a new emphasis on the part of the rabbis on encouraging the study of the Talmud, the most important canonical literary asset of the Jewish people and the key to its way of life.

This growing popular appeal of Talmud study is indicated by the increasing publication of *mishnayot* (subdivisions of tractates of the Mishnah). The number of editions published increased from 2 in the fifteenth century to 18 in the sixteenth, 53 in the seventeenth, and 65 in the eighteenth century, indicating that from the seventeenth century on, interest was extending beyond those learning in formal institutions.[4]

Interest in Midrash had begun earlier, in the sixteenth century, giving rise to many commentaries and to greater precision in the textual tradition. This in turn led to the consolidation of the midrashic text and its publication as the *Midrash rabah* in a format mirroring that of the printed editions of the Talmud, with the midrashic text framed by the most popular commentaries. But by the eighteenth century, interest was waning—or at least was not growing as fast as the interest in *mishnayot*: only 11 editions were printed, compared with the 26 editions printed prior to that.[5]

The reason for this was most probably that commentators and preachers could find all the midrashic material they needed in the anthologies of ethical literature that first appeared in the sixteenth century. These anthologies contained selections of midrashim organized by theme, saving people the effort of searching through the original midrashic texts in order to locate the sources

---

[4] Vinograd, *The Treasure of the Hebrew Book* (Heb.), i. 416. Sussmann, 'Manuscripts and Textual Traditions of the Mishnah' (Heb.), 215–50, states that, until the advent of printing, the Mishnah was studied as part of the process of studying the Talmud. Printing encouraged the publication of independent editions of the Mishnah and enlarged the circle of those studying it by itself as the circle of scholars also expanded. On the cultural implications of this development, see Gries, 'Between Literature and History' (Heb.), 155–6 and 174 n. 10.

[5] See my remarks in *The Literature of Customs* (Heb.), 71 and n. 106, and also Elbaum, *Openness and Insularity* (Heb.), 95–6, 118–27.

they sought. For about a hundred years, these anthologies seem to have satisfied the demand for midrashic material. Then, with the proliferation of commentators and preachers during the late seventeenth and eighteenth
centuries, partly as a result of Jewish migration to new areas and the establishment of new communities and partly as a result of social change and new
patterns of leadership, people sought more material than the old anthologies
could provide; interest in the original texts revived and new editions were
printed to meet the increased demand.[6]

BIBLE COMMENTARY AND HOMILETICS

For centuries, the only reading material available to the vast majority of Jews
who knew no languages other than Hebrew or Yiddish was the traditional
religious literature and the commentaries and homiletic texts that derived
from it. The literature circulating among the non-Jewish public by the seventeenth and eighteenth centuries, in contrast, bore the whiff of tantalizing new
worlds: scientific discoveries, folk tales, and chivalric romances, as well as
travel narratives and picaresque novels of an almost mythological character
such as *Don Quixote* and *Robinson Crusoe*. Jews had simply nothing comparable: virtually the only Jewish travel books published in the eighteenth century
were factual accounts: *The Travels of Benjamin of Tudela* and *The Round Trip of
Rabbi Petahyah of Regensburg*.[7] Their authors simply recorded descriptions of
their journeys; there were no imaginary heroes, through whose deeds readers
could experience exciting adventures, and whose only limits were those of
their authors' imaginations. When these roving heroes eventually found their
way into the Jewish literary repertoire in the eighteenth century through
Yiddish translations, they were eagerly devoured by a ravenous public that
included but was not limited to children and young people.

---

[6] See Gries, 'Between Literature and History' (Heb.), 157–8 and notes, 175–6 nn. 12–23.

[7] See above, Ch. 2 at nn. 8 and 32. It is no coincidence that Mendele Mokher Seforim called
the book about his picaresque and ridiculous protagonist *Masa'ot binyamin hashelishi* (The
Journeys of Benjamin the Third), for generations of readers in the 18th and 19th centuries were
nourished by *The Travels of Benjamin of Tudela*. On the travels of the second Benjamin,
see Gries, 'Definition of Shabatean Hagiographical Literature' (Heb.), 356–7 at n. 16, and the
bibliography there.

It would be a mistake, however, to assume that curiosity and an open-minded approach to the world led to the total abandonment of religious literature in favour of the new secular literature. Despite the availability of books in new genres, such as travelogues, the Jewish reading public maintained a constant and growing interest in traditional literature, such as commentaries on the Torah. The conservatism of the extensive adult reading audience, consisting mainly of men, was expressed in several ways. Thus, when Eleazar Zussman Rudelsum tried, in the mid-eighteenth century, to circulate a new systematic book for teaching the Torah in Hebrew, the response was not enthusiastic. In contrast, his more traditional text *Magishei minḥah*, on presenting offerings, saw 17 editions within a hundred years.[8]

Conservatism was not only evident in matters of education; it is also shown in the continued interest in the traditional commentaries on the Torah by scholars of greater and lesser reputation. Things began to change in the eighteenth century, however, with a growing interest in the publication of the genre of commentaries on commentaries (the technical term is 'supercommentaries'), particularly on the staple commentary on the Bible by the eleventh-century French commentator known as Rashi, and many such works circulated. Vinograd lists 26 editions in the eighteenth century, in contrast to 31 earlier printings. Comparison of the information in Friedberg's *The Library* with the data collected by Jacob Toledano and Israel Schapira identifies at least a further 13 different editions from the eighteenth century.[9] Judging from the number of eighteenth-century editions, however, the favourite book of this literary genre among the Jews of central and eastern Europe was the commentary of the Sephardi rabbi Elijah Mizrahi (*c*.1450–1526), *Peirush al peirush rashi al hatorah* (A Commentary on Rashi's Commentary on the Torah), first published in Venice in 1545.[10] Only one new edition of this work was published in the Mediterranean lands in the eighteenth century (as compared with four in central Europe), but the information I have gathered on the editions of supercommentaries and glosses published in the eighteenth century shows that nine of the twelve commentaries on this work published then were published

---

[8]   See Turniansky, '*Mikra mefurash* by Eleazar Zussman Rudelsum' (Heb.), 497–517.

[9]   See Toledano, *Canopy* (Heb.); Schapira, *Commentators on Rashi on the Pentateuch* (Heb.).

[10] Printed in Amsterdam, 1718, and in Constantinople in 1726 with the addition of *Naḥalat ya'akov* (The Inheritance of Jacob) by Jacob ben Benjamin Selnik; then in Zolkiew (1754), Fürth (1763), and Prague, in an abbreviated version called *Mizraḥi uma'aravi* (Eastern and Western), in 1793.

in Italy and the Ottoman empire, indicating that it must nevertheless have had a wide readership in those lands.[11]

In the context of study outside the yeshiva of commentaries and super-commentaries on the Torah, the study of Rashi was considered basic. A modest offshoot of this field was the supercommentaries on Abraham ibn Ezra (1089–1164), dating mainly from before the eighteenth century; however, these were regarded as less important and thus did not find their way into print.[12] In a similar vein, of the various attempts to interpret the secrets of Nahmanides' commentary on the Torah, which posed a challenge to kabbalists in the generations close to his lifetime—authors such as Bahya ben Asher, Meir ibn Sahula, or Isaac of Acre—only the work of Bahya ben Asher was committed to print. Few new works on Nahmanides' commentary appeared in subsequent generations, either in manuscript or in print, until the nineteenth and twentieth centuries.[13]

The commentators on Rashi, writing in Hebrew, developed a capacity for precision and for exegesis that was very different from the work of earlier sages. For example, the tenth-century scholars Sa'adiah Gaon, Samuel ben Hofni Gaon, and their associates, were an example (which remained unparalleled until modern times) of how it was possible, by means of a Torah commentary in a vernacular language (Judaeo-Arabic), to convey information to a broad reading public and discuss matters of faith and opinion, with an admix-

---

[11] In chronological order, the twelve editions published were: Solomon ben Abraham Algazi, *Shema shelomoh* (The Fame of Solomon; 1710); Vidal Zarfati, *Hasagot al perush haram* (Critiques on the Commentary of Haram; 1718); Jacob ben Yirmiyahu Ibn Naim, *Mishkenot ya'akov* (The Dwellings of Jacob; 1731); Levi ben Shelomo, *Ateret shelomoh* (The Crown of Solomon; 1739); Barzilai ben Barukh Ya'avets, *Leshon arumim* (The Language of the Cunning; 1747); Judah Ayash, *Lehem yehudah* (The Bread of Judah; 1748); Isaac Karbalio, *Sefer hazikhronot vehayei yitshak* (The Book of Remembrance and the Life of Isaac; 1761); Isaac Lombroso, *Zera yitshak* (The Seed of Isaac; 1768); Nathan ben Abraham Burgil, *Hok natan* (The Law of Nathan; 1776); Abraham Amarilio, *Berit avraham* (The Covenant of Abraham; 1796–1802); Judah Tanugi, *Erets yehudah* (The Land of Judah; 1797); Eliyahu ben Abraham Ventura, *Kokhba deshavit* (The Comet; 1799).

[12] See Ben-Menahem, 'Commentators on Ibn Ezra' (Heb.), 149–81.

[13] The only editions printed in the 18th century were: Samuel ben Abraham Zarfati, *Nimukei shemuel* (The Reasonings of Samuel; 1718); Bahya ben Asher, *Be'ur al hatorah* (Commentary on the Pentateuch; 1726); and *Kuntres harav shem tov gaon* (The Booklet of Rabbi Shem Tov Gaon), as transmitted by Rashba (Solomon ben Adret) and containing an interpretation of the secrets of the Torah of Nahmanides, in *Likutim mirav hai gaon* (A Compilation of Rav Hai Gaon's Writings; 1798).

ture of philosophy and the interpretation of dreams.[14] Their successors in writing Torah commentaries in the vernacular, however, adopted a very different approach. *Tsena urena*, for example, the sixteenth-century Yiddish commentary on the Bible intended for a broad readership—women as well as men who were outside the world of Torah study—gave readers a strong dose of legends and tall tales but a minimal amount of scientific or critical information of any kind.[15]

Some might argue that the publication of *Mikraot gedolot* (the text of the Bible printed together with digests of the most popular commentaries—Rashi, ibn Ezra, Nahmanides—abbreviated so that they could fit on the same page) would have had a deleterious effect on the publication of other Torah commentaries, but in my opinion they were intended for very different audiences. The purchasers of *Mikraot gedolot* were people whose demand for insights into the text was satisfied by an abridged and condensed version of the popular commentaries, whereas those who wished to delve more deeply into the sacred texts wanted to have the full versions of these works and other extensive commentaries; but the size of this latter group appears to have dwindled during the eighteenth century. In the nineteenth century, the renewed interest of Christian commentators and critics in the scriptural text led to a similar revival on the part of Jewish religious reformers, such as Moses Mendelssohn and his circle, the fathers of *Be'ur* (commentary from an Enlightenment perspective), and Abraham Geiger, one of the founders of the Wissenschaft des Judentums movement. In consequence, supporters of traditional approaches rose up in opposition and produced their own new commentaries on the Torah. Among them were Samson Raphael Hirsch, who also wrote in German, as well as scholars who wrote in Hebrew: Meir Loeb ben Jehiel Michael (the Malbim); Meir Simhah Hacohen of Dvinsk (author of *Meshekh hokhmah*—The Pouch of Wisdom—and *Or same'ah*—Joyous Light); Naphtali Zvi Yehuda Berlin of Volozhin (author of *Hamek davar*—Search the Matter Profoundly); and Jacob Zvi Mecklenburg (author of

[14] There has been no in-depth critical academic discussion of the contribution of biblical commentaries to the dissemination of traditional norms, ideas, and attitudes through the ages, either from a Sephardi perspective, from the time of Sa'adiah Gaon onwards, or from an Ashkenazi perspective, from the time of Rashi onwards.

[15] On the history and many editions of *Tsena urena*, as well as on the linguistic changes that editors introduced over the generations in order to make it appropriate for its readers at a particular time and place, see Shmeruk, *Yiddish Literature in Poland* (Heb.), 147–64.

Haketav vehakabalah—The Writing and the Tradition). In addition to these there is *Mikra kifeshuto* (The Bible According to its Plain Meaning), a book written by Arnold Ehrlich under the pseudonym Shabetai ibn Boded and later published under his own name in an expanded German version.

An interesting offshoot of the supercommentaries on the Torah is the rather more homiletic Torah discourse or sermon. According to Vinograd's list,[16] there was again an increase in the number of these published in the eighteenth century compared to earlier periods, as the following figures show:

	Pre-18th century	18th century
(*a*) Discourses following the order of the *parashiyot*	49	114
(*b*) Discourses for festive occasions and eulogies	43	74
(*c*) Other discourses	17	32

Although collections of rabbinical discourses in which sermons on the Torah are central (*a* above) appear to have been less popular in the eighteenth century than new commentaries on the Talmud by a factor of almost one to four (114 versus 464 editions), this is a somewhat problematic comparison since in practice it is often difficult to distinguish between rabbinical discourses on the Torah and commentaries on the Torah, which Vinograd lists separately. His figures show that the number of editions published decreased from 86 prior to the eighteenth century (12 in the fifteenth century, 52 in the sixteenth, and 22 in the seventeenth), to 33 in the eighteenth century.[17]

Even if the two above categories—Torah discourses and Torah commentaries—are combined, however, we see that new commentaries on the Talmud were still much more numerous than commentaries and sermons on the Torah. Are these figures sufficient to enable us to conclude that there were indeed far more regular readers and students of the Talmud than readers of discourses, commentaries, and supercommentaries on the Torah? I doubt it. In my view we are dealing with two distinct groups. The increasingly numerous groups of people who avidly read Torah discourses and commentaries belonged mainly to a stratum of Jewish society which, even if fairly learned in comparison with the broad masses, did not themselves aspire to the writing of commentaries. The availability of the literature they were interested in encouraged them to read more, but not to write. In this they differed from those

---

[16] *The Treasure of the Hebrew Book* (Heb.), i. 397–8.   [17] Ibid. 422.

who were interested in the new commentaries on the Talmud. The latter were unquestionably members of the learned stratum of society, which was a small minority of the reading public. Such people saw the expansion of printing and the decreased cost of producing books as an opportunity to communicate their own ideas to their contemporaries and to succeeding generations, and it is for this reason that the number of books they published was so great.

FOUR

Ethical Literature in Hebrew and Yiddish

JEWISH ETHICAL LITERATURE, which includes a number of different genres, began to appear in the tenth century under the influence of similar literature from Islam. Like Judaism, Islam is a religion of law, making it easy for the rabbis to adopt Islamic literary models and to fill them with content from Jewish sources and traditions. From this basis, Jewish ethical literature developed to include a broad spectrum of genres: wills, handbooks of recommended behaviour, hagiographies, epistles, anthologies of ethical ideas, proverbs, sermons, and polemics, as well as commentaries on books of the Bible deemed to offer moral lessons, such as Job, Proverbs, Psalms, and Ecclesiastes. Within this spectrum, rabbinic, philosophical, and kabbalistic approaches were all represented. This marvellous literature, which has been in existence now for more than a thousand years, is a source of encouragement and solace for many Jews. It is also a source for many folk religious customs that have their origin in tales, legends, and parables.

It is worth emphasizing that Jews did not have any collections of purely secular stories until the second half of the seventeenth century. These early publications were mainly in Yiddish; it was not until the end of the eighteenth century that such works began to be published in Hebrew. Prior to the mid-seventeenth century, then, the only books available for those who wanted to read material that was literary rather than strictly religious were works of an ethical nature.[1] True, some works of a more religious nature also contained parables and stories, beginning with kabbalistic commentaries on the Bible

---

[1] See the extensive treatment of this subject in Dan and Tishby, *Selected Ethical Literature* (Heb.), and also my remarks on page 104 below.

(of which the Zohar is a prime example); and similarly, in the sixteenth century, Jacob ibn Habib compiled a collection of stories from the Talmud called *Ein ya'akov* (The Spring of Jacob). However, these works were written for the most part in high rabbinic Hebrew or Aramaic, and were thus inaccessible to the majority of the reading public because their Jewish education and literary skills were insufficient to allow them to read such works.

As the changes that occurred in the eighteenth century meant that literacy was no longer restricted only to a privileged elite, people began writing books that would appeal to this wider readership; it is no coincidence that at the end of the century popular homiletic books became more numerous. An example is the work of Jacob Kranz, the Magid of Dubno; his books were the first commentaries on the Torah to contain homilies and short stories written to appeal to the new readership.

Against this background it is particularly interesting to examine the circulation of ethical literature in Hebrew and Yiddish during the eighteenth century. Vinograd's lists as published in *The Treasure of the Hebrew Book* separate secondary genres of ethical literature, such as wills and manuals of recommended conduct, from the primary genres, and frequently books that undoubtedly ought to have been included in a secondary genre of their own —such as abridged editions of ethical works—have disappeared entirely.[2] According to Vinograd, however, whereas 285 ethical works were published before the eighteenth century, 516 were published in the course of that century. But this is not the full picture. A close inspection shows that works published in Yiddish hold pride of place, and foremost among these is *Lev tov* (A Good Heart) by Isaac ben Eliakim of Posen.[3]

I have mentioned elsewhere that ethical works of a kabbalistic nature, most of which were written in Safed during the sixteenth century, were first published mostly in Italy and Turkey in the sixteenth and early seventeenth

[2] See the list of abbreviated books in the index of Gries, *Literature of Customs* (Heb.), 399–400.

[3] On *Lev tov* see Erik, *History of Yiddish Literature* (Yid.), 291–304. According to Vinograd, 24 different editions of this book were printed during the 18th century; according to *The Library* the number was 23. On another popular book, *Simḥat hanefesh* (The Joy of the Soul) by Elhanan Kirchan, see Erik, *History of Yiddish Literature*, 301–9, and Zinberg, *The History of Jewish Literature* (Heb.), iv. 103–7, and 144–8, where he discusses the second part of the book, which is entirely different in character. According to Vinograd, 18 different editions of *Simḥat hanefesh* were published during the 18th century (*The Library*'s figure is 11).

3. Title page for *Menorat hama'or* (Amsterdam, 1722)

centuries and then published again only a hundred years later, in the eighteenth century.[4] These books included *Sefer ḥaredim* (The Book of Those Who Fear God) a short guide for people striving to achieve communion with God by Eleazer Azkari (Venice, 1601; Constantinople, 1753); *Igeret shemuel* (The Epistle of Samuel), a mystical commentary by Samuel Ozeidah, a disciple of Isaac Luria, on the book of Ruth (Constantinople, 1597; Amsterdam, 1712); and his *Leḥem dimah*, a mystical commentary on the book of Lamentations (Venice 1600; Amsterdam, 1710). Especially prominent in this category is *Reshit ḥokhmah* (The Beginning of Wisdom) by Elijah de Vidas, an anthology of texts arranged by subject. First published in Venice in 1579, it was then published twice more before the end of the sixteenth century—in Venice again, in 1593, and in Cracow, also in 1593. In the seventeenth century it was published only once (Constantinople, 1660), but in the eighteenth century it was published in 17 editions, half of them in eastern Europe in the latter half of the century, after the recovery of Jewish printing there. This increase partly reflects the growing demand for the printed word as books became cheaper, but in the particular case of *Reshit ḥokhmah* it also reflects the expansion of the hasidic movement as hasidic preachers in particular frequently used this work in preparing their sermons.

Anthologies like *Reshit ḥokhmah* constituted a genre of ethical literature that flourished because of the great riches it offered people who needed to write sermons and rabbinical discourses. Another example is *Menorat hama'or* (The Lamp of the Light) by Isaac Aboab, first published in 1514 in Constantinople, with a further 37 further editions appearing before the end of the eighteenth century.[5] It was an abridged version of a work of the same title by Israel Al-Nakawa which remained in a manuscript form until the twentieth century when Heiman Gershom Henelau published it in four volumes (New York, 1929–32). A small extract of Al-Nakawa's work was copied by de Vidas and printed at the end of *Reshit ḥokhmah*;[6] it was only two chapters of the many that Al-Nakawa wrote. The most widely circulated of the anthologies was *Shevet musar* (The Staff of Morality), by the prolific author Eliyahu

---

[4] See Gries, 'Between Literature and History' (Heb.), 158, 175–6 nn. 17–23.

[5] This book was printed in many editions, notably in Amsterdam in the 18th century. See Gries, *Literature of Customs* (Heb.), pp. xviii, 54 n. 56.

[6] On its abbreviation as *Sefer hamusar* (The Book of Ethics) by Judah Khalaz, see Ya'ari, *Hebrew Printing in Constantinople* (Heb.), 22, 94–5 (no. 124).

Hacohen Ha'itamari, who was suspected of Shabateanism.[7] According to Friedberg, after the first edition was published in Amsterdam in 1712 a further 17 editions appeared in the course of the eighteenth century; according to Vinograd, there were 33 editions in Hebrew or Yiddish.

Ethical literature of a lighter nature was also popular, particularly during the eighteenth century. According to Vinograd's listings, *Orḥot tsadikim* (Paths of the Righteous), also known as *Sefer midot* (Book of Virtues) in its bilingual Hebrew–Yiddish version,[8] was printed in 27 editions during the eighteenth century, and only 10 times prior to that. According to Friedberg there were 13 Hebrew editions, 2 in Hebrew with a Yiddish supplement, and 3 in Yiddish only.

Another much-loved book was *Sefer hayashar* (The Book of the Upright), which has been attributed to a number of authors, including Rabenu Tam and Jonah Gerondi.[9] According to Vinograd, it was published 6 times before and 13 times during the eighteenth century; according to Friedberg, there were 6 editions before the eighteenth century and 11 during it.

These books, which had been cherished by previous generations, were not intended to disseminate customs but rather to combine the discussion of certain moral virtues, according to the teachings of the sages, with stories and fables. They were widely considered as worthy books to be read in idle moments—at home, in one's shop, or while travelling—to prevent distraction by sinful thoughts. The same role was also successfully filled by miniature (and thus highly portable) editions of the book of Psalms and other ethical works, which also became popular at this time.

It is not possible to discuss in this brief survey all the various genres of ethical literature and characterize their appearance and use, or their reception by the reading public, particularly in eastern Europe, during the eighteenth century. It is clear, however, that works in certain literary genres grew rapidly in popularity and were therefore published more frequently during the eighteenth century than in earlier periods. An example of this is the interest in wills. Although they did not make history or shape the behaviour of the

[7] See Scholem, 'R. Eliyahu Hacohen Haitamari and Shabateanism' (Heb.), 451–70.

[8] See my remarks on this book in *Literature of Customs* (Heb.), 14 n. 56 and the references there to the works of Pachter, Halamish, and Shohet.

[9] See *Literature of Customs* (Heb.), 23 n. 194 and the additional bibliography there.

masses, they sometimes included details of burial customs and ceremonies for the dead which are of interest to those studying the spread of such customs.[10]

Among the more popular and widely circulated books we must also include bilingual editions of laws and customs in Hebrew and Yiddish, a phenomenon that dates from the end of the sixteenth century.[11] As in other bilingual volumes, there is great disparity between the elevated style of the Hebrew and the popular tone of the Yiddish. They were directed at two different readerships: the Hebrew was for educated people, while the Yiddish was for those without a formal education. (Members of these separate audiences were likely to be living under a single roof as man and wife.) The eighteenth and nineteenth centuries saw many editions of such volumes; the great demand for them can be illustrated with reference to two: *Kav hayashar* (The Honest Measure), an ethical work by Tsevi Hirsh Koidonover (d. 1712) that was published in Frankfurt am Main in 1706, and *Sefer haḥayim* (The Book of Life), by Simon Frankfurt, which was published in Amsterdam in 1703.

Koidonover, the author of *Kav hayashar*, was influenced by *Yesod yosef* (The Foundation of Joseph), the work of Joseph ben Yehuda Yudl of Dubno (greatgrandfather of the Jewish historian Simon Dubnow), which he knew in manuscript form. (It was eventually published in Shklov in 1785.) Because of the important information *Kav hayashar* contains about changes in the lives of the Jews, Azriel Shohet made use of it in his important study *With the Change of Epochs* about the beginnings of the Haskalah in Germany.[12] According to Vinograd, 11 bilingual editions of *Kav hayashar* were printed in the eighteenth century, plus 8 editions in Yiddish and 8 in Hebrew—a total of 27 editions. Vinograd chose to end his listing of books in 1863. However, a comparison with Friedberg's data reveals that, for the nineteenth century, 8 bilingual Yiddish–Hebrew editions are listed, 2 in Yiddish alone, 2 bilingual editions with Ladino, and 24 Hebrew editions—a total of 36. Neither Vinograd nor Friedberg saw the books they listed with their own eyes; their listings are based on catalogues and earlier lists. From their lists, it certainly seems that the eighteenth century was a period when bilingual editions flourished, as

---

[10] See *Literature of Customs* (Heb.), 51–3 and additional bibliography. Avriel Bar-Levav has written about the literature of wills: see his 'Rabbi Aaron Berakhyah of Modena and Rabbi Naphtali Hacohen Katz' (Heb.), 201, and id., 'Jewish Ethical Wills as Egodocuments'.

[11] See Gries, *Literature of Customs* (Heb.), 59–62.

[12] See Shohet, *With the Change of Epochs* (Heb.), index s.v. Koidonover, 341.

4. Title page for *Kav hayashar* (Koshtandina, 1732)

opposed to the nineteenth century, when Hebrew editions predominated; but until the books themselves can actually be inspected it is impossible to be certain. The National and University Library in Jerusalem does not contain copies of all the books listed (and nor does any other single collection), so it will take a great deal of work before a definitive pronouncement can be made.

A second bilingual (Hebrew–Yiddish) book in great demand (as exemplified by the number of editions) is *Sefer haḥayim*,[13] a book intended to help those caring for the sick and advise those dealing with the dead. In the eighteenth century this book was printed in 15 bilingual editions, 2 Yiddish editions and 8 Hebrew editions—a total of 25 editions. During the nineteenth century, however, there appear to have been significant changes in demand, in consequence of which there were 3 Hebrew–German editions,[14] 1 Hebrew–Dutch edition,[15] 1 Hebrew–English edition,[16] 1 Hebrew–Yiddish edition,[17] and 9 monolingual Hebrew editions. Again, only inspection of actual copies can confirm the accuracy of this information so I refrain from drawing firm conclusions from these data.

In the sources we have listing publications of ethical literature, commentaries on Proverbs and Ecclesiastes are grouped together with commentaries on the Ethics of the Fathers (*Pirkei avot*). Detailed examination, however, shows that the number of ethical works written as commentaries on Proverbs and Ecclesiastes is minuscule compared to the number of commentaries on *Pirkei avot*. I have noted elsewhere in this context that the streams of commentators who followed in the footsteps of Maimonides and of Rashi were less concerned with variant readings of the text and emendations than with eliciting moral lessons.[18]

It is difficult to determine from Vinograd's lists (which are arranged by place of printing), the number of editions of commentary on *Pirkei avot*, and for this one must consult the lists of Isaac Joseph Kohen.[19] My own research suggests that one commentary was printed in the fifteenth century, 14 in the sixteenth century, 10 in the seventeenth century, 32 in the eighteenth century,

---

[13] See Bar-Levav, 'On the Concept of Death in *Sefer haḥayim*' (Heb.); the dissertation also considers the many bilingual editions of this work.

[14] Frankfurt am Main, 1834; Hanover, 1863; Fürth, 1865.

[15] Amsterdam, 1851.   [16] London, 1847.   [17] Sulzbach, 1837.

[18] See the appendix to Gries, 'Rabbi Israel ben Shabetai of Kozienice' (Heb.), 163–4.

[19] See Kohen, '*The Ethics of the Fathers*' (Heb.), 104–17, 277–85. I compared his listings with those of the Hebrew Bibliography Project of the National and University Library in Jerusalem.

and 84 in the nineteenth century. Thus, although there was a decided increase in the popularity of such works during the eighteenth century, the peak of their popularity came later; and only in the nineteenth century do we find titles being printed in multiple editions. Foremost among these is *Midrash shemuel* (The Midrash of Samuel) by Samuel Ozeidah of Safed, who anthologized the most popular commentaries on *Pirkei avot* and added his own incisive and rather pleasing commentary.[20]

Similar popularity was accorded to the works of Ozeidah's contemporary, Moses Alsheikh, who was also from Safed,[21] and to the work *Derekh hayim* (Way of Life) by the sixteenth-century rabbi of Prague, Judah Loew ben Bezalel (known as the Maharal).[22] It should also be pointed out that most editions of commentaries on *Pirkei avot* during the eighteenth century were printed in towns in German-speaking lands, including Amsterdam and Prague—due to the decline in Poland's importance as a centre of Jewish printing at that time. Commentaries on *Pirkei avot* were always popular because of the widespread custom of studying one chapter each week on Shabbat afternoons between Pesach and Shavuot, and rabbis always liked to consult new sources in preparing their public discourses.[23] In any event, like the early ethical works mentioned above, works offering moral insights and explanations of the ethical injunctions of *Pirkei avot* were undoubtedly favoured reading material. Both genres were part of a body of literature intended to offer its readers spiritual sustenance and help them overcome human weaknesses so they could maintain the high ethical standards of a Jewish way of life. Some commentators derived their approach from medieval philosophy and others from kabbalah, but in the main they related directly to the tradition of the sages and the rabbis from the Midrash on the tractate from the *Avot derabi natan* (The Fathers According to Rabbi Nathan) onwards.

Another important genre of Jewish ethical literature was the letter or epistle conveying moral or other didactic messages. From the sixteenth century on, under the influence of Italian humanism, Jews made use of epistles, especially as a tool for teaching the correct path of action in a variety of cir-

---

[20] By my count, 14 editions of *Midrash shemuel* appeared during the 19th century.

[21] Though in far fewer editions. By my count, three editions were printed during the 19th century.   [22] By my count, five editions were printed in the 19th century.

[23] See Sharvit, 'The Custom of Reading *The Ethics of the Fathers* on Shabbat' (Heb.), 169–78.

cumstances.[24] In eighteenth-century Europe the epistle formed the basis of a new literary genre, the epistolary novel. In the Jewish community the latter genre did not develop, but collections of epistles were certainly published for educational purposes (viz. as a guide to how to write different sorts of letters to a variety of recipients), as polemical tools (for example, in response to the vicissitudes of the Shabatean movement), or as a way of conveying the experience of divine revelation. A prime example of the latter category is the well-known letter from Israel Ba'al Shem Tov, the founder of hasidism, to his brother-in-law, Gershon of Kutow, which was first printed at the end of Jacob Joseph of Polonnoye's *Ben porat yosef* (Joseph Is a Fruitful Bough).[25]

According to detailed lists prepared by Dov Rappel,[26] a total of 19 epistolary collections were published by collectors in the eighteenth century, including those published for purposes of instruction. In the nineteenth century, however, there was a huge increase in the publication of works of this genre; as the Haskalah movement gained strength and attempted to spread its message to the masses, some 80 such collections were published, most of them new titles.

One needs to be wary in interpreting these figures, however; they are less indicative of popular demand than of the intense efforts of a small group of people determined to spread their new ideology. Although not a few respectable scholars seem to think that the sheer number of books published —especially in eastern Europe, or in western Europe for an east European readership—indicates their broad influence, I am not convinced. The fact is that during most of the nineteenth century the maskilim did not even manage to persuade the government school system newly established for Jews in Russia to accept their approach, despite its predisposition to the Haskalah ideology; it is unlikely that they would have had much influence on the traditionally educated Jewish masses. On the contrary: the multiplicity of titles, with no repeated editions, proves only that this was a propaganda exercise, not that the propaganda was effective.

[24] See Gries, *Book, Scribe, and Story* (Heb.), 31–2, 117–18 nn. 80–1.

[25] Korets, 1781. This letter has been discussed at length by scholars. Idel, *Hasidism: Between Ecstasy and Magic*, 291–2 n. 202 (Hebrew edn pp. 147–8 n. 196), mentions most of the scholarship on this subject, including further bibliography. See also the discussion in Gries, 'The Historical Figure of the Besht', 418–20, where further bibliography is listed. In addition, see Rozhni, 'The Epistle on the Elevation of the Soul by Rabbi Israel Ba'al Shem Tov' (Heb.).

[26] See Rappel, 'Bibliography of Jewish Letter Collections' (Heb.), 53–79, 134–62; id., 'On the Literature of Letter Collections' (Heb.), 119–35.

It must also be borne in mind that figures on the printing of Jewish books in general during the nineteenth century, and especially in the main centres of Jewish printing—Vilna, Lemberg, and Warsaw—demonstrate unequivocally that Haskalah books of various types and genres, though mostly in Hebrew, were a drop in the ocean compared to traditional Jewish literature. The only secular literature which had a major influence on the masses during the nineteenth century was in Yiddish, especially during the second half of that century and towards its end, and in the 1880s Yiddish fiction positively flourished. I shall return to this subject in Part II.

FIVE

On Libraries Private and Public

THE INCREASED AVAILABILITY of printed books brought with it an increase in the number of libraries, both private and institutional.

The growth of private Jewish libraries consequent on the spread of printed books is, unfortunately, an area in which little information is available. However, the published will of the eighteenth-century rabbi Pinhas Katzenellenbogen, who served in communities in east Galicia, southern Germany, and Moravia, which appeared at the beginning of his auto-biographical work *Yesh manḥilin* (There Are Bequeathers), shows that he purchased books, that he gave them to his son, and that he bequeathed them to his wife. This suggests that he saw them as valuable belongings and not only as a vehicle for study. One can assume that it was because he saw books in this way that he owned several editions of important works as well as manuscripts.[1]

The catalogue of books in Katzenellenbogen's library gives us information both about the extent to which ethical literature in Hebrew had penetrated Jewish communities and about how far Yiddish literature and kabbalistic works had expanded their readership. Most were talmudic and halakhic works, but a considerable number were neither required reading in the estab-lished system of Torah study nor the halakhic works favoured by scholars: there were also kabbalistic works, ethical works, and books in Yiddish. His holdings in these latter categories are summarized below. The list of works in Yiddish shows that literature generally regarded as being aimed at women and children was nevertheless important enough for an eighteenth-century rabbi to list in his library. However, while these books may indeed have been read by

[1] Katzenellenbogen's *Yesh manḥilin* (There Are Bequeathers) is a goldmine still awaiting researchers, and the late Yizhak Feld, who edited it, has earned our gratitude.

other members of Rabbi Katzenellenbogen's household, it would be wrong to think that the contents of a collector's library would accurately reflect the type of books that were read by the Jewish masses. Even so, the relatively large number of more popular pamphlets and books in Katzenellenbogen's library—ninety-three, to be precise—does tell us that the interest in such publications was not necessarily limited to the lower strata of Jewish society. Likewise, the availability of books in Yiddish describing and explaining various rituals and other customs of kabbalistic origins would have undoubtedly influenced the spirituality of the members of the household as they related to actions that were part and parcel of everyday life. Conversely, the fact that kabbalistic works were technically available to the women and children of the household does not mean that they necessarily read them; in any case they would probably not have had the linguistic skills to cope with the rather esoteric style.

PINHAS KATZENELLENBOGEN'S LIBRARY

The books in Katzenellenbogen's library are to be found in his autobiographical work *Yesh manhilin* (There Are Bequeathers); I used Feld's 1986 edition of this work. The categories below are my own, and within each category I have arranged the works alphabetically for ease of reference. The page and item numbers and other locational identifiers are from Feld's edition; note that several works may share the same page and item numbers because they are listed in the same place. Where I have been able to find additional information on the editions cited it is given in square brackets.

Ethical Books

Derekh tov (The Right Way) [(Fürth, 1697)]: p. 51, foot of page.

Even bohan (The Touchstone) [by Kalonymos ben Kalonymos; according to its place in the lists, apparently an edition with a translation into Yiddish (Sulzbach, 1705)]: p. 50, no. 122.

Hovot halevavot (Duties of the Heart): p. 42, no. 12, bound with *Vayakhel moshe* (And Moses Convened) [by Moses Alpeles (Venice, 1597)], a book of sermons. Among the books he gave to his son. *Another copy* p. 48, no. 28; *another copy* p. 48, no. 52, bound with *Ruah hen* (Spirit of Grace) [an explanation of philosophical words and concepts by Y. ibn Tibbon].

Igeret ba'alei ḥayim (Epistle of the Animals) [by Kalonymos ben Kalonymos; according to its place in the lists, it was apparently an edition with a translation into Yiddish (Hanau, 1718)]: p. 50. no. 122.

Igeron yehudit [apparently a collection of letters in Yiddish—*a brivshteler*, the name of which is not listed]: p. 51, foot of page.

Kitsur ma'avar yabok (an abridged version of The Crossing of the Yabok): p. 49, no. 65.

Kitsur shenei luḥot haberit (an abridged version of The Two Tablets of the Covenant) [by Yehiel Mikhel Epstein]: p. 43, no. 30. Among the books he gave to his son. *Another copy* p. 49, no. 64, printed in Fürth; *another copy* p. 49, no. 65.

Kur lezahav (Melting Pot for Gold) [an abridged version of *Mivḥar hapeninim* (The Choicest of Pearls)]: p. 42, no. 14. Among the books he gave to his son.

Masa gei ḥizayon (Journey into the Valley of Vision) [an ethical poem, apparently the edition of Riva di Trento, 1560]: p. 51, no. 74.

Menorat hamaor (The Lamp of the Light) with the commentary *Nefesh yehudah* (Soul of Judah): p. 42, no. 15. Among the books he gave to his son. *Another copy* p. 51, no. 59.

Meshal hakadmoni (The Parable of the Ancient): p. 51, no. 90.

Midrash shemuel (The Midrash of Samuel) [by Samuel Ozeida]: p. 46, no. 112.

Mivḥar hapeninim (The Choicest of Pearls): p. 51, no. 81.

Orḥot tsadikim (The Ways of the Righteous): p. 51, foot of page.

Reshit ḥokhmah (The Beginning of Wisdom): p. 42, no. 8. Among the books he gave to his son. *Another copy* p. 50, no. 16.

Sefer hamusar (The Book of Ethics) [by Yehuda Khalaz; an abbreviated version of *Menorat hamaor* by Israel Al-Nakawa]; p. 49, no. 83.

Sefer ḥasidim (The Book of the Pious): p. 49, no. 99.

Sefer hayashar (The Book of the Upright), attributed to Rabenu Tam: p. 49, no. 100.

Sefer hista'arut (The Book of Assault) (Amsterdam, 1737): p. 49, no. 105.

5. Title page for *Sefer karnayim* (Zolkiew, 1709)

Sha'arei teshuvah (The Gates of Repentance) by Jonah Gerondi: p. 49, no. 99.

Shevet musar (The Staff of Instruction):   p. 49, no. 93.

Tsori hayagon (The Balm of Grief) [by Shem Tov ben Falaquera; apparently an edition with the Epistle of Nahmanides (Hanau, 1713)]: p. 51, no. 76.

Yesh nohalin (There Are Inheritors): p. 48, no. 55.

Yoreh hataim (Instructor of Sins): p. 51, foot of page.

Kabbalistic Books

Asarah ma'amarot (Ten Sayings): p. 48, no. 26.

Avodat hamikdash (The Temple Service) [by the Rama (R. Menahem Azariah) of Fano and M. De Lonzano, apparently printed in Fürth, 1726]: p. 50, no. 45.

Berit menuhah (The Covenant of Rest): p. 49, no. 70.

Derekh hayim (The Way of Life) [the *Shulhan arukh* for wayfarers (Sulzbach, 1713)]: p. 49, no. 90.

Erev yom kipur katan (Minor Yom Kippur Eve): p. 51, no. 102.

Igeret hatiyul (The Epistle of the Journey): p. 51, no. 105.

Kavanot ha'ari (Meditations of the Ari): p. 47, nos. 14–17. *Another copy* p. 48, no. 36; *another copy* p. 48, no. 55.

Livyat hen (A Graceful Wreath) [abridged version of *Ma'avar yabok*, apparently printed in Hanau, 1744]: p. 51, no. 69.

Magid meisharim (Who Announces What Is True): p. 48, no. 28.

Megaleh amukot (Revealer of the Depths): p. 43, no. 33. Among the books he gave to his son. *Another copy* p. 49, no. 64.

Mekor hokhmah ve'imrei binah (The Source of Wisdom and Sayings of Intelligence) [on the Zohar, by Yissakhar Beer of Kremenets]: p. 48, no. 29.

Me'orot natan (The Lamps of Nathan) [= *Me'orei or* (Lamps of Light) by M. Poppers]: p. 48, no. 28.

Migdol david (The Tower of David) [a kabbalistic commentary on Ruth by David Lida, 1680]: p. 50, no. 116.

Mishnat ḥasidim (The Doctrine of the Pious) [by Immanuel Hai Riki]: p. 50, no. 17. *Another copy* p. 50, no. 18. Prayers with hasidic teachings.

Ne'edar bakodesh im sefer yetsirah (Glorious in Sanctity *with* The Book of Creation) [*Ne'edar bakodesh* is *Idra raba* from the Zohar arranged for reading on Shavuot. This appears to be the first printing of it together with *Sefer yetsirah* (1723)]: p. 50, no. 43.

Nishmat adam (The Soul of Adam) [by Aharon Shmuel ben Moshe Shalom of Kremenets]: p. 48, no. 55.

Nishmat shabetai halevi (The Soul of Shabetai Halevi): p. 48, no. 55.

Or ne'arav (Pleasant Light) [by Moses Cordovero (Ramak), with an introduction consisting of *Eshel avraham* (The Tamarisk of Abraham) (Fürth, 1701)]: p. 51, no. 80.

Otserot ḥayim (Treasures of Life) [apparently a manuscript of Lurianic kabbalah, 1st printed in Korets, 1783]: p. 47, no. 18. [Five precious Lurianic manuscripts are listed separately in Katzenellenbogen's collection; see the foot of p. 47 and the top of p. 48.]

Pa'amon verimon (Bell and Pomegranate) [by the Rama (R. Menahem Azariah) of Fano]: p. 48, no. 53.

Pitḥei yah (The Entries of God) [by Yissakhar Beer of Kremenets]: p. 49, no. 91.

Sefer hagilgulim (The Book of Reincarnations): p. 49, no. 84.

Sefer haḥayim (The Book of Life) [by Simon Frankfurt]: p. 51, no. 86.

Sefer hakaneh (The Book of the Reed): p. 51, no. 88.

Sefer kanah ḥokhmah kanah binah (The Book: He Who Acquires Wisdom Acquires Understanding): p. 50, no. 136.

Sefer karnayim (The Book of Horns): p. 49, no. 99.

Sefer tola'at ya'akov (The Book of the Worm of Jacob): p. 49, no. 100.

Sefer yetsirah vesefer raziel (The Book of Creation and the Book of Raziel) in a single volume: p. 48, no. 25.

Sha'arei orah (The Gates of Light): p. 43, no. 32. Among the books he gave to his son. *Another copy* p. 48, no. 27; *another copy* p. 48, no. 28, *another copy* p. 49, no. 86.

Shefa tal (Abundance of Dew): p. 46, no. 125.

Shulḥan arukh ha'ari z'l (The *Shulḥan arukh* of the Ari of Blessed Memory): p. 51, no. 68.

Tikunei zohar (Midnight Services Based on the Zohar): p. 50, no. 15.

Tikun keriyat shema (Prayer Service for the Recital of the Shema): p. 51, no. 102.

Tikun leil shavuot vehoshana rabah (Midnight Prayer Service for Shavuot and Hoshanah Rabah): p. 43, no. 47. Among the books he gave to his son. Other midnight services for the first night of Shavuot: p. 51, no. 58; p. 51 at the foot.

Tikun sukot (Prayer Service for Sukkot): p. 49, no. 83.

Tomer devorah (The Palm Tree of Deborah): p. 51, no. 67.

Yalkut reuveni katan (The Small Compendium of Reuben): p. 48, no. 53. *Another copy*: p. 49, no. 68.

Yonat elem (The Silent Dove): p. 49, no. 70.

Zera kodesh (Holy Seed) [penitential services based on *Pegam ot brit* (Flaw in the Sign of the Covenant) by Moses Graf (Fürth, 1696)]: p. 51, no. 69.

Zohar: among the books he gave his son: p. 42, no. 44–6.

Zohar ḥadash (New Zohar): p. 48, no. 30.

Zohar rut (The Zohar of Ruth): p. 49, no. 86.

Yiddish Books

Birkat hamazon (Grace after Meals), called *Benshin* in Yiddish: p. 50, no. 122. *Another copy*: p. 50, no. 130.

Boba ma'aseh (Grandmother's Tale): p. 51, no. 110.

Deitsh kinot (Lamentations in Yiddish): p. 50, no. 124.

Deitsh minhagim vederekh yesharah (Yiddish Customs and the Correct Way) [by Yehiel Michel Epstein]: p. 51, no. 102.

Deitsh perakim (Chapters in Yiddish): p. 51, no. 108.

Deitsh seliḥot (Penitential Prayers in Yiddish): p. 50, no. 123.

משלי

שועלים

להחכם השלם

רבי ברכיה הנקדן

נדפס פעם שנית בתכלית
היופי

בק״ק ברלין

להכין מ׳של ומליצה.

דברי חכמים וחידותם

תק״ף

6. Title page for *Mishlei shu'alim* (Berlin, 1756)

Deitsh beukhl [?] (lit., 'little book in Yiddish'): p. 47, no. 138.

Even bohan (Touchstone): p. 50, no. 122 [see also above, under 'Ethical Books'].

Hovot halevavot deitsh (Yiddish translation of *Hovot halevavot*) [see also above, under 'Ethical Books']: p. 50, no. 131.

Igeret ba'alei hayim (Epistle of the Animals): p. 50, no. 122 [see also above, under 'Ethical Books'].

Kav hayashar deitsh (*Kav hayashar* in Yiddish): p. 50, no. 127. *Another copy*, in Hebrew and Yiddish: p. 50, no. 128.

Kehilat ya'akov (The Congregation of Jacob) [like *Tam veyashar* mentioned below, apparently an adaptation of *Sefer hayashar* (1st printing, Fürth, 1692)]: p. 50, no. 126.

Ma'aseh beit david (The Story of the House of David) [Yiddish translation of the Hebrew work of Yitshak Akrish (Amsterdam, 1700)]: p. 51, no. 74.

Ma'aseh buch (Story Book): p. 50, no. 129.

Ma'aseh hashem (The Work of God): p. 51, no. 109.

Ma'aseh yudit, yehudah hamakabi uma'aseh tuviah (The Story of Judith, Judah the Maccabee, and the Story of Tuviah) [Yiddish translation of works from the Apocrypha, apparently printed in Frankfurt, 1714]: p. 51, no. 98.

Mahzor deitsh (Yiddish Festival Prayer Book): p. 50, no. 130.

Meshal hakadmoni beyidish (The *Hakadmoni* Parables in Yiddish) [on the printing of *Mashal hakadmoni* in Yiddish, see Haberman, *The Yiddish Version of Mashal hakadmoni*, 95–101)]: p. 51, no. 91.

Nahalat tsevi (The Goodliest Inheritance) [Yiddish translation and adaptation from the Zohar]: p. 47, no. 137.

Orhot tsadikim deitsh (The Ways of the Righteous in Yiddish): p. 50, no. 122.

Parliament [I have been unable to ascertain what this book is]: p. 51, no. 107.

Sefer meshalim (Book of Parables) [an anthology translated into Yiddish of the *Hakadmoni* parables and animal fables by Moses ben Eleazar Wallich (Frankfurt am Main, 1697)] p. 50, no. 122.

Simhat hanefesh (Joy of the Soul): p. 50, no. 122.

Sod hashem (The Secret of God) [by David Lida; included here because most of its editions contain laws and customs in Yiddish relating to ritual circumcision; sometimes with the addition of charms]: p. 50, no. 44.

Tam veyashar (Innocent and Upright) [Yiddish translation of *Sefer hayashar*, a compendium of medieval legends in the order of the books of the Bible; translated by Jacob Treves ben Yirmiyahu Matitiyahu Halevi (1st printing, Frankfurt am Main, 1674)]: p. 50, no. 125.

Tefilah im perush ashkenaz (Prayers with Yiddish commentary): p. 50, no. 19. *Another copy*, with a new prayer with Yiddish commentary: p. 50, no. 20.

Yosifon deitsh (Yiddish translation of *Yosifon*): p. 51, no. 95.

The institutional libraries of the Jewish world, by contrast, were established to make the important works of talmudic and halakhic literature available to the more learned members of the community, the educated male elite. This was especially so in the case of the *batei midrash* in Poland. However, from the eighteenth century they began to expand their holdings to include certain types of book that were not specifically required for study according to the traditional curriculum—viz., books of kabbalah and Jewish philosophy—becoming in consequence important agents in the diffusion of knowledge and in fomenting social change.[2] The phenomenon is well known from a general historical perspective; in France, for example, the opening of public libraries during the second half of the eighteenth century had enormous impact, creating a reading audience that extended far beyond the nobility and the educated, ecclesiastical elite.[3] We must therefore assume that the fact that rabbinic religious literature, ethical works, and books on kabbalah and customs were to be found in the libraries of the *batei midrash* had a similar impact, helping to communicate new ideas and new ways of thinking. They

---

[2] See Gries, *Book, Scribe, and Story* (Heb.), 61–2; id., 'Between Literature and History' (Heb.), 158–9; id., 'Between History and Literature' (Heb.), 120 n. 36.

[3] On the status and function of private libraries versus public ones, including lending libraries and university libraries, see Darnton, 'History of Reading', 145–9; Martin, *The History and Power of Writing*, index s.v. 'libraries'. See also Corbin, 'Backstage', iv. 535–9; the remarks in Chartier, *The Order of Books*, 61–86, 108–12, on 'libraries without walls', and id. (ed.), *The Cultural Uses of Print*, 183–239, on 'Urban Reading Practices 1660–1780', which discusses customs of reading and types of reader in public libraries as opposed to private ones. See also the remarks on the development of libraries in the 16th–18th centuries in Schottenloher, *Books and the Western World*, 226–38, 275–83, 375–86.

were in any case popular meeting places for the men of the congregation (this was long before the emancipation of women), who would go there to study in a congenial atmosphere before and after prayer.

By the end of the sixteenth century, the libraries of the *batei midrash* were not the only source of knowledge for the curious. This was because a development ostensibly aimed at strengthening traditional religious society in fact contributed, almost inadvertently, to increasing and broadening the circle of the reading public. I am referring to the practice of publishing prayer books, compilations of religious customs, and abridged versions of ethical works, hitherto available only in Hebrew (and thus only available to scholars) together with a Yiddish translation.[4] This important development in the history of the Jewish book reached its peak in the eighteenth century. Furthermore, individual Jewish communities were not content with collecting general customs and traditions relating to such ceremonies as circumcision, marriage, or burial,[5] but took, in addition, to publishing their own particular customs.[6] Publication of such works marks an important stage in the transition from oral to written culture as a way of preserving customs for future generations. It also provided an intellectual stimulus for the nascent intelligentsia, prompting people to look into the halakhic basis for the customs and rituals that were the basis of communal life and that they could now read about. The significance of this development, which expanded the stratum of society familiar with customs and rites far beyond the narrow segment of the scholarly elite to include a large number of people—women as well as men—who knew how to read Yiddish but not Hebrew, will be discussed in the next chapter.

The scholar Zalman Shazar (later third president of the State of Israel) sought to explain the growth of popular literature in Hebrew and Yiddish from the second half of the seventeenth century onwards as being a consequence of the great spiritual upheaval caused by Shabateanism. He believed that the rabbis, alarmed by the influence of this movement, encouraged the

---

[4] See Gries, *Literature of Customs* (Heb.), 59–62.

[5] The foundations for extensive research into rites of passage were laid by the Dutch scholar Arnold Van Gennep, in *The Rites of Passage*. Victor Turner is the most prominent scholar to follow in his footsteps: his study of rites of passage in contrast to other rituals further develops the concept of liminality coined by Van Gennep. See especially the chapter, 'Passage, Margins, and Poverty: Religious Symbols of Communitas' in his *Drama, Fields, and Metaphors*, 231–70.

[6] See Gries, *Literature of Customs* (Heb.), 64–9, and also Ch. 7 at nn. 5–6 below.

translation of the Bible into Yiddish in order to reclaim the hearts of the people. My account so far of events in the world of the book, both non-Jewish and Jewish, before and during the period of Shabateanism, disagrees with Shazar's interpretation.[7]

[7] See Shazar's introduction to Leib ben Ozer, *Sipur ma'asei shabetai tsevi* (The Story of the Deeds of Shabetai Tsevi), pp. xxvii–xxx.

SIX

Kabbalistic Literature and its Role in Hasidism

KABBALAH is the form of mysticism that developed among the Jews at the end of the twelfth century. While long consigned to the margins of scholarship as a strange phenomenon originating in hallucinations and culminating in illusions, as a result of the pioneering scholarship of Gershom Scholem it has come to be recognized as an integral part of Judaism which requires thorough study if we are to understand its place in Jewish culture.

So far, however, little scholarly attention has been given to the history of kabbalistic works in manuscript and print, their diffusion, and their public reception. The study of such factors could be highly significant in determining the role played by kabbalah in formulating the Jewish world-view and encouraging the longing for messianic redemption, as well as helping us understand the rituals and customs known to have been an important factor in stimulating the spiritual dimension of Judaism, which is essentially a religion of law. It would likewise help determine the role that kabbalah has played in shaping Jewish history, both through the spiritual leaders who adopted its tenets and through its influence on the general public. An examination of the diffusion and reception of different types of kabbalistic books and of the testimonies of those who read them, for example, could help us to evaluate the status and motive power of kabbalah in Shabateanism (the mass messianic movement of the seventeenth century), or in the hasidic movement established by Israel Ba'al Shem Tov in the eighteenth century. It may enable us, too, to flesh out the figure of the charismatic leader, who with one hand clung to halakhah, studying and observing it just like his ancestors and teachers, while in the other he clasped kabbalah, with, for the most part, no obvious tension between the two. Finally, such a study could provide a definitive answer as to whether kabbalistic works, by offering alternative approaches to Judaism, paved the way to the changes in Jewish consciousness that allowed the Haskalah and the spirit of modern times to take root, or whether they impeded the move towards modernity by enveloping Jewish consciousness in myths and superstitions, the forces of evil, demons, magical charms, and amulets.

Elsewhere I have discussed in detail the information we have on kabbalistic works from the origins of printing,[1] and I shall here summarize the essence of those earlier remarks as a basis and background for the present discussion. Gershom Scholem, with his great love of books, knew that there could never be a firm basis for scholarship in kabbalah or an understanding of its status among the Jewish people and its contribution to their spiritual life without a study of the history of its books. Unfortunately, however, whenever his bibliographical knowledge proved unequal to the power of his historical conception, he abandoned the history of the book as a yardstick for cultural history. One of Scholem's first projects was an annotated bibliography of the collection of kabbalistic works in the National Library in Jerusalem. To facilitate the study of this new subject, he also assembled everything he knew about those who had written on it in his *Bibliographia Kabbalistica*.[2] Nevertheless, he never used his immense intellect to provide readers and scholars with information on the history of kabbalistic books, or to draw conclusions from that history on the development of Hebrew culture in general. These comments are, of course, not intended to detract in any way from his extraordinary achievement, or to reproach him for leaving certain tasks undone.

The list of titles published by Hayim Dov Friedberg at the end of *The Library* shows that, from the beginnings of printing in the mid-fifteenth century until the end of the eighteenth century, some 300 different kabbalistic works were printed.[3] A comparison of this figure with the holdings of the world's great libraries, starting with the National and University Library in Jerusalem, reveals that, at most, 20 to 30 per cent of the existing books are not mentioned in Friedberg's list, indicating that the vast majority of such works had already been published by the end of the eighteenth century.

---

[1] See Gries, 'The Copying and Printing of Books of Kabbalah' (Heb.), 204–11. In the present chapter I have added notes and expanded the discussion.

[2] Leipzig, 1927.   [3] See *The Library* (2nd edn), under 'kabbalah', 1219–20.

The number of manuscripts, both copies and autographs—the original manuscripts on kabbalah—far exceeds the number of printed books. Surprisingly, the important kabbalistic works, most of which were first printed in the sixteenth century, were hardly reprinted at all in the seventeenth century. Only a small number are extant in dozens of manuscript copies and several printed editions from the sixteenth and seventeenth centuries. An example of this is the classic *Sha'arei orah* (The Gates of Light), by Joseph Gikatilla, which was first printed in 1561 in two different editions, in Mantua and in Riva di Trento, and again in 1600 in Cracow. It was then not printed again for more than a hundred years until it was republished in Offenbach in 1715 and 1721. It was then republished three times in Zolkiew: in 1739, and then again twice more at the end of the eighteenth century, in 1771 and 1782.

In contrast, most texts exist only in a few copies in manuscript form and a small number of printed editions. Thus, Moses Cordovero's *Pardes rimonim* (The Pomegranate Orchard) was first printed in Salonika in 1584; a second edition was published in Venice in 1586 and a third in Cracow in 1592, but thereafter it was not reprinted until 1712, in Frankfurt-am-Main, more than a hundred years later, with further editions appearing in 1780 and 1786 in Korets. There are 20 extant copies of the sixteenth-century printed editions and 6 manuscript copies dating from the seventeenth century, when there were no printings; not an impressive inventory. Cordovero's other works were hardly printed at all, and seldom copied in manuscript.

A similar situation obtains with regard to the books of another important kabbalist, Meir ben Gabai. His *Avodat hakodesh* (The Holy Service) was published in Mantua in 1545, then again in Venice (1567), and in Cracow (1577). It was not printed again for 150 years until it was republished in Slavuta in 1827. His *Derekh emunah* (The Path of Faith) was published in Constantinople in 1560 and then again in 1563 (Padua) and 1577 (Cracow); it was next reprinted 201 years later, in 1778, when two different editions appeared, in Zolkiew and in Korets. His *Tola'at ya'akov* (The Worm of Jacob) was first published in 1560 in Constantinople, with a second edition appearing in Cracow in 1581. It was not reprinted for 216 years, until a new edition appeared in Shklov in 1797.

Regarding the literature of kabbalistic ethics from Safed, avidly studied by later scholars wanting to glean new ideas for their own writings, the situation is similar: after their first printing in the sixteenth century, these titles were not printed again for a hundred years, and there are few extant copies in manuscript. Printed booklets of recommended kabbalistic and other practices and *tikunim* (midnight-prayer services) that were intended to supplement the regular liturgy fared somewhat better, however. From time to time, additional booklets of this kind are discovered dating from the seventeenth century; indeed, one such was reported as recently as 2001 by Jacob Barnai.[4] It is almost certain, however, that this literature of kabbalistic customs and the literature of kabbalistic doctrines mentioned above was not a factor in making Jews receptive to the advent of the messiah in the person of Shabetai Tsevi. Moshe Idel has noted the restricted circulation of Lurianic teachings during the seventeenth century and the small number of students of Lurianic kabbalah, and I have demonstrated the limited circulation of books recommending the adoption of Lurianic customs and ritual at that time. We both concluded that the interest in Lurianic kabbalah that developed among the rabbis was therefore a consequence of the spread of Shabateanism—because its leaders were known to engage in kabbalah in general and in Lurianic kabbalah in particular—rather than its cause.[5]

From assessment not only of the numbers of kabbalistic manuscripts and printed books but also of their content, I have since come to an even more far-reaching conclusion. Looking at the three hundred and fifty years from the beginning of printing until the end of the eighteenth century, we find that the number of titles printed doubled from century to century: very roughly, 40 titles were published in the sixteenth century, 80 in the seventeenth century, and 180 in the eighteenth century. This might suggest that my earlier claim regarding the restricted study of kabbalah was mistaken. However, of these 300 titles, most focus on very specialized topics that cannot be understood without prior knowledge and were printed in just one or in very few editions; the basic works of kabbalah form only a very small part of the total body of printed kabbalistic books during the period in question. This finding supports the thesis that, during the sixteenth and seventeenth centuries and the first half of the eighteenth century, no effort was made to disseminate the study of kabbalah widely, for it is only through mass circulation of the basic works that widespread education is possible. If we look, for example, at the Zohar, the classic work of kabbalah (which I shall discuss at length below), there are hardly any complete manuscript copies in existence—quite different from the

---

[4] In the paper he presented at the twelfth Congress of Jewish Studies in the summer of 1997.   [5] See my comments in Chapter 2 above.

case of *Sha'arei orah*, as discussed above—and there were few printed editions before the eighteenth century. This situation also contrasts with that of the works of Abraham Abulafiah, which were rarely printed, but of which there are many more complete manuscript copies than there are of the Zohar. This was noted early on by Moshe Idel.[6]

I do not deny that kabbalistic ideas and customs seeped into Jewish life during the seventeenth century, both in books of biblical exegesis and sermons and in works of halakhah, as Jacob Katz and Meir Benayahu have shown.[7] The information that I have presented, however, regarding extant manuscripts and printed books, especially the basic works of kabbalah, strongly suggests that the kabbalists made no concerted effort to communicate their teachings to the Jewish people as a whole, or to introduce the study of kabbalah as standard. I am not unmindful of the intense, extra-curricular study of the Zohar and other kabbalistic books practised in certain yeshivas, such as those of Moses Isserles in Cracow and Joseph Caro in Safed, or by certain groups of kabbalists in Safed and Italy, which left its mark in written books of recommended conduct based on kabbalistic practices, such as *Mareh kohen* (Cracow, 1589), written by Isserles's disciple Yissakhar Baer of Shebreshin (Szczebrzeszyn). These, however, were local, isolated phenomena, which do not reflect the general situation of the study of kabbalah prior to the second half of the eighteenth century.

I must nonetheless modify my claim to some degree, since in estimating the number of those who read and studied books of kabbalah regularly one must take account of the fact that, from the sixteenth century onwards, the number of what we may regard as Jewish public libraries in *batei midrash* may well have grown, as discussed in the previous chapter. In consequence, while the number of books they contained was not large, they could have served a large reading public since the *beit midrash* was an open institution.[8] Regrettably, there is no information regarding the growth, status, and function of these primary cultural institutions. Moritz Steinschneider, the greatest of Hebrew bibliographers, does not discuss this; since it is inconceivable that he would have ignored data that he found on the subject, the fact that he doesn't discuss the subject leads one to conclude that there were simply insufficient data available.

[6] In Idel's doctoral thesis; his comments were published in his *Mystical Experience in Abraham Abulafiah*, 4–5. [7] See above, Ch. 1 n. 4. [8] See above, Ch. 5 n. 2.

We do have partial information on some libraries, however. The magnificent collection of the Ets Hayim Portuguese synagogue and *beit midrash* in Amsterdam, amassed over many generations, is well known. A considerable portion was donated to the National Library in Jerusalem, but was eventually returned to Amsterdam following the ruling of a Dutch court that the collection is a Dutch national asset and should not be removed from Holland. From the sixteenth century, we know of the library of the *beit midrash* in Cracow, to which, as discovered by Hayim Hillel Ben-Sasson,[9] David Darshan ('David the Preacher') donated four hundred of his books in return for the right to teach a regular class and have a steady income. From the mid-eighteenth century we know of the collection of books in the *beit midrash* in Mezhirech, which also included kabbalistic manuscripts that had not yet been published. Those subsequently printed included a book of Lurianic kabbalah, *Maḥberet hakodesh* (The Holy Notebook), edited by Solomon Lutsker and published in Korets in 1783. Lutsker also oversaw the printing of the first edition (Korets, 1781) of *Magid devarav leya'akov* (He Speaks his Words to Jacob) by the famous *magid*, Dov Ber of Mezhirech. Another kabbalistic manuscript found there and subsequently published was *Kanfei yonah* (The Wings of the Dove) by Menahem Azariah (known as 'the Rama of Fano'), which was brought to press by Eleazar Leib (Korets, 1786).[10]

All of these are isolated droplets, however, which tell us nothing about the size or nature of the ocean, if, indeed, there was an ocean at all. We know of the existence of vast private libraries during the eighteenth century, such as the collection of David Oppenheim of Prague, and of large private collections such as that of Pinhas Katzenellenbogen discussed in the previous chapter. It is thus possible that, during the eighteenth century, with the increase in the printing and circulation of Hebrew books (including books of kabbalah in the second half of that century), that the libraries of the *batei midrash* served less frequently as centres for the study of kabbalah than they had in the sixteenth and seventeenth centuries. Here too, however, there is reason for circumspection, for we do not know how many libraries there were in *batei midrash* during

[9] See Ben-Sasson, *Ideas and Leadership* (Heb.), 165–8, 254–6. On the libraries of yeshivas in Spain, especially as centres for the copying of manuscripts from the mid-15th century until the expulsion, see Riegler, 'Were the Yeshivas in Spain a Centre for the Copying of Books?' (Heb.), 411–26.

[10] See Gries, *Book, Scribe, and Story* (Heb.), 59–62 and 130–2, nn. 35–40. See also Hundert, 'The Library of the Study Hall in Volozhin 1762', 225–44.

the sixteenth and seventeenth centuries, nor what they may have contained. It is my belief that, even if it were possible to prove that during that period there was a substantial number of public libraries in *batei midrash*, the inventories of books and manuscripts would lead one to conclude that the study of kabbalah was still limited to a few individuals. If there was propaganda to increase it, that propaganda did not produce its desired effect until the second half of the eighteenth century.

During the sixteenth century about half of the kabbalistic books to be published were printed in three cities—Cracow, Venice, and Constantinople; only a few isolated titles were printed in other cities, chiefly Salonika and Mantua. The reasons for this can only be speculated. During the seventeenth century, once again, the majority of titles were printed in a small number of cities, principally Venice, followed by Prague, while printing in Cracow decreased, in keeping with the general hundred-year-long decline of Hebrew printing in Poland, from the mid-seventeenth to the mid-eighteenth century, as already discussed. In the eighteenth century Zolkiew stands out as the city in which many dozens of kabbalistic books were printed; trailing far behind were two other cities: Korets, also in eastern Europe, where, as in Zolkiew, printing was re-established in the second half of that century, and Leghorn (Livorno) in Italy. In addition, isolated books of kabbalah were printed in many other cities in central and eastern Europe during the eighteenth century. It is also important to note that in Amsterdam, the great international centre of printing, whose output competed with that of Italy at that time, few kabbalistic books were printed.[11] As we have seen, the major cities involved in printing distributed their wares far beyond the borders of their country of origin, and sometimes competed aggressively with local printers by flooding the market with books that were cheaper and of better quality. We must therefore ask why, if there was increased demand for kabbalistic books in the eighteenth century, it did not affect the market strategies of the astute printers of Amsterdam, or the majority of printers in Italy.

The printing of kabbalistic works on a large scale during the last quarter of the eighteenth century, and particularly in Zolkiew, would seem to be a belated response to the renewal of interest in kabbalistic customs and practices in consequence of the Shabatean movement. At the same time, in Italy and especially in Amsterdam, printers were increasingly exposed to the spirit

[11] See Ch. 2 n. 32 above.

of Haskalah and rationalism, which pervaded their world and the lives of Jewish intellectuals in the same way that the spirit of the Enlightenment influenced the non-Jews there. In Zolkiew, Korets, and other cities of eastern Europe, the Zohar was printed alongside books of Lurianic kabbalah and works of kabbalah that came from the Ottoman empire, such as Isaac of Kiev's *Shoshan sodot* (Rose of Secrets). Followers of the Ba'al Shem Tov, such as Solomon Lutsker (who was involved in publishing activity in the 1780s in Korets), took a key part in this, along with scholars of the well-known *kloyz* of Brody,[12] and the maskil Isaac Satanow.[13]

It might be postulated that the Haskalah movement that had swept through the Jewish communities of western Europe and parts of central Europe had not yet had a major impact on the Jews of eastern Europe, who lived under a regime which offered no rights or emancipation; as a consequence they were attracted to the occult in general, and to kabbalah in particular. Such a conclusion, however, would be overstated. Anyone who has read the history of the upper classes and the enlightened intelligentsia of Paris at the end of the eighteenth century will be aware of the appearance of Franz Anton Mesmer, and his promise of the redemption of body and soul by means of occult doctrine. This interest in mysticism was not a local phenomenon characterizing the supposedly backward region of eastern Europe, but rather a characteristic of the period in general, when educated and enlightened people all over Europe were being drawn to investigate the occult.[14]

What, then, can be learned from the information I have presented regarding the status of kabbalah and its contribution to the formation of Jewish life and culture from the beginning of printing until the end of the eighteenth century? Before drawing any conclusions, it is worth considering, as a valuable example, the fate of the Zohar, to this day the most important work of kabbalah in general, and of Sephardi kabbalah in particular.

Many scholars claim that the Zohar is a canonical work to be set alongside the Bible and the Talmud. Gershom Scholem was the first to do so, and Isaiah Tishby followed in his footsteps.[15] But today epithets for people and phe-

---

[12] On this institution see Reiner, 'Capital, Social Class, and the Study of Torah' (Heb.).

[13] On Satanow and his work see the discussion at Ch. 10 n. 21 below.

[14] See Darnton, *Mesmerism and the End of the Enlightenment in France*. For more on Mesmer and the spirit of the age, see Berlin, *Roots of Romanticism*, 47. For an English translation of Mesmer's works, see Bloch, *Mesmerism*.

[15] The following discussion expands on and modifies remarks first made at a conference of

nomena are commonly trivialized, both by the way in which they are used, and by the users themselves. Through a lack of knowledge, through cynicism, or sometimes as a result of the life-cycle of the spoken language and the expansion of a word's semantic field, the original meaning of a concept becomes shallower. This is what has happened to the word 'canon'. The Bible and the Talmud have been accepted for generations as holy books—the literary canon—of the Jewish religion in the same way that the New Testament is accepted by Christians. In recent generations, however, scholars seem to have expanded the concept of the canon to include every book that they and a few friends and relatives admire. Thus, included in the 'canon' we may find a book that was printed only three times in a hundred years, or a book that was rejected by the reading public and favoured only by a group of critics of refined taste—for how could the ignorant masses determine what deserves to be included in the canon?

This touches on a subject that I can only begin to address here: the public reception of literary works, an aspect of the history of the book in the Jewish world that has been sorely neglected. In my own bibliographical excursions I have found no one who has attempted to define the canon of Jewish literature. I shall therefore propose my own definition in the hope that it will assist in this and other areas, and prevent, at least on the part of scholars, inflated use of the concept which brings together under one roof both the giants of culture and its dwarfs.

There are international yardsticks for the history of the reception of books that should be applied to every nation and culture. For example: how many editions of a particular book were printed? How many copies were there in each edition? Where was it circulated, and what was its target audience? The last of these can be determined according to lists of owners, censors' lists, the contents of books, statements by the authors, and the like. These questions are difficult to answer with respect to the history of books in the Jewish world before the modern period, for writers and printers did not usually preserve

the Departments of Jewish Thought held at the Open University in Israel in the spring of 1993, and on comments I have written elsewhere. See Gries, 'Between Literature and History' (Heb.). Boaz Huss has published a long and comprehensive article about the process of sanctification of the Zohar: see '*Sefer Ha-Zohar* as a Canonical, Sacred, and Holy Text', 257–307. While he did not respond to my definition of the canon in Jewish literature, he extensively analysed the reception of the Zohar, its authority, and its sanctification. See my extended response in 'Kabbalah and Halakhah' (Heb.), 191.

quantitative data, and they did not leave descriptions of their work and its goals.

There are, on the other hand, additional criteria which are intimately related to the culture and characteristics of a given nation, and these are often difficult—sometimes impossible—to apply to other nations. This is the case with regard to the changes undergone by the Jewish people, especially from the end of the nineteenth century, when most of those who identified themselves as Jews no longer observed the biblical commandments, and were not guided in their daily lives by Jewish law. As a result, it is hard to set criteria for including a book in the canon in the modern age. We who are living in the midst of this change still lack the perspective needed to determine what the new 'canon' is and whether, indeed, one has been formed at all. It is, however, possible to state that in a religion of law, such as Judaism is (even in modern times), any book must satisfy two criteria to be considered for inclusion in the canon. The first is whether the work is required for the stages of the traditional educational system, which would ensure that it is firmly established in the common consciousness of the nation. The second relates to the influence of the book on the actions of the people, by its inclusion for generations within the cycle of their life in ritual—here, the ceremonies observed by the Jewish nation.

The Bible passes both tests; it is studied from an early age, and has served for generations as the authoritative basis for the study of Talmud. It is also required reading (although not in its entirety) in the synagogue service. The Talmud also passes both tests since it is required reading in the educational system, and is also the primary source for Jewish laws, ceremonies, and rituals.

Does the Zohar pass this double test? Judged by its copying and printing up to the eighteenth century, the answer is no. Added to this, the compilation of its supposed religious laws in *Yesh sakhar* (There Is Reward), a sixteenth-century work by Issachar Beer of Kremenets, had no great impact; it was rarely reprinted, suggesting relatively little demand.[16] Customs derived from the Zohar did not affect Jewish life on a large scale via the prayer book, daily rituals, or religious ceremonies until the eighteenth century. The same is true of its influence on rituals associated with the final stages of life—kabbalistic customs relating to death. These are based on *Ma'avar yabok* (Traversing the

---

[16] On this book and its author, see Gries, *Literature of Customs* (Heb.), 76–80, and the additional bibliography there.

Yabok) by Aaron Berakhyah of Modena, which was first printed in the six-teenth century but then not again for about a hundred years; the main influ-ence of this work and its various abridgements dates from the eighteenth century.[17]

Major changes in the attitude towards kabbalah took place in the eight-eenth century—changes expressed both by the increasing circulation of pam-phlets on customs and by the number of editions of the Zohar itself. This growth in the study of kabbalah and its dissemination in eastern Europe from the middle of the eighteenth century was expressed in a greater demand for books, which was met with many printings in the last quarter of the century, particularly in Zolkiew and Korets.

Among scholars and the educated public it is generally accepted that the Zohar was regarded as sacred mainly in the Mediterranean Basin, from North Africa as far east as Iraq and Yemen, and this view is substantiated by the oral and written evidence available. This evidence, however, refers simply to the level of popular consciousness. It remains very doubtful, when judged by the figures on printing, that the book was included in the broad framework of required reading and study there at the end of the eighteenth century and dur-ing the nineteenth century. For the twentieth century, there is good evidence that it was required reading in the synagogues of Yemen on the sabbath.[18]

In 1740 *Hok leyisra'el* (A Law for Israel) was published anonymously in Egypt. This is a textbook for the daily study of what I would refer to as canon-ical literature. The book is divided into sections of the Bible according to the weekly Torah portion, the prophets, the writings (Hagiographa), the Mishnah, and a daily portion of the Talmud. At the end there is also a daily portion of the Zohar. An examination of the printings of *Hok leyisra'el* in the eighteenth century shows that, with the exception of three editions published in Italy (Venice, 1777; Leghorn, 1788 and 1792) almost all were printed in east-ern Europe. Until recently, the first printing there was thought to be that of Korets in 1785, but in 2001 Sarah Frankel found a copy printed in Korets in 1781 in a collection of books from Romania.[19] For the nineteenth century, Friedberg lists in *The Library* 27 editions from eastern Europe and another 2

---

[17] See ibid. 63–9, and Bar-Levav, 'Rabbi Aaron Berakhyah of Modena' (Heb.).

[18] See Etstah, *The Life of Joseph* (Heb.), 28.

[19] In her lecture at the twelfth Congress of Jewish Studies in the summer of 1997 she reported on a copy that had reached Bar-Ilan University Library.

from Italy (Leghorn). In the National and University Library in Jerusalem, however, I have counted 43 nineteenth-century editions from eastern Europe, and 12 from Italy and other places.

The many editions of *Ḥok leyisra'el* produced during the nineteenth century seems to testify to the expansion of hasidism because its leaders made it clear, in their insistence on its daily study, that they considered the Zohar to be as sacred as the Bible, the Mishnah, and the Talmud. For them it had become part of the canon. Since it is well known that the Vilna Gaon and his disciples were deeply involved in kabbalah, and were also counted among the greatest scholars and teachers of halakhah of their generation, it is evident that the dissemination of daily study of the Zohar through *Ḥok leyisra'el* was not limited to hasidim. It was clearly intended for everyone who regarded kabbalah as holy, or who regarded the practices of the leaders and teachers of the generation as holy, seeing them as role models whose deeds were to be emulated. If these individuals studied the Zohar extensively, a simple Jew should at least study a small section each day, to become familiar with it and to absorb it as he would the Bible, Mishnah, and Talmud.

My friend Amos Goldreich has drawn my attention to strong evidence of the widespread adoption of the custom of studying *Ḥok leyisra'el* in the late nineteenth century. In Bialik's story *Ariyeh ba'al guf* (Arieh the Strong Man) the hero makes fun of those who sit in the *beit midrash* and synagogue and 'chew on the *Ḥok*' after their prayers. Reb Arieh explains to a wagon-driver there what the *Ḥok* is: 'It's a book that lies in the *talit* and *tefilin* bags of fine Jews, and they study from it after Aleinu—a kind of dessert after prayers.'[20] He does not speak about hasidim exclusively, but about Jews in general, confirming that at the end of the nineteenth century many Jews adhered to the custom of studying *Ḥok leyisra'el*.

If we study the dissemination of Lurianic kabbalah during the nineteenth century, it becomes apparent that during the second half of that century, in contrast to the first, hardly any books of kabbalistic doctrines were published. In the 1870s and 1880s, however, two adepts made an effort to reinvigorate the study of Lurianic kabbalah. The first, Isaac Haver, a disciple both of the famous rabbi Menahem Mendel of Shklov and of the Vilna Gaon, who had a deep interest in kabbalah, wrote a work of Lurianic kabbalah entitled *Pitḥei*

---

[20] See Bialik, *Ariyeh ba'al guf*, 17. Aleinu is a hymn recited near the end of all three daily prayer services.

she'arim (The Openings of Gates).[21] To this day, however, it lies untouched by scholars because the father of research into kabbalah, Gershom Scholem, concluded his study with what he considered to be the final stage of kabbalah in modern times—the hasidic movement—and ignored later works. A second attempt was made by Jacob Meir Spielman, who attempted to combine old kabbalistic teachings with new ones in *Tal orot* (Dew of Lights).[22] Scholem wrote at the start of his own copy of the first volume of this work: 'This is a most marvellous book and very interesting; a hasidic-psychological interpretation in the style of the Magid of Mezhirech using the method of the Rashash [Rabbi Shalom Sharabi], *Emek hamelekh* [Valley of the King]!! and *Sha'ar gan eden* [The Gate of the Garden of Eden].'[23] Regarding the circulation of ethical kabbalistic works in nineteenth-century eastern Europe, we find demand for the anthology *Reshit ḥokhmah* (The Beginnings of Wisdom) by Elijah de Vidas, *Sefer ḥaredim* (The Book of Those Who Fear God) by Eleazar Azkari, and, of course, *Shenei luḥot haberit* (The Two Tablets of the Law) by Isaiah Horowitz, together with its abbreviated versions in Hebrew and Yiddish: *Kitsur shenei luḥot haberit* and *Ets ḥayim* (Tree of Life), both by Yehiel Mikhel Epstein.[24]

[21] See Friedlander's remarks about Haver in the Foreword to Haver's *Magen vetsinah* (Shield and Buckler), 1–20. At the end of this book is a photo-offset of the eulogy published by his son Joseph after his death. Entitled *Nefesh naki* (Pure Soul), it is more hagiography than biography. *Pitḥei she'arim* was first published from Haver's manuscript more than fifty years after his death, through the efforts of his son Moses, the chief rabbinical judge of Jedwabne, who added a short introduction entitled 'The Proposal of the Son of the Rabbi–Author'.

[22] The book was published in four volumes (Lemberg, 1876–85). At the beginning of vol. i is an approbation by the rabbi of Lemberg, Joseph Saul Nathanson, author of *Sho'el umeshiv* (Ask and Answer). He authorized the person who prepared the book for the press, Noah Tsevi Lernovitsh, to publish the collection of Spielman's works that was in his possession. He apologizes that, in contrast to his normal practice, lack of time and frequent interruptions meant that he could only give the works a superficial examination, 'and while it is my usual practice to make some remarks with my approbations of books, time is pressing so perhaps, God willing, when the aforementioned books are printed, I will peruse them, if at all possible. That with which God favours me, I will write here briefly.' I have found none of his comments in the other printings. I discuss his approbations below: see Ch. 9 at nn. 7–9.

[23] See National and University Library, Jerusalem, Gershom Scholem Collection, no. 1773. He adds in Hebrew in his own hand: 'Based mainly on the book *Sha'arei gan eden*, see fo. 32a, and he joins the tradition of the disciples of the Besht with that of the disciples of Rabbi Shalom Shar'abi.'

[24] On Epstein, see Gries, *The Literature of Customs* (Heb.), 58–64, and Shohet, *With the Change of Epochs* (Heb.), index, s.v. 'Epstein, Yehiel Mikhel' (p. 337).

We must therefore assume that the main interest of the public was in popular literature on kabbalah and in the customs associated with it, as in the case of the Zohar itself. The masses could relate to these customs, whereas deep study of the doctrines of kabbalistic literature remained the province of a select few, as it had throughout the generations.

Kabbalistic influences were certainly to be found in the widely circulated books of sermons and homilies of the nineteenth century. They also underlay messianic hopes: for example, the Sephardi rabbi Judah Alkalai (1798–1878) attempted to prove that the year 5600 (1840) would be the year of Redemption,[25] an expectation of the end of days that was based on the Zohar's commentary on the biblical portion 'Vayera' (Gen. 18–22).[26] When this expectation was disappointed, he became instead a fervent supporter of the proto-Zionist Hibat Zion (Love of Zion) and Hovevei Zion (Lovers of Zion) movements that began to take shape in the 1880s. The authority of kabbalah was also called upon to support other ideologies too: references to kabbalah, and in particular to the Zohar, are dispersed throughout Rabbi Hillel Lichtenstein's *Avkat rokhel* (The Pedlar's Powder) in an attempt to convince his readers that they should refrain from following the path of religious innovators who were trying to change the Jewish way of life.[27] Similarly a younger ultra-orthodox leader, Rabbi Hayim Eleazar Shapira of Munkacs, then in Hungary, regarded the Zohar as an authority on the requirement for every Jew to combat Zionism and the efforts of its adherents to settle in the Holy Land.[28] Shapira and men like him, who barked at the Zionist puppy because they were unable to contend with the monsters of emancipation and emigration to the American continent, are discussed below.

[25] Several studies have been written about Judah Alkalai and his programmes for redemption. See the extensive treatment, with bibliographical references to other academic studies, in Morgenstern, *Messianism and the Settlement of Erets Israel* (Heb.), 26, 38–40.   [26] See ibid. 39.

[27] Lichtenstein, also known as Hillel Lash, served as a rabbi in Hungary and finished his career as a rabbi in the Galician town of Kolomya. His son-in-law was Akiva Joseph Schlesinger, on whom see Cohen, *The Sages of Transylvania* (Heb.), index s.v. 'Schlesinger' (p. 587). See also Lichtenstein, *Avkat rokhel, passim.*

[28] On Shapira and his battle against Zionism, see Ravitzky, *Zionism and Jewish Religious Radicalism* (Heb.), 60–110, and Nadler, 'The War on Modernity of R. Hayyim Eleazar Shapira of Mucachevo', 233–64. It should be pointed out that, if these scholars had examined his collection of responsa, *Minḥat eleazar* (The Offering of Eleazar), they would have found that his voice, when addressing his community, was soft and considerate: see his *Divrei torah* (Words of Torah), which contains useful indexes, and also his *Sha'ar yisakhar* (The Gate of Yissakhar).

Does the use of kabbalistic books by these important authors contradict my assumption that the study of kabbalah was not widespread at this time? Not necessarily. A decrease in the price of books during the second half of the nineteenth century associated with the increase in demand made it easier for authors to draw on a wide variety of sources in their attempt to make their works more attractive to various communities of readers. As I noted in Chapter 4, during the nineteenth century, and especially in the second half of that century, dozens of commentaries on *Pirkei avot* were printed: these made use of a variety of sources, including kabbalistic books, for the same reason. In certain hasidic circles, such as those of Komarno, Zhidachov, and Spinka, a large number of kabbalistic works were written, which might convince us that in those courts kabbalah was widely studied in the nineteenth century. Even if that were true, it is certainly not the case with regard to the followers of Hillel Lichtenstein and Hayim Eleazar Shapira of Munkacs, in whose publications the kabbalistic content is insignificant.

An interest in practical kabbalah—kabbalistic ritual, as opposed to kabbalistic doctrine—certainly flourished in central and eastern Europe during the nineteenth century. For example, Rabbi Akiva Joseph Schlesinger of Pressburg, one of the most vocal advocates of the staunch halakhist Moses Sofer (known as the Hatam Sofer), relates that during Passover of 1865 a mysterious guest from Tibet, Eliezer ben Rabbi Simon Moses, came to the home of his father-in-law Rabbi Hillel Lichtenstein. The guest was introduced to Rabbi Lichtenstein and the members of his household as a great kabbalist, with a profound mastery of both theoretical and practical kabbalah. He was careful to eat only vegetables, and he spoke to his hosts in Hebrew. He told them that he had been sent on the orders of his rabbis in Tibet to spend Passover with them in Hungary. The guest noticed that a dog was clinging to Rabbi Lichtenstein, following him wherever he went and insisting on remaining with him at all times. When he sat, the dog sat with him, and when he walked, the dog walked beside him. The guest whispered something into the dog's ear, and it immediately curled its tail between its legs and ran away, never to return. After it had gone, the guest told his hosts that, with his whisper, he had repaired the sinful soul that had been reborn in the dog.[29]

[29] See the preface to Lichtenstein, *Avkat rokhel*. On the vitality of practical kabbalah, the widespread interest in it, and the imaginative ferment of those drawn to it through reading about it, see Gries, *Book, Scribe, and Story* (Heb.), 74, 136 nn. 15–17, and id., 'The Historical Figure of the Besht' (Heb.), 425 n. 43 and 441.

The revival of Hebrew printing in Poland from the second half of the eighteenth century onwards was due to an effort on behalf of the authorities to encourage greater productivity among the Jews and a concomitant decrease in the number of books imported from abroad.[30] As I have said, the energetic production of kabbalistic books in eastern Europe at this time was a response to an existing demand rather than an attempt to produce one. This claim is supported by analysis of the inscriptions on the walls of wooden synagogues in Poland built at the beginning of the eighteenth century, such as in Gwózdziec (northwest of Przemysl) which provides evidence of kabbalistic influences on the liturgy decades before such texts found their way into daily and festival prayer books.[31] Most of the prayer books produced in the second half of the seventeenth century and at the beginning of the eighteenth century contain no trace of such influences, whereas the evidence from Gwózdziec suggests that we must consider dating the oral kabbalistic tradition and its influence on the masses to the end of the seventeenth century.

Another important conclusion follows from this: we must carefully re-appraise historical patterns of Jewish literacy discussed in the Introduction and opening chapters of this book. This conclusion does not in any way con-tradict my earlier claim that the interest of Shabateans in kabbalah in general and Lurianic kabbalah in particular was responsible for its later influence on the general public and their desire to study it. Kabbalistic literature did not attract the masses to the Shabatean movement. It served, rather, to arouse tra-ditional messianic expectations, which were whipped into a frenzy by the events of the 1660s, when Shabetai Tsevi was proclaimed the messiah.[32] These remarks suggest that the increase in printing activity in Poland, and especially Zolkiew, in the second half of the eighteenth century was a response to the increasing demand for books on kabbalah from the end of the seventeenth century. In consequence the kabbalists were no longer able to control the number of people studying kabbalah nor what they read, as they had done when kabbalistic texts were only available in manuscript. The dissemination of kabbalistic practices and ceremonies, as well as the circulation of books of

[30] See id., *Book, Scribe, and Story* (Heb.), 110–11 n. 4, and especially the articles by Emmanuel Ringelblum mentioned there.

[31] I refer to an article written jointly with Thomas Hubka and Avriel Bar-Levav to be pub-lished elsewhere. The article by Hubka has now been published: see 'The Synagogue of Gwózdziec' (Heb.), 272.   [32] See my comments in Chapter 2 at n. 9.

kabbalistic lore, also undoubtedly increased in the second half of the eighteenth century, and even more so in the nineteenth century, as a consequence of the growth of hasidism. It has almost been forgotten, however, that even in Vilna, that scholarly stronghold regarded as the great centre of opposition to hasidism, the revered Gaon himself was deeply interested in kabbalah. The contribution of the Gaon and his disciples to kabbalistic literature has been largely ignored by scholars to this day, despite the fact that we possess important writings by them on the subject.

The publication during the eighteenth century of a large number of pamphlets on customs, many of them originating in kabbalistic ideas, illustrates the way in which Jewish religious practice developed, and how Jewish spirituality increased as a result of kabbalistic influences. This literature on customs, which served both hasidic and non-hasidic communities, does not include instructions for visionary, mystical journeys to a state of *devekut* (cleaving to the Infinite); explicit formulas for seeking closeness to God are mainly to be found in homiletic kabbalistic literature, both hasidic and non-hasidic. It is regrettable that the kabbalistic homiletics of the Vilna Gaon and his disciples have been neglected by modern scholars despite the fact that they were an important focus of study and instruction, whereas the hasidic homiletic literature, which has been a frequent subject of modern scholarship, was of less importance in hasidic culture than the hagiographic accounts of the miracles wrought by tsadikim, which modern scholarship has largely ignored.[33] While oral transmission of such stories in hasidic circles continued, from the middle of the nineteenth century onwards they were increasingly written down and published. This literature does not focus on esoteric activity which acts to isolate the individual from the togetherness that characterizes hasidic society; its purpose, rather, was to bond individuals into a single group around the figure of the tsadik, like lovers who cling to one another without barriers.[34]

Moshe Idel's *Hasidism: Between Ecstasy and Magic*, which contains a more comprehensive discussion of hasidic ecstasy and mysticism than can be found in the work of his predecessors,[35] makes no reference to the literature of customs, or to the testimony of stories, memoirs, and the like. It does not therefore provide information on the extent to which the quest for *devekut* was part

[33] See Gries, *Book, Scribe, and Story* (Heb.), *passim*.
[34] See id., 'From Myth to Ethos' (Heb.), ii. 117–46.
[35] e.g. Rivka Schatz-Uffenheimer's *Hasidism as Mysticism*.

of the everyday life of the hasidim. In a study of my own, I have shown that the dominant theme of hasidic stories and hagiographies of the great tsadikim is the traditional demand for spiritual humility and self-awareness as the means of self-realization and spiritual fulfilment; they lack all trace of a demand for transcending the self (*bitul hayesh*) and going beyond the seeming reality of the material world so as to achieve the oneness with the Infinite that is the goal of *devekut*. Similarly, there is no call to make prayer more effective as a way of communion with God by means of the kabbalistic meditations known as *yihudim* and *kavanot*, nor any advocacy of these practices for the hasidic public; they were intended only for a select few within the hasidic community. Rather, there is severe criticism of those who are concerned with self-redemption by means of such practices while forgetting their duties towards the Jewish community as a whole. In the letter known as the *Igeret hakodesh*, the Holy Epistle, written by Israel Ba'al Shem Tov to his brother-in-law Gershon of Kutow as mentioned in Chapter 4, there appears to be a tendency to advocate the use of Lurianic *kavanot* among the wider community of hasidim: the Ba'al Shem Tov says that the messiah told him that he will not appear until the teachings of the Ba'al Shem Tov have been disseminated throughout the world, and until other people are able to use *yihudim* and *kavanot* as he does. The Ba'al Shem Tov expresses his regret that the messiah's appearance will be delayed because of the length of time this will take, suggesting that, in reality, only a very few of the Ba'al Shem Tov's followers—a small minority within a minority—had the knowledge and ability to use these special techniques of prayer.[36]

In their effort to characterize the spirit of hasidism and its message, many scholars refer only to the literature of hasidic homiletics, which was intended for a small number of individuals within the hasidic community. Little attempt has yet been made, however, to compare the messages conveyed in the homiletic literature with that of the hasidic hagiographies which, in both oral and written form, were the prime source of religious inspiration for the masses of hasidim. Within that literature there was a constant effort to instil in the minds of readers and listeners—by means of parable, story, advice, or

---

[36] See my extensive treatment of this subject in 'Hasidic Stories of Prayer' (Heb.), 219–35. On the letter of the Besht to Gershon of Kutow, see Ch. 4 n. 25 above. The portion of the letter cited here is missing from the manuscript version printed by Frankel and Bauminger. One cannot exclude the possibility, therefore, that it was a later, tendentious addition, intended to strengthen the letter's messianic message.

recommended practice—that the behavioural norms appropriate for hasidim were those recommended in traditional Jewish ethical literature.

It is of course possible to claim, and with ample justification, that a subject of such intimacy as the way one should take in order to approach God will not be mentioned casually, but only by those who propose to follow it. It is also possible to claim that instruction on how to undertake this mystical journey has been esoteric. In an area which has still been revealed to us only in part, as in the ancient *heikhalot* literature and other kabbalistic writings over the generations that Moshe Idel has done so much to recover, the texts doubtless give details of just a tiny part of the knowledge that was vouchsafed to individuals. Most instruction regarding these practices must have been given orally and, again, only to a restricted number.

I still maintain, however, that it is difficult to accept that the demand or the desire for closeness to God became widespread among the masses at any stage in the history of hasidism. On the contrary, the fact that a yearning to cleave to God appears within the homiletic literature—which was and remains inaccessible to the masses—only emphasizes what I have repeatedly argued: that the principal intimate mystical experience for most ordinary hasidim was that of the intimacy within their hasidic community. Intimate connection with others—in study, in the mystical third meal of the sabbath, in dance, or in song—was the force responsible for bringing the individual and the multitude together in going beyond the bounds of corporeality. The power unleashed through these communal activities is clearly quite unlike the dynamic created in individual communion with God.

It could be that the essential difference between Moshe Idel's arguments and my own resides in our view of the relationship between literature and life. In my view, the history of the printing and circulation of kabbalistic books among the hasidim and their opponents during the eighteenth century shows that the way to the intimate mystical experience of merging with God (and practical instructions for reaching this state) was usually communicated, as it always had been, by one individual to others who were considered worthy of joining the select minority.

Another question arising from the wide circulation in eastern Europe of books by kabbalists and books of customs is the degree to which the tendency towards openness to change and the modern world (which, as I shall outline in the next chapter, is mainly found in Yiddish literature) could coexist with traditional myths and symbols, kabbalistic and other, and with magic spells and superstitions. Today it is still possible to find individuals who, while working at the forefront of modern science and technology, are able to combine these talents with the study of the esoteric and the mysterious. How much more must this have been true in the eighteenth century, a time when the Enlightenment was gathering strength and industrial and political revolutions were beginning but science and technology as we know them today were still in their infancy, and when human helplessness in the face of disease and death was still widespread. Furthermore, one must take account of the fact that expansion of the circle of readers and their use of the literature of kabbalistic customs would undoubtedly have led the nascent Jewish intelligentsia to delve more deeply into rabbinic literature, which contains the primary linguistic and conceptual foundations of kabbalistic works. From here they would have progressed to more advanced treatises of kabbalistic teaching.

While the wide circulation of kabbalistic customs and ceremonies was very probably responsible for encouraging the belief in ghosts, imps, spirits, and dybbuks, and while the remedy for such visitations was to be found in a constant preoccupation with spells and amulets to keep them at bay, it undoubtedly inspired the nascent Jewish intelligentsia to study the nature of divinity as taught in classical Lurianic kabbalah, and to try to transcend their corporeality by studying the prophetic kabbalah of Abraham Abulafiah and the paths to ecstasy communicated by adepts or in esoteric texts that centred on the Zohar. Those who occupied themselves strenuously in these matters were doubtless few in number but, as in all societies, the intelligentsia functioned as a catalyst for wider social development and change. In our case, a penchant for deep study of kabbalah sharpened the conceptual abilities of those involved and developed their capacity to manipulate ideas. This intellectual stimulus was undoubtedly responsible for advancing the thinking of the nascent intelligentsia and preparing it to enter a new era.

What conclusions can be drawn from all this? In an article on kabbalah that Gershom Scholem wrote for the *Encyclopaedia Judaica*, he says that while there is some disagreement regarding the nature of the influence of kabbalah on Jewish history, no one doubts that its influence was profound.[37] He fails, however, to locate this influence in time or space through precise examination of the history of the reception of its literature and customs. Perhaps his vast

---

[37] This was printed separately in a book published by the editorial board of the encyclopedia, which includes all of the articles on the subject of kabbalah written for it by Gershom Scholem. See Scholem, *Kabbalah*, 190 ff.

bibliographical knowledge was unconsciously set aside when it came into conflict with his conception of the place of kabbalah and its adherents in Jewish history. As early as his fine article 'Redemption through Sin',[38] he repeatedly emphasizes the importance of the 'spiritual brethren' (he calls them 'the salt of the earth in our history' and 'the agents of fertility and ferment'), even though for long periods their number was small. In his view, the kabbalists formulated their esoteric system into a matrix for the doctrine of messianic redemption as a response to their expulsion from Spain; this revolutionary doctrine, eagerly accepted by the downtrodden and poverty-stricken masses, opened people's hearts to the promises of the false messiah Shabetai Tsevi and led to the rapid spread of his movement.[39]

My intention here is not to correct Scholem's statements regarding the background to the growth of Shabateanism on the basis of the importance of Lurianic kabbalah and the status of its leaders; rather, I want to put into perspective the influence that kabbalah in general, and its literature in particular, exerted in the Jewish world from the beginning of printing in the mid-fifteenth century to the end of the eighteenth century and the threshold of the modern era.

I have concentrated here on books that are profoundly kabbalistic in nature, and have ignored the many commentaries on the Torah, books of sermons, and halakhic works—from *Beit yosef* (The House of Joseph) by Joseph Caro onwards—in which kabbalistic ideas and customs are merely present but not the core. These latter works, however, influenced the penetration of concepts and customs among those who frequented the *batei midrash* and, perhaps as a result of this, paved the way for the interest in kabbalah that we find in the eighteenth century. A comprehensive examination of this literature would certainly refine my own figures and conclusions. It is unlikely, however, that it would change the main thrust of my argument, namely, that until the eighteenth century, the process of popularization of kabbalah was slow and confined to small circles.

This conclusion, based principally on the paucity of editions and the limited circulation of the basic books that are the main source for the development of a broad network of study, counters Gershom Scholem's assertion that the freedom adopted by the kabbalists in probing the source of the divinity and attempting to influence the flow of divine bounty entering the world had

---

[38] 'Mitsvah haba'ah be'averah', printed in the 1930s in *Sefer bialik* (Tel Aviv, 1937), 347–92.
[39] See Scholem, *Studies and Texts Concerning the History of Shabateanism* (Heb.), 19–20, 31–5.

the effect of liberating their thinking more generally. Thus, according to Scholem, the kabbalistic enterprise had the paradoxical effect of loosening the shackles of religion and enabling the Jew to enter the modern world. While it may certainly be argued that kabbalah, with its transformatory approach to the world, influenced both the Haskalah movement and Zionism, in my opinion the main factor impelling the Jews towards modernization derived from quite different sources. These include the important role of books as an agent of change in the intellectual lives of the majority of the Jewish population, who until the eighteenth century had been largely deprived of reading matter. As for the other major factors, I need only refer to Jacob Katz, who tried, in his pioneering work *Tradition and Crisis*, to describe the stages in the transition from a traditional society to the modern world and its causes, and to the revolutionary book by Azriel Shohet, *With the Change of the Epochs*.[40] I hope that my remarks will counterbalance those of Scholem, whose approach to kabbalah influenced Katz in *Tradition and Crisis* and other of his early publications.[41]

In concluding this chapter it is important to recall the contribution of the Israeli literary critic Baruch Kurzweil (1907–72), who expressed doubts before I did as to whether the interest in kabbalah indeed led to the Haskalah, as Scholem believed. Although Kurzweil went to extremes when he accused Scholem of anchoring secularity in the very heart of Judaism, it is hard not to agree with him when he says that Scholem's tendency towards anarchism and intellectual revolution coloured his study of Shabateanism.[42] In this context it is worthy of note that Scholem's deepest friendship was with Walter Benjamin, whose Marxist and dialectical views undoubtedly had a significant influence on Scholem's thinking, but this is not a topic which can be addressed in the present book.[43]

[40] Not only did Shohet's book pre-date the work of contemporary scholars of Jewish studies by a generation, it was also an important innovation in the study of history in general in that he was the first to understand that the study of Jewish social history has to include popular literature written for the masses as well as high literature written for the elite.

[41] See Gries, *Book, Scribe, and Story* (Heb.), 95, 143 and nn. 49–51.

[42] See Kurzweill, *In the Struggle for the Values of Judaism* (Heb.), 100, 111, and 173–6 ('On the Anarchistic Foundation of his Teaching').

[43] See Scholem's *Walter Benjamin*, and also his testimony in his memoirs, *From Berlin to Jerusalem*, 70–1.

SEVEN

Literature for Women and Children Only, or for Everyone?

T HE IMAGE of the nascent intelligentsia as a kind of Sleeping Beauty, awakened by the magical kiss of the literature made available by enterprising printers and booksellers, has been a recurrent theme in this book. Despite the great importance of those genres of Hebrew literature—mainly ethical and kabbalistic works—that flourished during the eighteenth century and were read avidly in the great Jewish centres in Poland, it appears that the most powerful stimulus, culturally speaking, came not from Hebrew literature but from Yiddish literature.

The absence of Jewish printing from Poland for some hundred years from the mid-seventeenth century did not lessen the demand for books among the Jewish population there. As we have seen, this demand was met by printers in Amsterdam and elsewhere in the German-speaking lands. But the silencing of the Polish presses nevertheless had important consequences. First, the extensive changes in eastern Yiddish in this period, in consequence of the introduction of Slavic words and for unrelated reasons, were never recorded. Second, as Chone Shmeruk has correctly noted, the continued printing of Yiddish books in Germany preserved in print the language and style of western Yiddish literature, and it was these works that circulated in eastern Europe.[1]

---

[1] See Shmeruk, *Yiddish Literature* (Heb.), 176–87. Studies of the Hebrew story in the Middle Ages have not compared its subsequent circulation in print to that of the Yiddish story. The majority of Hebrew works that included stories of various kinds were hardly printed at all in the 18th century. This was the fate of *Midrash aseret hadibrot* (The Legend of the Ten Commandments), *Alfa beita deben sira* (The Alphabet of Ben-Sira), *Sefer ḥasidim* (The Book of the Pious), *Shalshelet hakabalah* (The Chain of Kabbalah), and *Shevet yehudah* (The Staff of

The books most frequently published in Yiddish were ethical works with stirring titles such such as Isaac ben Eliakim of Posen's *Lev tov* (A Good Heart)[2] and Elhanan Kirchen's *Simḥat hanefesh* (Joy of the Soul), and books of popular exegesis and homily such as *Tsena urena*. Because they were published in Yiddish, which was the vernacular language, they were read by a much wider circle of readers than books in Hebrew; most certainly they were accessible to women in a way that Hebrew texts were not. As such they gave an eager public of women as well as men a taste of rabbinical legends and the teachings of medieval rabbis that stimulated their thirst for knowledge. Then, in the mid-seventeenth century, as Chava Turniansky has shown, this awakening took a more serious and critical turn. Even before that time, cultural entrepreneurs and translators had published books that combined commentaries on the Bible and popular *midrashim* (legends) in Yiddish; now, however, they started to translate the Bible itself into Yiddish.[3] The publication of books in the old style, such as *Tsena urena*, did not cease, but there was a move towards translating the texts themselves.[4] There was also an increasing demand for books of prayers in Yiddish for women (a genre known as *tekhines*), which was eagerly met by women authors keen to demonstrate their creativity in this field.[5] Similarly, Yiddish-language publications served to reinforce local custom; thus, the circulation of literature in Yiddish on kabbalistic customs legit-imized local ritual practices, as did the printing of booklets, known in Yiddish as *bentsherlekh*, which contained the grace after meals as well as those sabbath table-hymns current in the locality where the booklets were printed. Turniansky has shown that 14 such booklets were printed in the seventeenth century, whereas in the eighteenth century this number more than doubled, to 32.[6]

Judah). The only book that enjoyed greater circulation is *Yosipon*, although its main circulation during the 18th century was in Yiddish. See Dan, *The Hebrew Story in the Middle Ages* (Heb.); Yasif, *The Hebrew Folk Tale* (Heb.), 271–399.

  [2] See Ch. 4 n. 3.

  [3] See Turniansky, 'The History of the Yiddish Translation of the Pentateuch' (Heb.). See also Ch. 2 n. 28 and Ch. 5 n. 7 above.

  [4] Though, as outlined in Chapter 3 above, these changes took place against a background of conservatism: see p. 41.

  [5] See Weissler, 'The Traditional Piety of Ashkenazi Women', ii. 247–75, and her remarks in *Voices of the Matriarchs, passim*.

  [6] See Turniansky, 'The Grace After Meals and Sabbath Hymns in Yiddish' (Heb.), 51–92. The numbers accord with her bibliographical lists in the same article (pp. 69–92). See also Ch. 5 at nn. 4–6 above.

Very little attention has been given to the nature of reading material for Jewish children and young people. For many generations no literature directed specifically at these groups was written or printed, nor did young people serve as role models in either sacred or secular literature. Haym Soloveitchik once said to me that the reason we know the date of death, but not the date of birth, for many great rabbis is that when they were born they were considered unimportant—'just children'. In this, of course, the Jews were no different from other nations, and it was only with the advent of modern times that a writer of genius such as Rudyard Kipling could compose stories 'just' for children.[7]

In wider European society, the absence of literature aimed specifically at young people meant that once children had learned to read, their literary fare was simple adult books and illustrated books. These would have included popular ethical and historical works, but above all, children read fables, tales, and chivalric romances. As long as books were written in Latin, the language of high culture, they were inaccessible to this lively and curious young readership. When the Reformation brought about a revolution in the use of the vernacular in writing and printing, children gained a measure of independence from the adults in their household upon whom until then they had relied to tell them stories; they also gained intellectual satisfaction from the use of language as a basis for abstract, conceptual thought.

Uriel Ofek, an outstanding scholar of Hebrew literature for children, has made the description of the early development of children's literature in Hebrew his principal focus.[8] According to Ofek, the first children's book in

---

[7] Kipling's *Just So Stories* was first published in 1902 with illustrations by the author, embellished with his amusing comments. Thirty-three years elapsed before Avraham Regelson produced an abridged Hebrew translation, entitled *Ken hayah* (So It Was) (Tel Aviv, 1935). A new edition published in 1798 was retitled *Stam sipurim*. Nahum Guttman, author of tales of a similar type in Hebrew, supplied young readers with serialized stories in the magazine *Davar leyeladim* describing his trip to Africa, and like Kipling's stories they were illustrated with drawings with amusing captions. These were eventually published as the popular and much-acclaimed children's book, *In the Land of Lubengulu the Zulu King, Father of the Metabulu Nation, in the Mountains of Bulavaya*.

[8] See Ofek's *Give Them Books* (Heb.), 18–28, where he notes the kind of books that children read before people began to write books for them in Hebrew, and also his *Children's Literature in Hebrew* (Heb.). In this context, we should also note the work of Zohar Shavit and others: see Shavit and Ewers (eds), *Deutsch-Jüdische Kinder und Jugendliteratur von der Haskala bis 1945*. These last two books are both of great bibliographical importance.

Hebrew was *Avtaliyon*, written in the late eighteenth century.[9] He does not, however, deal with the question of what Jewish children read before the modern period.

Chone Shmeruk has noted that illustrated Yiddish books were published with the idea that children would be among their readers.[10] This insight has unfortunately not been followed up by Jewish cultural historians. Scholars of European culture and literature, in contrast, have approached children's literature, including books whose main characters are children, from several directions. The well-known thinker Paul Hazard dedicated a touching essay to children's literature in which he noted the pioneering work of Charles Perrault (1628–1703), the author of the *Mother Goose Rhymes*, which Hazard did not regard as a mere offshoot of Perrault's better-known contribution to European thought in that period.[11] Of the many studies of Perrault's children's stories, the scholarly treatment of its place in the popular literature of France at that time, the Bibliothèque Bleue, is of particular interest.[12] Children's literature in revolutionary France at the end of the eighteenth century has also received attention,[13] as has the literature of that time whose main characters were children and which was read avidly by women, young people, and children.[14]

There is, of course, no essential difference between the needs of Jewish and non-Jewish children: all children yearn for good books. Prior to the publication of Yiddish story books, Jewish children (and adults too, in areas where Yiddish was the vernacular) relied mainly on the oral transmission of stories. This tradition was neither repressed nor diminished by the spread of printed Yiddish because every society always has a social and cultural need to transmit

[9] Ofek, *Children's Literature in Hebrew: The Beginning* (Heb.), 28–37 n. 8.

[10] See Shmeruk, *Illustrations of Yiddish Literature in the Sixteenth to Seventeenth Centuries* (Heb.), 39 ff. See also the important insights in Shavit, 'The Function of Yiddish Literature in the Development of Children's Literature in Hebrew' (Heb.), 148–53, and her *Poetics of Children's Literature* (a Hebrew version of this appeared in 1996, with the collaboration of B. Even-Zohar: *Childhood Story: Introduction to the Poetics of Children's Literature*).

[11] *Mother Goose* was published in 1697 under the name of Perrault's son Pierre; Hazard's essay appears in his pamphlet *Books, Children, and Men.* See also his fascinating book *The European Mind 1680–1715*; it is noteworthy that this great scholar of European thought gave special attention to books for children.   [12] See Velay-Vallantin, 'Tales as a Mirror', 92–135.

[13] See Krammnick, 'Children's Literature and Bourgeois Ideology', 11–43.

[14] See Hunt, *The Family Romance of the French Revolution*, 171–81. On changes in reading during the 19th century among supposedly marginal sectors of the population, see Lyons, 'New Readers in the Nineteenth Century', 313–44.

stories orally: people want a tale that has a teller, someone who uses voice and gesture to act the part. Thus the process of creating and shaping stories for the pleasure of new generations of listeners is maintained, and natural storytellers emerge to attract audiences.

The eighteenth century saw a great increase in the publication of story books in Yiddish: 112, or three times the number published in the seventeenth century. Sarah Zfatman-Biler's excellent doctoral dissertation on Yiddish narrative, with its comprehensive list of the titles of books and pamphlets published (mostly in Amsterdam, though also elsewhere in the German-speaking lands), reveals that the intended readers were unquestionably children and young people.[15]

Below I present two lists of eighteenth-century publications in Yiddish: the first contains stories from Jewish sources or about Jewish subjects; the second contains stories from general sources. Both reveal certain educational trends, and the desire to import fiction and general information from the outside world. They also illustrate how the horizons of the Yiddish reader were expanded through access to popular sources of information. This was not simply a stimulus for increased learning as reading in the vernacular introduced people to new patterns of thought; it also served to shape their conceptual and literary world. The first to respond was the readership otherwise most deprived of books: children, young people, women, and men outside the scholarly elite who could not read Hebrew but had acquired the ability to read Yiddish. I am convinced, however, that one must add to this list the scholarly elite, for, as we have seen from the discussion of the writings of Jacob Emden and Solomon Maimon in Chapter 2, they too yearned for contact with and knowledge of the outside world.

At the conclusion of this chapter I should also mention, for the sake of comparison, the place of Judaeo-Arabic literature which, like Yiddish and Ladino, was written in Hebrew characters. It opened windows on the world during the Golden Age of the Jews in Spain, and between the tenth and twelfth centuries, some of the greatest Jewish scholars—from Sa'adiah Gaon to Maimonides—wrote their best works in Judaeo-Arabic. Maimonides in particular made a point of writing in this language, including his commentary

[15] See Zfatman-Biler, 'Narrative in Yiddish' (Heb.), esp. i. 23–54, and the notes on it at ii. 22–42, where the reader will find additional bibliography on the research of her predecessors and teachers. The figures on printing in Yiddish come from Zfatman-Biler, *Narrative in Yiddish: Annotated Bibliography* (Heb.).

on the Mishnah. This process was undoubtedly responsible for placing speakers of Judaeo-Arabic in the front rank of thinkers at that period. Neither then nor for hundreds of years afterwards did Yiddish acquire a similar status; it achieved its status and influence in a different way, as I have shown. The decline of Judaeo-Arabic literature began halfway through the late Middle Ages, in consonance with the general decline of culture in those lands where it was used—the lands of Islam.

A SUMMARY OF EIGHTEENTH-CENTURY LITERARY WORKS IN YIDDISH

The descriptions of the work are my own. Page and item numbers refer to the listing in Zfatman-Biler, *Narrative in Yiddish: Annotated Bibliography* (Heb.).

Stories from Jewish Sources or on Jewish Subjects

1. *Ma'aseh beit david* (Amsterdam, 1700), tales of the kings of Israel; a translation of the Hebrew work by Isaac Ekrish: pp. 78–9, no. 61.

2. Translations from the Apocrypha, including *Dash ma'aseh fun Mordekhai un Esther* and *Dash ma'aseh fun Shoshanah un Daniel* (both Germany, early eighteenth century): p. 82, no. 67; *S[efer] tuviyah* (Prague, 1703), p. 86, no. 71; *S[efer] shoshanah* (Ofibach, 1715), pp. 106–7, no. 96; *S[efer] yehudit, yuda makabi vetuviyah* (Frankfurt, 1715), pp. 107–8, no. 97.

3. Stories from the Talmud and about Hasidei Ashkenaz (German pietists), in many editions of *Ma'aseh bukh* (for example, Amsterdam, 1701; Frankfurt am Main, 1703): pp. 83–5, nos. 68–9; pp. 94–5, nos. 81–3; see also p. 148, no. 149.

4. *Sipur adam ba'al shem* (Amsterdam, 1700):[16] p. 79, no. 62; pp. 88–9, no. 75.

5. Stories from the Zohar and *Zohar hadash*, following the versions to be found in the many printings of *Ma'aseh hashem*: pp. 91–4, no. 80; see also other references there. Stories from the Zohar also appear in *Ein vander-*

---

[16] On the stories about Rabbi Adam, see Shmeruk, *Yiddish Literature in Poland* (Heb.), 119–46; for further sources on recent discussions see the references in Gries, 'The Historical Figure of the Besht', 426 n. 46, 435 n. 72. Etkes, *Master of the Name* (Heb.), 78–81, rejects my identification of the Joshua ben Nun who is mentioned as possessing writings from Rabbi Adam as being a rich Jewish merchant who lived in Safed in the sixteenth century. His reasons are surprising, for I point out that the hasidim felt that their right to possess and study the writings of the Holy Ari, the kabbalist Rabbi Isaac Luria, should be recognized, especially after the

likh shin ma'aseh oyz den Zohar (Prague, 1640), p. 89, no. 76; *Ma'aseh geshakh ein grosher* (*Talmid ḥakham*) (Frankfurt am Main, 1728), p. 124, no. 118.

6. Translation of *Ma'aseh yerushalmi* (Homburg, 1711), the story of the marriage of a Jew to the daughter of Ashmedai the King of the Spirits: pp. 98–9, no. 86.

7. *S*[*efer*] *ma'aseh gadol* ((?)Halle, 1711), a tale of the tribulations of an orphan girl sold into slavery by the Cossacks: pp. 100–2, no. 88.

8. *Ma'aseh fun ein yung* (Prague, 1713), a story about the drunken son of rich people who refused to repent: p. 102, no. 89.

9. *Ein vanderlikh maaseh dez geshehn iz tun di nakht fun shavuot* (Amsterdam, 1714), the story of a *tikun* (midnight prayer and study session) for Shavuot, and of Joseph Caro and Solomon Alkabetz: pp. 103–4, no. 91, where there is also another reference.

10. *Ein shein ma'aseh fun hagaon hagadol rabi Yitsḥak Tirna zts'l* (Frankfurt am Main, 1715), the story of the love of a king's daughter for Rabbi Yitshak Isaac Tirna: pp. 108, no. 98.

11. *Ein shein ma'aseh* [*ma'aseh Prague*] (Prague, 1705), a story about the establishment of the Jewish community in Prague: pp. 87, 88, no. 74, where there are also other references.

ban of Brody in 1772 restricted the study of Lurianic kabbalah to the rabbis of the Brody *kloiz*. Use of *Shivḥei ha'ari* (The Praises of the Ari) as an authority is clear, because of its wide circulation and acceptance. Moreover, Etkes argues that a source of which I was not aware indicates that Joshua ben Nun was in the possession of secret knowledge, and that he was the heir of Moses. Thence, supposedly, derives the proof that it cannot be known whether the reference is to the Joshua ben Nun who lived in Safed, or Joshua ben Nun of the Bible. The text upon which Etkes relies comes from Schaeffer, *Synopses of Heikhalot Literature* (Heb.), 673–8. In contrast to *Shivḥei ha'ari*, however, the *heikhalot* literature that Etkes quotes was known until modern times to only a very few people, and only from manuscripts. Moreover, the authors of that ancient esoteric doctrine incorporated in their texts the opening passage of *Pirkei avot*, which cites the train of transmission of the oral tradition, so as to legitimize the study of esoteric doctrine. They did so in order to make their readers believe that it was a tradition given from heaven, like the Written and Oral Torah, which Moses received and transmitted to Joshua, the elders, and so on. I presented the tradition according to *Merkavah shelemah* (The Entire Chariot), fo. 4a, in 1978, in a handbook on the early kabbalah which I wrote for Israel's Open University; that is to say, I did not need Shefer's synopses in order to be aware of this text. The programme on the kabbalah was unfortunately never published, for reasons unconnected with my involvement, but the handbook was, and was circulated for use by the students at Oranim Teachers' Seminary. See Gries, *The Early Kabbalah* (Heb.), 14.

12. *The Scroll of Antiochus* [for Hanukah] (Amsterdam, 1708–30): pp. 119–20, no. 105.

13. An abridged version of *Gelilot erets yisra'el* (The Regions of the Land of Israel) by Gershon Halevi printed in *Ma'aseh bukh* under the title *Bashraibung fun Eretz Yisroel* (Amsterdam, 1724):[17] p. 122, no. 110.

14. *Ma'aseh gadol venora* (n.p., 1767), the story of the exorcism of a spirit by the Master of the Name Rabbi Moses Prager: pp. 140–1, no. 138; see also pp. 151–2, no. 154.

15. *Die oybige libshaft* (Fürth, 1778), a love story concerning the Prince of Naples and the daughter of Rabbi Azriel the merchant: p. 142, no. 140.

16. *Historie die iz geshen in Amshterdam* (London, 1782), the story of a bride and groom who were born on the same day: p. 149, no. 150.

17. *Ein sheine historia fun dreie leit* (Fürth, 1789), tales of the Prophet Elijah: p. 154, no. 157.

18. *Ein vahre geshikhte velkht in Amshterdam geshehn izt bishnat taf-kuf-nun-zayin* (Amsterdam, 1798), the story of the tribulations of a woman who asks her husband for a writ of divorce: pp. 163–4, no. 170.

19. *Sefer emanuel* (Fürth, 1728), adaptation of *Maḥberet hatofet veha'eden* (The Joining of Inferno with Paradise) by Emanuel of Rome: pp. 126–7, no. 117.

Stories from Non-Jewish Sources

1. *S[efer] ma'aseh fun ein kalah* (Amsterdam, 1700), adaptations from Boccaccio's *Decameron*: p. 81, no. 65.

2. *Shildburgir zeltsami unt kortsveilige geshikhti* (Amsterdam, 1700), humorous stories, such as that of the Wise Men of Chelm: pp. 77–8, no. 60.

3. *Ma'aseh fun Shlomo Hamelekh* (Amsterdam, 1700), tales of the king's son and the monk: p. 80, no. 64.

4. *Der zibn veizn meinshter* (Amsterdam, 1707), selections from the tales of Sindbad and others: pp. 81–2, no. 66, and in the index, p. 187.

5. *Ein shein ma'aseh* [*Ma'aseh foyar mit nemi gril*], translated from Dutch

---

[17] See Shmeruk and Bartal, 'The Trials of Moses' (Heb.), 121–37, which shows that this book drew on *Igeret orḥot olam* (Epistle on the Paths of the World) by Abraham Parizol, and various German works.

(Amsterdam, 1707), the pranks of a villager who amuses himself by telling the truth: pp. 90–1, no. 79.

6. *Shpinisha heiden oder tsigeinrsh*, translated from Dutch (Amsterdam, 1713–25), after Cervantes, a story of the daughter of aristocrats who is abducted by Gypsies: pp. 102–3, no. 90. According to the title page, it was intended to help readers improve their Yiddish.

7. *Die beshtendigi libshaft fun Floris un' Flankinfeld* (Offenbach, 1714), a Dutch folk tale of the love of Floris and Flankinfeld: pp. 105, no. 93; see also other references there.

8. *Marot hatsovot* (Wansbeck, 1718), a translation of *A Thousand and One Nights*, apparently from the French: pp. 109–17, no. 100. The author planned to publish 365 stories in groups of seven per booklet at the rate of one booklet a week, but no more were printed.

9. *Vanderlikhi un kamishe geshikhti fan Eiln Shpigl* (Frankfurt am Main, before 1721), German folk tales, some taken from the popular German book *Eulenspiegel*: p. 119, no. 104, and see further references there.

10. *Historie hertsag hoiz halendish flandren* (Prague, 1762), the story of Elizabeth, daughter of the count of Flanders, who was accused of witchcraft: pp. 135–6, no. 131.

11. *Beshreibung dash lebnsh fun Robinsahn Krizah* (Metz, 1764), some tales of Robinson Crusoe said to have been translated from the French, but which appears to have been translated from German: p. 138, no. 134.

12. *Historie oder moralishe ertsehlung* (Frankfurt am Main, 1789), stories of King Arthur: p. 153, no. 155.

13. *Boba ma'aseh* (Frankfurt am Main, 1796), the well-known work by Eliyahu Bahur, based on the Italian narrative tradition; an abbreviated version of *Bobe Antona*:[18] pp. 161–2, no. 167

---

[18] See, in addition to the bibliography in Zfatman's *Narrative in Yiddish: Annotated Bibliography* (Heb.), the remarks in Shmeruk, *Yiddish Literature* (Heb.), 89–104. Shmeruk published a critical edition in Hebrew of the Yiddish novel *Pariz un' vienna*, which is attributed to Eliyahu Bahur (Jerusalem, 1996). In his introduction (pp. 11–38) Shmeruk reconsiders the identity of the author, concluding, against the generally held view, that it was not Bahur but rather one of his faithful students and admirers. However, an appendix by Shmeruk's co-editor Erika Timm—'A Different Hypothesis Regarding the Identity of the Author' (pp. 39–41)—argues in favour of Bahur.

PART II

THE BOOK

Guardian of the Sacred or Herald of Secularization?

The New Hebrew Literature: Continuity or Revolution?

IN THE AUTUMN OF 1979, when my wife and I were in England, we took the opportunity to visit the spiritual community of Findhorn. This settlement is located in a region of northern Scotland noted for its fierce storms; yet the community, which follows a unique way of life, had succeeded in cultivating the land in an area where everyone else had given up. As a son of farmers who had failed in his efforts to make agriculture his profession and source of livelihood, I had been attracted for some time by the fabled achievements of this community. The story of the great harvests of Findhorn appeared in brochures and leaflets which were circulated worldwide. According to the reports, the members of the community had worked wonders, growing cabbages the size of pumpkins and squash the size of melons on its barren soil. This miracle was said to be less a blessing from heaven than a direct result of meditation—combined with music specially composed for the process of personal, inner concentration—practised in the fields, especially at night. When we reached Findhorn, I found to my astonishment that the fields were miserable. The 'gigantic' vegetables were closer in size to lemons than the massive specimens promised in the literature. On the other hand, to my surprise, the community's publishing house, from which material flowed in profusion, was impressive in both its size and its activity.

Relying on current accounts without examining in detail the craggy soil on which modern Hebrew literature grew in the second half of the nineteenth century, it might appear that it flourished in a manner similar to that of the vegetables described in Findhorn's brochures: a harvest that provided the Jews of the period with their spiritual nourishment. I would contend, however, that here too there is a huge discrepancy between the true situation and the way in which it has been interpreted. Scholars claim that the impact of the Haskalah and secular literature, particularly during the second half of the nineteenth century, was such as to start a revolution in reading habits whose impact is felt to this day. This assessment is based on an implicit assumption that the fathers of modern Hebrew literature took an ideological stance with regard to the traditional literature in which they had been educated, a literature that came from the world of Torah and its commandments, and which encouraged those who studied and read it to cling to that world.

For more than a century, scholars of Jewish literature have communicated the message that modern Hebrew literature is secular in essence and therefore different from the Jewish literature of earlier periods and from contemporary literature in the traditional mode. For generations the world of Jewish literature and the world of the Jewish religious tradition, with its own peculiar vocabulary and values, were synonymous. Jewish literature spoke to all Jews who had received a traditional religious education, whether in the second century or the nineteenth century. This was the view of Simon Halkin, who regarded traditional literature as not being bound by place or time, since its central theme was God and his connections with the world and with mankind.[1]

According to this view, even those works that were written by Jews in secular literary genres in the period when the world of the Jew was essentially sacred—whether poetry, parody, or the fables and tall tales of the Middle Ages and Renaissance—derived from the world of traditional language and imagery. Though authors may have intended to write about a secular world, the language in which they wrote confined them to the discourse of the Bible and rabbinic literature, with its characteristic expressions and subjects. As a consequence, readers needed a traditional Jewish education in order to fully understand this literature.

Halkin regarded modern Hebrew literature as marking a fresh start—a

---

[1] See Halkin, *Conventions and Crises in our Literature* (Heb.), 15. Halkin's major study is *Modern Hebrew Literature*; see also his *Currents and Forms in Modern Hebrew Literature* (Heb.), and cf. the remarks in Kurzweil, *Is Our New Literature a Continuation or a Revolution?* (Heb.). I shall return to Kurzweil and his words below. See also the work of the preceding generation of scholars: Klausner, *History of Modern Hebrew Literature* (Heb.); Lachower, *History of Modern Hebrew Literature* (Heb.); Shapira, *History of Modern Hebrew Literature* (Heb.). Their principal followers are Gershon Shaked and Dan Miron (see below).

revolutionary reaction to the past, both in language and in the way of think-ing.[2] To the best of my knowledge, the only scholar of Hebrew literature who has doubted this discontinuity between modern Hebrew literature and its progenitor, the traditional Hebrew literature, was Dov Sadan.[3] In his intro-ductory essay to *Avnei bedek* ('Touchstones'), Sadan argues that the gap between modern and traditional Hebrew literature is not as wide as is com-monly assumed, since many writers of the modern movement borrowed abun-dantly from hasidic literature and other traditional religious sources. Regrettably, his words have largely been ignored. In my opinion, modern Hebrew literature is far more traditional than is generally thought by scholars, in terms of both the language and background of its creators and their concep-tual world. Thus, modern Hebrew literature coexists with its ancient, tradi-tional, and self-renewing sister.

According to the literary critic Baruch Kurzweil,

the languages of Europe were unquestionably the languages of secular life. In the Catholic world, the language of liturgy was Latin. The process of secularization in the literature of the non-Jews was, therefore, self-evident. It did not endanger their national foundations. On the contrary, it strengthened them, by freeing literature and science from the custody of the Church, which was international in character. Furthermore, the national essence of the non-Jews was never in doubt. Their land and state testified clearly to it.[4]

This is in contrast to the secularization of Jewish literature which, according to most scholars, began in the eighteenth century. Kurzweil takes a position which is reminiscent of that of Balaam in Numbers 23: 9, that the Jewish people 'shall not be reckoned among the nations', since their literary history is quite different.

The foregoing is part of a basic argument, frequently reiterated in Kurzweil's writing, that has been influenced by Max Wiener's important book, *The Jewish Religion in the Period of the Emancipation*. Wiener argues that the great crisis in Jewish life and literature was the transition from a homogen-ous society, where religion sanctified life, to a divided society where some continued to adhere to religion and to the sacred writings as canonical litera-ture while others abandoned religion and instead sanctified secular life. In

---

[2] See *Modern Hebrew Literature*, 17.   [3] See Sadan, *Touchstones* (Heb.), Introd.

[4] Kurzweil, *Continuation or Revolution?* (Heb.), 30–1.

Kurzweil's view, the Hebrew literature of the time was an expression of this crisis and the consequent undermining of Jewish religious life. Yet despite is miserable beginnings in an assortment of pamphlets written by early advocates of the Haskalah, it became a developed form of artistic expression, culminating in the writing of Nobel prizewinner S. Y. Agnon.[5]

This argument is easily refuted, since, from as early as the sixteenth century, Christian reformers emerged whose first act was to transform vernacular languages such as French and German into a language of sacred texts and prayer. This change was accompanied by a growth in secular literature in those languages, and by a new approach to life and education. The great difference between the Christianity of those who were innovators in the field of secular literature in the non-Jewish world and the Jewishness of those Jewish writers who abandoned their religion, or who were drawn to the secular world, stems from the fact that Judaism is a religion of law. As such, it permeates every aspect of life and imposes a context of religious sanctification or profanation upon the acts of those who adhere to it. Until the modern period, therefore, the entire spectrum of Jewish life—material and spiritual—was completely immersed in the realm of the sacred.

Jews were capable, of course, of distinguishing between sacred and profane and between holy and secular objects. Among other things, they recognized the difference between sacred books, which had to be preserved (and buried with reverence if their pages were damaged), and secular texts, which were influenced by the genres of secular literature current in the non-Jewish world, and did not have a sanctified status among the Jews. Thus the many books and pamphlets of secular literature published during the eighteenth century, especially in Yiddish, were never regarded as holy.

It is difficult to accept Baruch Kurzweil's sweeping criticism of Simon Halkin for identifying manifestations of secular literature in periods when the world of the Jew was supposedly sacred. Furthermore, both Halkin and Kurzweil ignore Yiddish literature, which, decades before the formal emancipation of the Jews of Europe, was already transmitting secular knowledge from the non-Jewish world to an eager Jewish public. This was in addition to its function in disseminating Jewish customs and ritual, and thereby also helping to reinforce the traditional Jewish way of life. Thus, alongside the sacred literature—which is not bound by the strictures of time and place, for it

---

[5] Kurzweil, *Continuation or Revolution?* (Heb.), 32–6.

is part of a chain of creation that is independent of time—there developed a literature of time and place. This literature, even though it bore the hallmarks of the 'ordinary' and the 'temporal', was very popular among the Jews. If this is so, it is not unreasonable to ask why three generations of critics and scholars in modern Hebrew literature—Joseph Klausner, Hayim Nahman Shapira, and Fischel Lachower, from the first generation, Simon Halkin and Baruch Kurzweil from the second, and Gershon Shaked and Dan Miron from the third[6]—all ignored its traditional characteristics and motifs.

The answer, in my opinion, is that ideology played as important a role in literary criticism as it did in literature itself. Because of their Zionist commitment, the critics and scholars I have mentioned appear to have been convinced that the emergence of modern Hebrew literature marked the birth of Jewish nationalism. It was therefore unnecessary to study it in relation to the traditional literature that preceded it or was contemporaneous with it. In order to promote the Zionist ideal, modern Hebrew literature was described as having been created *ex nihilo*, as it were, from the writers' uncontrollable Nietzschean drive to alter the spiritual image of Judaism.

Halkin was a step ahead of the other literary critics when he attempted to develop his research within a broad social and cultural analysis of the life of the Jews of eastern Europe. In this way he was able to show the extent to which the period of the birth of modern Hebrew literature—between 1880 and 1920—was a time of revolutionary social change, during which more than a third of the Jews of eastern Europe—then the largest centre of world Jewry—saved up to emigrate to America.[7] While we may be impressed by Halkin's uniqueness in making this observation, we may equally wonder why he never examined how contemporary Hebrew literature responded to this central development in Jewish life, and how it documented it.

Erets Yisra'el attracted only a minority of this mass Jewish emigration, which was directed mainly toward the United States. However, because of the symbiotic relationship between Zionist ideology and literary modernism, the gentle sound of that trickle of immigration reverberated in modern Hebrew literature as though masses of Jews had taken their staves and knapsacks and made their way to the Holy Land. In actual fact, only a few thousand found

[6] See Shaked, *Modern Hebrew Literature*, vol. i: *In Exile* (Heb.). See also Miron, *Between Vision and Truth* (Heb.), and *When Loners Come Together* (Heb.), pt. i, pp. 23–111.

[7] See Halkin, *Currents and Forms*, 9–18.

their way there, in search of national advancement; yet literally millions of others set their sights and their hopes for advancement of a more personal nature in the land where gold was said to line the streets. We may well ask whether, when modern, national Hebrew literature first flourished, there was a large readership in eastern Europe which responded to it and identified with its protagonists. It appears likely that, while those whose education had been based on modern literature, and those who wrote and criticized it in the generations following the mass immigration, were charmed by Zionist ideology, the great majority of the Jews in eastern Europe themselves did not waver between Zion and the United States. They had no doubts as to whether personal problems or national problems should take precedence. They simply wondered how, when, and what to pack for the trip to America.

It is possible to find evidence of criticism of modern Hebrew literature both before and during the emigration, but scholars have generally ignored this. Historians of modern Hebrew literature have not paid serious attention to early critics such as Abraham Uri Kovner and Abraham Jacob Papirna,[8] or to the better-known early twentieth-century critic Joseph Hayim Brenner. Were they to do so, they would need to reconsider their conviction that modern Hebrew literature records modern Jewish experience, hopes, and longings more than any other literary corpus of the time.[9]

Abraham Kovner, as an observer of events and their impact on Hebrew literature some fifteen years prior to the start of the emigration, states categorically that it is a florid literature without life or vitality, bombastic from start to finish, while saying nothing to its readership.[10] Elsewhere in his writings Kovner rejects the dogmatic attitude of the Hebrew writers of his day and chides their constant return to it in their texts. He thus supplies the first example in modern Hebrew writing of a protest against the gap between literature and life itself. He writes:

For about a decade now, authors—who have multiplied like the fish of the sea—*have been raising their voice like a trumpet*, calling to the Hebrews to rouse from their slumber. Everyone who is capable of writing three or four lines in the Hebrew language becomes a castigator of the people of Israel, demanding that it emerge from darkness

---

[8] On literary criticism in the Hebrew press see Ch. 10 n. 11 below.

[9] The most comprehensive and profound study of Hebrew literary criticism in the period under discussion is the doctoral dissertation by Arnah Golan, 'Hebrew Literary Criticism' (Heb.). [10] See his *Collected Writings* (Heb.), 45.

into light, from vain belief to Enlightenment, and the like. If we take almost all the books that have left the hands of the maskilim during the past ten years—all the articles that have been printed in magazines—we will be amazed to see that 'they are of one language and of one speech' [Gen. 11: 1], and they cry out: 'My people, my people, why do you slumber! Awaken! Arise toward the new morning! Do not rebel against the light! Do not turn away from the path of Enlightenment! Enlightenment will not hinder faith! Torah and wisdom are sisters; tradition and knowledge are twins! How lovely is the fruit of Enlightenment! How great are its deeds! How great is its utility! All who find it have found life!' etc. etc. etc. Not one of them, however, turns his mind to contemplating and probing the factors that impede the Enlightenment of the Hebrews in Russia. In the opinion of those who *raise their voice like a trumpet*, the reason is the stupidity of the Hebrews. For they *hate* Enlightenment, and they say there is death in it. They think of it as an enemy and traitor, whose home is in the underworld, and leads to Gehenna and to eternal damnation; and having found, in their opinion, the illness, some search in this direction, some in that, to find an effective cure. Some sought to prove that Enlightenment would not violate fear of God, that its home is not in the ways of the underworld, that he who has found it has found *life*, for it brings a myriad things that are useful for life. So they cried in a loud voice: 'Grasp the horns of Enlightenment, so that it will go well for you, so that you will live, so that you will enjoy all the benefits that result from Enlightenment!' In point of fact, all of these men erred in their vision, and in the thought that they had found the disease, and that once it was cured, that which they wished to bring to them would indeed come.[11]

Kovner goes on to write that the Jews of his time who maintained their traditions and were in dire distress found consolation in traditional ethical literature, 'which leads to life in the world to come'. Alongside the sarcasm he directs towards the evil, spirit-ridden world of his contemporary brethren we find a reliable description of their inner feelings, showing the extent to which the maskilim ignored the existential distress of the average unsophisticated Jew. As long as it remained unaddressed it would prevent awareness of the need for Enlightenment. And what was that distress? It was not only an absence of the emancipation of western Europe, but also the backwardness and lack of progress that characterized Jewish social and economic life.

For some reason, scholars of modern Hebrew literature have not taken Kovner's words seriously. Were they to take the trouble to look at the advocates of the new revolutionary poetry and compare their descriptions of everyday Jewish life and that life itself, they would have to revise their opinion

[11] Ibid. 182–6.

of their literary outpourings. Consider, for example, the famous poem by Judah Leib Gordon, *Kotzo shel yod* (The Dot of an I),[12] on which generations of Israeli high school students have been educated, and examined at matriculation. This poem contrasts progress—in the figure of Fabi (originally Feibush), the 'engineer', who is actually a supervisor, the Jew who lays railroad tracks, the path to the future—with the conservative world of tradition, represented by the 'rebellious husband' in Russia who has abandoned his wife and by the rabbis who refuse to force him to initiate a divorce. For Gordon, the rabbis in Russia insist on living in darkness even though progress has already brought light to their doorways. Anyone who reads the memoirs of Laurence Oliphant's trip to Russia in the mid-nineteenth century, and anyone who travels in the heart of that country today, will see that progress—not to mention the railway—which had not arrived there then, has still not arrived today.[13]

Some decades later, Joseph Hayim Brenner drew a picture of the modern Hebrew literature emanating from Palestine as a literature of 'memoirs', some of which, like the stories by Solomon Tsemah, offered a romantic depiction of the miserable new Jewish villages as though they were as full of vigour as the villages of Germany.[14]

The astute thinker Max Wiener has noted that the image of modernism that influenced the writing of Jewish history was based mainly on the post-Haskalah experience of German Jewry: literary modernism began there and spread from there to eastern Europe. As Wiener correctly notes, however, the

[12] On Gordon see Stanislawski, *For Whom Do I Toil?*; *Kotzo shel yod* is found in Gordon's *Writings* (Heb.), 129–40. See also Feingold, '*Kotzo shel yod*: The Anatomy of a Satire' (Heb.), 73–103.

[13] See Oliphant, *Russian Shores of the Black Sea* (Heb.). There is insufficient space in the present volume to describe this amazing man—visionary, adventurer, and prophet of the return to Zion—who employed the author of *Hatikvah*, Naftali H. Imber, as his personal secretary, but see the detailed biography by Anne Taylor (*Laurence Oliphant, 1829–1888*), which includes additional bibliography; on the reception of his travel book, see p. 24. For comparative purposes, see *Encyclopaedia Britannica* (1990), xxviii. 766, s.v. 'Transportation'. This highlights the lack of a good rail network in mid-19th-century Russia, but does also mention the enormous project involving the laying of thousands of miles of track on the trans-Siberian railway between 1891 and 1916 (p. 788).

[14] See Brenner, *Collected Writings* (Heb.), ii. 268–9. For a comprehensive study of Brenner's literary criticism see Parush, *Literary Canon and National Ideology* (Heb.): the third part of the book (pp. 261–366) is devoted to Brenner.

historical experience of the German Jews was completely different from that of the Jews of eastern Europe during the nineteenth century.[15]

The Jewish satirist Sami Gronemann has given us a vivid description of the course of events in Germany at the end of the nineteenth century:

The orthodox often carried the Torah and the severity of the practical commandments to a grotesque degree . . . and the tendency grew, from the cult of mere external forms, to forget any deeper meaning. Women in those circles wore wigs, 'so as not to find favour in the eyes of other men', but not, for example, in the way that the Jewish women of Poland wore them. Rather, they wore charming, elegant wigs, abundant with all the virtues and ornaments of Parisian coiffeurs, which beautifully suited the rules of honest décolletage, while yeshiva students scrupulously avoided using money on the sabbath, and arranged credit in houses of ill repute for that day . . . that is to say, *right and left, the Holy One, blessed be He, became profanely secular.*[16]

Gronemann's understanding of the distinction between the Jews of Germany and Poland at the turn of the nineteenth century is important, since it is a record of the distinction between the forms of Judaism practised in those two countries. The lack of emancipation and the concomitant lack of any impetus to assimilate encouraged the continued vitality of traditional Jewish life in Poland. The community was devoted to the traditional way of life and clung to the literature that was intended to conserve it.

In the next chapter I will discuss in depth the literary diet of the Jews of eastern Europe, the great centre of Jewry during the eighteenth and nineteenth centuries. I will also comment on those who created and disseminated that literature, and with the audience it addressed. In east European Jewish society, the Jewish tradition and its literature served as highly important cultural agents, binding the Jewish community together and giving succour to the individuals within it. It is no coincidence, therefore, that most Jewish literature in the eighteenth and nineteenth centuries, both in Hebrew and in Yiddish, came from this Jewish tradition. Most of the literature wore a traditional guise, reflecting the world through the lens of religion, in line with the Talmudic dictum (Rosh Hashanah 2*a*) 'See this and sanctify it!'

Precursors of the miraculous resurrection of the Hebrew language can be found in the eighteenth and nineteenth centuries, but the miracle that transformed the Hebrew language into a powerful tool for the fulfilment of Jewish

---

[15] See Wiener, *The Jewish Religion in the Period of the Emancipation* (Heb.), 40, 62, and esp. pp. 204–83. See also Gries, 'Heresy', 347–8.   [16] Gronemann, *Memoirs of a Yekke* (Heb.), 29.

national aspirations in the Land of Israel is a twentieth-century phenomenon. The opening of fissures in the traditional world, and the new image of the Jew and of his dreams for the reparation of his world are, of course, to be found in Jewish literature before the twentieth century. The renewal of sovereign national life in the Land of Israel, however, required more than the enthusiastic creativity of linguistic zealots in devising and implementing a national language that would meet the needs of modern society; we must not forget that a willingness to migrate and the changes in the civil and political status of the Jews of Europe during the twentieth century, especially after the rise of fascism, were equally important factors in achieving this goal.

NINE

Jewish Books and their Authors in the Nineteenth Century

THERE IS FIRM EVIDENCE that until the end of the nineteenth century, the prime factor encouraging intellectual activity in the great Jewish cities of eastern Europe was religious literature. Although today it is not fashionable to consider how this literature of rabbinic responsa, epistles, commentaries on the Talmud, homiletics, and exegesis served the lives of the Jews in a changing world, there is no doubt that it was intended to offer solutions in times of distress and to fulfil yearnings for spirituality and closeness to God.

It is interesting to compare the output of two major centres of Jewish publishing in the nineteenth century, Lemberg and Vilna. Lemberg in the 1860s accommodated the hasidim, the maskilim, and the traditional halakhic authorities without excessive friction. Vilna, in contrast, was home to an impressive array of both traditional scholars and maskilim and had supposedly been the centre of opposition to hasidism in earlier generations. We find testimony to this in the memoirs of the literary critic Abraham Jacob Papirna, who recounts that, when he was a student at the Vilna yeshiva, an itinerant rabbi called Tsevi Hermann Schapira (who ultimately became a professor of mathematics in Heidelberg, and later conceived the idea of a Jewish National Fund for the purchase of land in Palestine for the Jewish people) read excerpts from his anti-hasidic satirical writings there. One of these satires, which Schapira called both *Masekhet ḥasidim* (Tractate of the Hasidim) and *Masekhet shirayim* (Tractate of the Tsadik's Leftovers), was eventually published with a commentary by Isaiah Tishby.[1]

---

[1] See the references to Papirna's remarks in Tishby, 'Tsevi Hermann Schapira as a Haskalah Writer' (Heb.), 556–74, 696–712; see also id., 'The Conception of Haskalah' (Heb.), 263–80. On

בדפוס
סל הנגידים המוסלנים
מוהכ״ר
דוב בעריש לו״א
ומוהכ״ר
הירש שפע־לינג

7. The printers' mark used by Dov-Berish Luria and Hirsch Sperling in the
press they owned in Lemberg from 1860 to 1864. With its bear and deer, it is a
graphic representation of their names. This mark was taken from an
edition of *Mishnayot* that they published

Another literary critic in Vilna at this time was Abraham Uri Kovner, who recounts how he found, read, and enjoyed the manuscript of *Bohen tsadik* (The Examiner of the Holy Man). The author was not named, but Kovner assumed that it was Joseph Perl, the author of *Megaleh temirin* (The Revealer of Hidden Things), printed in Prague in 1838. Both books were critiques of the hagiographies of the tsadikim that were then popular.[2] Maskilim, who served as tutors in the homes of wealthy Jews, liked to read these satires; since they were hard to obtain they copied them by hand in their free time, as I heard from Shmuel Werses, who drew my attention in this context to a note by his teacher Professor Klausner on *Divrei tsadikim* (The Words of the Tsadikim) by Isaac Ber Levinsohn.[3]

The output of Vilna's main printers in the 1860s confirms the stereotype of the city as a stronghold of traditional scholarship and Haskalah ideology. The leading figure in promoting the Haskalah movement in Vilna was Samuel Shraga Feigensohn, who wrote under the pen-name Shafan Hasofer; yet Feigensohn was effectively the director of the Romm printing house, famed for its edition of the Talmud, from the second half of the 1860s until the early 1920s except for the fifteen-year period from 1888 to 1903.[4] Lemberg, in contrast, had the edge in publishing hasidic books, primarily hagiographies. *Shivhei habesht* was printed there in Hebrew and Yiddish, in edition after edition in the 1860s, as were hagiographies compiled by Menahem Mendel Bodek and Michael Frumkin-Rodkinson, together with books of hasidic exegesis, customs, and epistles.

It may be that there was no ideological division here, but rather a division of labour reflecting specialization of knowledge: Lemberg produced pietistic literature, kabbalah, and hasidic works for both Galicia and Russia, while

Schapira, see the wonderful article by Reuven Brainin, 'On the Life of Professor Tsevi Schapira' (Heb.), 181–9.

[2] See Kovner, *Collected Writings* (Heb.), 39–40; see also Werses, 'The Satirical Method of Joseph Perl' (Heb.), 45–9, and the edition by Avraham Rubinstein of Perl's book *Al mahut kat hahasidim* (On the Essence of the Sect of the Hasidim).

[3] On *Divrei tsadikim* and its editions, see Klausner, *History of Modern Hebrew Literature*, 2nd edn, vol. iii (1953), 40–1. He notes that Perl changed the first part of the book—which had been in the form of a conversation—into letters in order to obtain the censor's permission to print; ibid. 109–10.

[4] See the memoirs published in Bar-Dayan, *The Jewry of Lithuania* (Heb.) under the heading 'On the History of the Romm Printing House' (i. 282–302). On the trade in Jewish books in Vilna and other cities of Lithuania, see Zalkin, *Daybreak* (Heb.), 159–63.

Vilna produced books of halakhah and Haskalah, also for both regions. The chief product of Vilna, however, was the splendid edition of the Talmud published by the printing house established by David Romm and owned after his death by his widow and brothers. The first volume of this edition was published in the 1880s. David Romm had published an earlier edition in 1859, but this had brought him into conflict with a printing house in Slavuta (owned by descendants of Pinhas Shapira of Korets, one of the founding fathers of hasidism) that had started to publish their own edition the previous year.[5] The Romm edition of the 1880s was widely considered superior to the Shapira edition, because it contained dozens of new interpretations, including a commentary by the Vilna Gaon that the Shapira family had had access to but not published. Among the books published in Lemberg at this time it should be pointed out that hasidic teachings were relatively rare, for the main literary contribution of the hasidim in the second half of the nineteenth century was traditional rabbinical literature of the sort that had been known for generations.

While the information outlined here might suggest that there were clear-cut distinctions in the 1860s between the different groups within Jewish society, and between Vilna and Lemberg, the reality was not so simple. The memoirs of Abraham Papirna, for example, indicate internal divisions among the teachers at the Vilna rabbinical seminary: some were innovators, some conservative; some were belligerent, and some mild in their opinions.[6] It would therefore be wrong to depict Vilna as an anti-hasidic stronghold where hagiographies were rejected as fairy tales or figments of the imagination, as compared to Lemberg, where the soil for absorbing them was fertile. The

[5] See Israel Klausner, *Vilna, the Jerusalem of Lithuania* (Heb.), 380–4. A large number of articles have been written on the Romm printing house of Vilna: see Kohn, 'On the Romm Printing House' (Heb.), 244–50; and id., 'Towards a History of the Romm Printing House' (Heb.), 109–15, which gives information on the names of the books and their genre. Friedberg, *Hebrew Printing in Poland* (Heb.) devotes space to Vilna: see pp. 87–9 of the first edition and pp. 124–32 of the second edition; it was sharply criticized by Rivkind in 'History of Hebrew Printing in Poland' (Heb.), 97–8, 305. Friedberg published an expanded and corrected edition of his book (Tel Aviv, 1950), where pp. 124–32 are devoted to printing in Vilna. See also Liberman, 'On the Printing House of the Widow and the Brothers Romm' (Heb.), 527–8 (repr. in *Rachel's Tent*, i. 217–18). The best description is by Feigensohn, 'The History of the Romm Printing House' (Heb.), i. 268–97. On the controversy between the printers of Vilna and those of Slavuta concerning the rights for printing the Talmud, see the second edition of Friedberg, *Hebrew Printing in Poland* (Heb.), 107–9. [6] See Papirna, *Collected Writings* (Heb.), 175–93.

distinction between the two groups was not so clear cut. I first made this point in the 1980s when I took part in Rivka Schatz-Uffenheimer's project to create a new register of hasidic books, noting even then that most of the books written and published from the mid-1860s onwards by men known to be hasidim were in fact works of halakhah, new interpretations of the Talmud, and works of biblical exegesis and rabbinical homiletics that contained no explicitly hasidic motifs. The contribution of the hasidim to halakhic literature, and to rabbinic literature in the more general sense, should prompt us to look again at our understanding of the make-up of Jewish society during this period. This is not the proper place to trace the growth of modern Orthodoxy and its components in eastern Europe and the relative part played in this by the hasidim, their opponents from within the traditional community (known as mitnagedim), and the maskilim. We should, however, note that as the hasidic movement became increasingly established, especially in the area known as Congress Poland—hasidic courts arose, such as Przysucha, whose main focus was halakhic scholarship and study.

In the world of Torah literature of the nineteenth century, the writing of 'approbations' or endorsements for works prior to publication was very widely practised. This literary genre has not yet been studied in depth, and no attempt has been made to establish the personal connections between those who wrote approbations, and between them and the authors for whom they wrote them. The most prominent supplier of approbations in the nineteenth century was Joseph Saul Nathansohn, the rabbi of Lemberg. As a consequence of the prodigious number he wrote he was sometimes referred to as 'the minister of approbations' (*sar hamaskim*, a pun on the biblical phrase *sar hamashkim*, the chief of butlers, in Gen. 40: 2). The many hundreds of approbations he wrote give a fascinating picture of this prominent rabbi, who not only took the trouble to read a great many books but also included corrections and comments to their authors in his approbations.[7] We also learn of the

---

[7] See his approbations to the following books: Yehudah Rozanis, *Parashat derakhim* (*Crossroads*) (Lemberg, 1858); Yisrael Kahana, *She'elot uteshuvot beit yisra'el* (Questions and Answers of the House of Israel) (Zolkiew, 1858); Tsevi Hirsch Eichenstein of Zhidachov, *Beit yisra'el* (The House of Israel) (Lemberg, 1860); *Sefer haheshek* (The Book of Desire) (Lemberg, 1865); Avraham Naftali Herz Yener, *Tsiluta de'avraham* (The Prayer of Abraham) (Cracow, 1868) (in Friedberg, *The Library*, the city is erroneously listed as Lemberg); Shmuel Shmelke Horowitz of Nikolsburg, *Nezir hashem* (The Nazarite of God), and, by his son Tsevi Joshua, *Semikhat mosheh* (The Ordination of Moses) (both Lemberg, 1869); Elazar Azkari, *Sefer*

types of books he read and the authors with whom he was in contact. Considering the wide variety of books he reviewed, from studies in halakhah to works of piety, including books on hasidism and kabbalah, and comparing these to his own principal work, a book of responsa entitled *Shoel umeshiv* (The Asker and the Respondent), it is clear that, although he was very well read in a wider range of books, he continued unswervingly in his major role as a *posek* (a halakhic authority) in the tradition of former generations. Nathansohn's beloved disciple Menahem Mendel Bodek was a collector of hasidic stories, and the two debated subtle issues of halakhah. The rabbi read his student's works on halakhah,[8] and gave an approbation to his book of Torah discourses, *Einot mayim* (Fountains of Water). He also gave his approbation to *She'erit yisra'el* (The Remnant of Israel), by the God-fearing hasid Israel Dov Beer of Vilednik, even though its publisher, Michael Frumkin-Rodkinson, was widely considered a wanton good for nothing.[9]

Another prolific source of approbations, for halakhic works as well as hasidic writings, was Rabbi Hayim Halberstam of Sanz, a great hasidic tsadik. He was also very learned in halakhah, though his approbations, unlike Nathansohn's, did not include detailed corrections or commentaries. In the

ḥaredim (The Book of Those Who Fear God) (Lemberg, 1870); Ya'akov Tsevi Jolles, *Kehilat ya'akov* (The Congregation of Jacob) (Lemberg, 1870); Tsevi Hirsch Eichenstein of Zhidachov, *Ateret tsevi* (The Crown of Splendour) (Lemberg, 1871); Tsevi Hirsch of Sokolov, *Imrat hatseru-fah* (Pure Speech) (Lemberg, 1871); *Shemirat hanefesh* (The Guarding of the Soul) (Lemberg, 1872); Tsevi Gutmacher, *Naḥalat tsevi* (Beautiful Heritage) (Lemberg, 1873); Yehudah Asad, *Teshuvot maharia* (The Responsa of Maharia) (Lemberg, 1873); Aharon Tenenbaum, *Ḥadashim laketoret* (New Things for the Incense) (Warsaw, 1879); Avraham David of Buczacz, *Da'at kedoshim* (The Wisdom of the Holy) (Lemberg, 1880); Shneur Zalman of Vilna, *Matsav hayashar* (The Position of the Upright) (Vilna, 1881). The author added a note to Nathansohn's approbation of the latter book, stating that he had removed everything that Nathansohn had disagreed with in his approbation, and that he had therefore also removed Nathansohn's detailed critique on these matters.

   [8] As he says in many places in *Sho'el umeshiv*: see *Kama* 2. 110, 3. 93; *Tinyana* 1. 64, 2. 9, 71, 3. 129, 4. 111; *Talita'ah* 1. 449, 2. 152, 3. 133; *Reviah* 1. 185, 4. 28 (references are to part/section). In this context, see Meir Wunder, *Encyclopedia of the Sages of Galicia* (Heb.), s.v. 'M. M. Bodek' (pp. 416–17); Wunder takes the trouble to present the places where Bodek is mentioned in Nathansohn's writings. I have indicated here only those references where they are debating matters of halakhah.

   [9] Rodkinson is a colourful character worthy of a biography in his own right. See my remarks about him in *Book, Scribe, and Story* (Heb.) 37–8, 40, 48, 103, 123 n. 108, 128, n. 10, and 148 n. 87 and the additional bibliography there.

circumstances of nineteenth-century eastern Europe, and particularly the challenges from maskilic circles, the need to ensure the continuation of Jewish traditions in the old way drew prominent hasidic rabbis closer to those who were not hasidim. This social phenomenon dates from before the second half of the nineteenth century, by which time hasidism was an established presence in Jewish life—we can find indications of it far earlier, in the period of struggle between the hasidim and the mitnagedim. There is evidence of it, for example, in the approbations, written for the same works, by Hayim of Volozhin, a disciple of the Vilna Gaon, and by Levi Isaac of Berdichev, a disciple of the Magid of Mezhirech. I will return to this in Chapter 11.

THE PUBLISHING ACTIVITIES OF THE MASKILIM

The number of books and periodicals published by the maskilim has misled scholars into thinking that the Haskalah was the main factor explaining the growth of Jewish publishing in the nineteenth century. Few statistics are available to us, but the few that are suggest that this was not the case. Thus, Eugène Sue's *Les Mystères de Paris* was translated into Hebrew by Kalman Schulman (a God-fearing man in every respect) and widely circulated in maskilic circles as *Misterei pariz*, going into as many as six editions (regarded by present-day scholars as an enormous circulation). A Hebrew translation of Georg Weber's German-language *General World History with Special Attention to the Spiritual and Cultural Life of the People* was similarly successful.[10] At the same time, however, popular books of a religious nature such as *Ḥok leyisra'el* (A Law for Israel), which were intended to provide the Jew with ritual reading from the canonical literature—the Bible, Mishnah, Talmud, and Zohar—were printed in dozens of editions (see Chapter 6 above). The periodicals of the maskilim themselves, as well as the reports of their organizations and the complaints of printers and entrepreneurs such as Samuel Joseph Fuenn,[11] provide evidence of the muted response among the Jewish readership to their printed message.

[10] See Gries, *Book, Scribe, and Story* (Heb.), 39, 125 n. 120; see also Feiner, *Haskalah and History*, 205–10, where Feiner expresses reservations regarding exaggerated estimates of the circulation of various works by maskilim. On Schulman, 'The First Professional Popularizer', see ibid. 253–73. Georg Weber's book was published in German as *Allgemeine Weltgeschichte mit besunderer Beruckschictigang des Geist and Kulturlebens des Volkes*, 15 vols (Leipzig, 1882–90).

[11] See Feiner, *Haskalah and History*, 209, and also the testimony in Gottlober, *Zikhronot*

Similar testimony is found in the minutes of the Hevrat Marbei Haskalah (Society for the Promotion of Enlightenment), which were printed in book form by its secretary Judah Leon Rosenthal,[12] and in the feuilleton *Al hahaskalah umefitseiha* (On the Haskalah and Those Who Disseminate It), printed anonymously in *Hamelits* in 1892 (though it was widely assumed that the author was the activist doctor Judah Leib Katzenelson, known by the pen-name of Buki ben Yogli). The author complains that despite thirty years of hard work, the society still has only eight branches in the cities of Russia, with a tiny number of members in each branch (Vilna, for example, had only seventeen).[13] The leading members of the society did, however, provide massive support for the preparation, printing, and dissemination of books on history, geography, and natural science, some of which are discussed by Shmuel Feiner in his *Haskalah and History*. Its primary objective was to provide financial support for students of the sciences and medicine, but the report by a Dr Hirschhorn for the executive committee of Hevrat Marbei Haskalah in 1868 indicates that, despite these lofty intentions, most of the funds were distributed by the trustees to their friends and relatives, who, like them, had exchanged their seat in the *beit midrash* for the world of public activity in intellectual affairs. It would seem that, from time immemorial, blood ties have overcome plans for spiritual renewal of one kind or another—a situation that is unlikely to change.[14]

The reality of the Haskalah in eastern Europe in the nineteenth century is that of a small group of men who read and wrote for the journals and periodicals of their age such as *Hamagid*, *Hamelits*, *Kokhevei yitshak*, and *Hatsefirah*, and who occasionally managed to put together enough money to print one of

umasa'ot, ii. 181, on Fuenn's losses in producing his newspaper *Hakarmel*. In that newspaper Fuenn published an article by Adam Hacohen Lebensohn entitled 'Comments and Clarifications', at the end of which Lebensohn explains in a special supplement that he was unable to finance by himself the reprinting of his book *Shirei sefat kodesh* (Poems in the Holy Tongue), which had first been published in Leipzig, nineteen years earlier, saying with regret that the fate of his book was 'like the judgement of every book which only maskilim purchase' (*Hakarmel*, 1/28, 6 Shevat 5621 [1861], p. 224, in the *Hasharon* supplement). Lebensohn ultimately enlisted the help of subscribers, and an announcement of the appearance of his book appeared in the second volume of *Hakarmel*, 2/11, 13 Tishrei 5622 [1862], p. 84.

[12] See Rosenthal, *History of the Marbei Haskalah Society* (Heb.).

[13] See Katz, 'Y. L. Katzenelson: the Man and his Work' (Heb.), 220–1. On the activities of Katzenelson on the board of the Marbei Haskalah society, see pp. 218–25.

[14] See Rosenthal, *History of the Marbei Haskalah Society* (Heb.), 58–9.

their own works. It is a pity that those who write on the nature and identity of the supporters of the Haskalah do not usually refer to the important and thorough work of Getzel Kressel in his *Encyclopedia of Modern Hebrew Literature*. Looking through the entries there one is astonished to discover that many dozens of the authors mentioned were educated until maturity primarily in Jewish religious literature. This was the literature that shaped their outlook on the world and influenced their patterns of thought. In their family and community life, these men belonged to the traditional Jewish world, which they allegedly intended to replace by turning their pens into mason's trowels to build, *ex nihilo*, a literature and a world populated by a new kind of Jew.

In many instances, moreover, these writers earned their livelihood as teachers in old-fashioned *talmudei torah* and *batei midrash*. Occasionally, they served as private tutors in wealthy homes, or taught in the new style of semi-modern schools that combined the traditional religious curriculum with secular studies which were established in Russia after the 1860s. We also find these so-called revolutionaries working as typesetters and proof-readers in Jewish printing houses, which, as we have seen, were primarily involved in producing traditional rabbinic literature—that is, religious works. This occupation ensured they were in intimate daily contact with the literature they knew best and the people involved in the traditional Jewish way of life.

Many of them continued to write in the various traditional genres of rabbinic literature: commentaries on the Torah or on *Pirkei avot*; sermons based on the Torah portions, or on other common topics. It could be argued that the Hebrew autobiographies of the maskilim contradict my claims, for they declare clearly and with assurance that their authors had been banished from the tables of their ancestors.[15] I would reply that, as has been shown by Fischel Lachower, the motif of banishment in these autobiographies was a theme borrowed from the *Confessions* of Jean-Jacques Rousseau rather than a fact of life.[16] Lachower noted that it was first adopted by Solomon Maimon and appears again in Mordecai Aaron Guenzburg's *Aviezer*,[17] a model of maskilic Hebrew autobiography that was subsequently much imitated. According to

---

[15] See Mintz, *Banished from their Father's Table*.

[16] See Lachower's introduction to the autobiography, *The Life of Solomon Maimon* (Heb.).

[17] See Werses, 'The Paths of Autobiography in the Haskalah Period' (Heb.), 175–83; Bartal, 'Mordecai Aaron Guenzburg: A Lithuanian Maskil in the Face of Modernity' (Heb.), 109–25.

the rules of Romantic sensibility, struggle and revolt were integral to any autobiography of the Haskalah worth its salt; stylistically, the Hebrew auto-biographical literature of the Haskalah owed a significant debt to European literature of that time. The scholar who wishes to make a serious study of the literature of that generation must avoid being taken in by Romantic clichés.

Others whose autobiographies follow the model of *Aviezer* include Abraham Ber Gottlober, Judah Leib Levin, Moses Leib Lilienblum, Judah Leib Katzenelson, and others. All show clearly the influence of rabbinic cul-ture, thanks to the rabbinic literature mentioned in these works and the rab-binic language in which they were written; even Haskalah writers had no alternative way of writing, since modern Hebrew did not yet exist. Yiddish too was not really a viable alternative at this time for modern writing; the his-torian Simon Dubnow writes in his autobiography that until 1875, Yiddish was not yet the language of a new literature.[18] By the mid-1880s the picture had changed radically, however, with a large number of new works of modern fiction in Yiddish widely available.

In comparing the new Hebrew and Yiddish literature with the traditional literature, it is relevant to consider the extent to which the old literary genres supplied models for the new fictional creations. In the European literary tradition, new literary forms derive from earlier genres and forms; thus,

---

[18] See Dubnow, *The Book of Life* (Heb.), 67–8. Compare the data on the prevalence of Yiddish as a mother tongue among the Jews at the end of the 19th century in Russia to the statement in Leshchinsky, 'Autonomism and the Letters on the Old and New Judaism' (Heb.), 177–80. In this context, one should mention two books on Jewish fiction in Germany. The first, Shefi, *German in Hebrew* (Heb.), deals mainly with the transition to Hebrew translations: see esp. pp. 72–3. The second, Ben-Ari, *Romance with the Past* (Heb.), deals with the appearance of literature in German: see esp. pp. 187–242. See also the enlightening and fascinating comple-ment to these books and those of others by Werses, 'The Expulsion from Spain and Portugal in Yiddish Literature' (Heb.), 115–59, and the important remarks in Shmeruk, *Yiddish Literature* (Heb.), 147–97, and cf. Pines, *History of Yiddish Literature* (Heb.), esp. p. 47 and to the end of the book. It should be noted that Pines does not write as a historian of culture, but rather as some-one with literary taste. This is why he shares Sholem Aleichem's views on Nahum Meir Shaikevich (see below). Although Shaikevich was a popular and prolific author of romances in the late 19th century, Pines does not mention him favourably (see pp. 109–15). Here I must cor-rect Parush, *Reading Women* (Heb.), 120, who for some reason attributes *S[efer] haberit*, which was the daily reading material of Mordecai Aaron Guenzburg, to Moses Mendelssohn and not to its author, Pinhas Eliyahu Horowitz (see below, nn. 40–3). She also errs in attributing the commentary on Ecclesiastes to Mendelssohn: David Friedländer translated it and Aaron Wolfssohn and Yoel Brill wrote the commentary.

romances, folk tales, hagiographical accounts of heroes and saints, and the literature of epistles and other didactic genres all have their modern counterparts. Was this true of modern Jewish literature too, or were the traditional genres of Jewish literature relegated to an obscure corner while Jewish authors created something new?

The answer is quite surprising. The information we have regarding the printing of books in the nineteenth century shows clearly that the traditional epistolary collections were ten times more frequent than epistolary novels, and hagiographies of tsadikim were far more numerous than other kinds of Hebrew short stories. In fact this latter genre only became properly established at the start of the twentieth century; the short stories and romantic novels that conquered the late nineteenth-century Jewish book market were in Yiddish, and most of them were written by a single author, Nahum Meir Shaikewitz (known as Shmer). The latter were strongly attacked by Sholem Aleichem in his Yiddish work, *Shmers mishpat* (The Trial of Shmer).[19]

A fascinating article by Solomon Goldenberg in *Hashiloaḥ* shows that most of the readers using the libraries that Marbei Haskalah had taken so much trouble to establish were students who referred primarily to material in Russian, and moreover their numbers and their actual use of the books were unimpressive. In particular, he notes, they seemed to show little interest in the Haskalah and national reawakening.[20]

A later study by Dan Miron, which made use of Goldenberg's figures but chose to rely mainly on data collected by the journalist and editor of *Hatsefirah*, Nahum Sokolow, concluded that, beginning in the 1880s, there was a huge expansion in the readership for Hebrew literature.[21] Compared to the few hundred subscribers to newspapers and anthologies before the 1880s, Sokolow managed to sell 10,000 copies of the first volume of *Ha'asif* in 1884,

[19] See Kressel, *Encyclopedia of Modern Hebrew Literature* (Heb.), ii. 925–6, and also Pines, *History of Yiddish Literature* (as cited in n. 18 above).

[20] See Goldenberg, 'Are There Hebrew Readers?' (Heb.), 417–22. For a nice lesson on the difference between the image of the reader according to statistics (as provided by Goldenberg), and the reader's own self-image and wild imagination, see the delightful discussion in Bialik, '*Hamelits, Hatsefirah*, and the Colour of Paper' (Heb.), 133–9. For valuable information about the printing, circulation, and reading of books, the creation of collections, and private and public libraries, see Zalkin, 'Culture', in *Daybreak* (Heb.), 229–51.

[21] See Miron, 'On the Perplexing Background of Hebrew Literature' (Heb.), 419–87. See also id., *When Loners Come Together* (Heb.), 56–85.

and 12,000 copies of the second. Since the books would have been passed from hand to hand, Miron concludes from these figures that they would have reached some 100,000 readers.[22] However, my own examination of the titles of Hebrew books and the number of their editions compared to those of Yiddish literature and traditional rabbinic literature over these years suggests that there was an enormous difference between the two, with Yiddish literature alone exceeding Hebrew literature by a factor of ten. It was not until the 1890s that there was, for the first time, mass circulation of the 'penny books' written by Ben-Avigdor, the pen-name of Abraham Leib Shalkovich, in Hebrew.[23] He was the first to write stories that were free of the ponderous biblical expressions and rabbinic rhetoric that had hitherto characterized modern Hebrew literature.[24] In the introduction to the first two stories that he published, *Le'ah mokheret dagim* (Leah the Fishmonger) and *Shenei ḥeziyonot* (Two Visions), Shalkovich explains to his readers:

A great lack is evident in our Hebrew literature, and that is the lack of *belles lettres*. . . . We do not have literature for the masses, where the beautiful and the useful meet together, and in which is seen, as in a mirror, the life of our people, described not in articles full of ancient bombast and not in feuilletons full of witticisms, but living and clear pictures—true drawings taken from life.[25]

From a rough estimate of the numbers involved, it may be said that Shalkovich's books were prime movers in promoting the reading of modern Hebrew literature. Although he died young, he nevertheless managed to publish hundreds of books in the Hebrew Library series and the Great Library series of Tushiyah ('Resourcefulness'), the publishing house he set up in Warsaw. His policy of writing elegant literature that faithfully reflected everyday life must be taken seriously in any account of the Jewish literary accomplishments of his time, though there was nothing revolutionary in his content. After Shalkovich's death in 1921, his nephew Nahum Goldmann, later to become the president of the Zionist Federation, was asked by the fam-

---

[22] Miron, 'On the Perplexing Background to Hebrew Literature' (Heb.), 447. See the extensive discussion (which continues to p. 473) on the creation of an economic and social basis for modern Hebrew literature and the formation of a reading public. See also Shavit, 'The Rise and Fall of the Literary Centres' (Heb.), 423–9, and the amended version in ead. (ed.), *The History of the Jewish Community in Erets Yisra'el Since 1882*, 43–56.

[23] See Kressel, *Encyclopedia of Modern Hebrew Literature* (Heb.), i. 258–60.

[24] See Brenner, *Collected Writings* (Heb.), ii. 114.

[25] As quoted in Lachower, *History of Modern Hebrew Literature* (Heb.), bk. 3, ii. 15.

ily to take over the management of Tushiyah. He transferred the publishing activities from Poland to Germany, where working in partnership with his lifelong friend, the Zionist author and philosopher Jacob Klatzkin, he made it a base for their great project, the *Encyclopaedia Judaica*, which was to be published in German and Hebrew. The German arm of this project was more successful than the Hebrew one despite the Nazi interference, for only two volumes of the Hebrew edition, entitled *Eshkol*, were ever published.[26]

The spread of reading in Hebrew in the 1890s was accompanied, as we have seen, by the flourishing of Jewish public libraries. This impelled Samuel Leib Zitron, a Hebrew and Yiddish writer, to propose to those libraries— which he called 'treasure houses of books'—that they should classify their readers according to profession, occupation, and education, and compile a comprehensive list of the kind of books they favoured. In this way he hoped to advance the circulation of Hebrew books by giving readers publications on the topics that interested them.[27] However, I have found no evidence that his recommendation was acted upon.

Reviewing the discussion so far, it seems to me that throughout most of the nineteenth century there was no clear-cut distinction between authors with a religious orientation and those with secular leanings. Until the 1880s there was no change in the place of Yiddish secular writing, and Hebrew secular writing only really took off in the 1890s.

Two contemporaries of Abraham Shalkovich who were very popular at the time have been largely forgotten. One was Ben-Zion Alfas, who produced a series of writings known as *Ma'aseh alfas* (The Story of Alfas) that were published first in Yiddish and then in Hebrew.[28] No less important was Judah Yudl Rozenberg, a prolific, almost obsessive, writer of stories that purported to have been written in bygone times, who emigrated to Canada in mid-life and served as a rabbi in Toronto and Montreal.[29] Rozenberg collected folk

[26] See Goldmann, *The Autobiography of Nahum Goldmann*, 11, 14, 72, 75–80, 83–92.

[27] See Zitron, 'The People and Literature' (Heb.), 188–92.

[28] See Kressel, *Encyclopedia of Modern Hebrew Literature* (Heb.), i. 117; see also Luz, *The Meeting of Parallels* (Heb.), 167–8.

[29] See the introduction by Eli Yassif to his edition of Rozenberg's *The Golem of Prague* (Heb.), 7–72. See also Bar-Ilan, 'The Wonders of R. Judah Yudl Rozenberg' (Heb.), where, on pp. 181–4, there is an annotated bibliography of the writings of Rozenberg as an appendix. For the literary history of Rozenberg see Leiman's important article, 'The Adventure of the Maharal of Prague in London'. Leiman is unfamiliar with Yassif's work, published ten years earlier, but he certainly adds new material and stimulating insights.

tales transmitted by word of mouth, and translated the Zohar into Hebrew from Aramaic. He also wrote fiction in which he introduced literary devices which he had found in the detective stories of Conan Doyle translated into Yiddish and Russian. We can see these in his *Ḥoshen mishpat* (The Breastplate of Justice), the title of which would lead readers to expect a dry halakhic work, whereas in reality it is a mystery story in Hebrew.[30] He also adapted stories from the Zohar in a collection entitled *Niflaot hazohar* (The Wonders of the Zohar), published in Hebrew and Yiddish in the same volume. The English translation of the title appears there as *Niflous hazohar—A History of the Zohar from the Holy Bible*. The fact that this bilingual edition was published in Canada in the late 1920s is indicative of the large number of the Jewish immigrants there who still spoke and read Yiddish. At the beginning of the book Rozenberg takes pains to emphasize to his readers that his stories contain a moral message:

Why should you bring into your homes worthless books and stories that are full of poison—either the poison of *apikorsut* [heresy] or the poison of fornication—and read them? They pollute the brain and stupefy the heart, and a man's life becomes wanton. Is it not better for you to bring into your homes books of ethics and books of wisdom for your sons and daughters to read? Especially in these times, when the messiah's footsteps are seen, for *apikorsut* increases daily.[31]

Today, when the literary diet of the Jews of North America and Israel has changed, Rozenberg's books have been forgotten, but at the time he had a large readership. Michael Frumkin-Rodkinson, his predecessor in literary forgery, enjoyed similar popularity. Like Rozenberg, he emphasized to his readers that the stories of tsadikim and the hagiographies that he had collected were of exceptional moral utility.[32]

Recent important studies, and in particular, those of Brakhah Fischler and Iris Parush, have revealed the linguistic fabric of the writings of the maskilim, and the intellectual background to their programme.[33] In my opinion, how-

[30] See Rozenberg, *The Golem of Prague and Other Marvellous Stories* (Heb.), 27–8.

[31] *Niflaot hazohar*, 6.

[32] See *The Stories of Michael Levi Rodkinson*, ed. Gedaliyah Nigal (Heb.), 16–17 (author's foreword). In his opinion, too, the time was that when the messiah's footsteps first became apparent. Nigal (83 n. 25) explains this concept according to Lurianic kabbalah. However, the traditional epithet at the end of ch. 9 of tractate *Sotah* in the Mishnah seems to me to be sufficient.

[33] See especially Parush and Fischler, 'Considerations of Language, Literature, and Society

ever, their findings must be tempered with the realization that many of the subjects of their research lived, experienced, and internalized traditional literature and life according to the laws of the Torah as a vital component of their very being.

Chief among these was Mendele Mokher Seforim, who did not get his first steady job until the age of 41 (in 1881), when he became headmaster of the Odessa Talmud Torah, a seminary for teachers who were maskilim; according to the memoirs of his successor Hayim Tchernowitz (known as Rav Tsa'ir, the 'young rabbi'), it preserved much of the spirit of the old *beit midrash*. Mendele was a *talmid ḥakham* (a talmudic scholar), who constantly revisited his studies, and he was heartbroken when his son abandoned traditional Jewish ways. When Hayim Nahman Bialik and Chone Ravnitsky were preparing a new edition of his writings, they asked him for the sources of some of the apparently new or strange expressions that he used. Mendele, who was then an old man living in retirement in his daughter's house in Switzerland,[34] explained how he had coined the expression *sus mashkukhi* (a horse that leads the other horses) from the Talmud; why, when writing about a village dog, he wrote *kelev kufari* rather than the usual *kelev kafri* (because the former is the expression that appears in all the manuscripts of Mishnah *Kilayim*); and how he used the expression *tsipor hanefesh*, which can be misconstrued as 'bird of the soul', in its literal meaning of the windpipe, the vulnerable place on the neck, and thus by extension the thing most precious to the individual—this expression appears in the Babylonian Talmud in *Bava kama*, and Mendele's interpretation of the simple meaning of the words indeed agrees with that of scholars such as Hanokh Yalon.[35]

in the Controversy on Purism' (Heb.), 107–35, and their '"Hybrid" or "Unity"' (Heb.), 253–82. For more on criticism of Mendele, see Werses, 'Mendele in the Mirror of Hebrew Criticism' (Heb.), 34–62.

[34] See Shmeruk (ed.), *Correspondence between Abramovits, Bialik, and Ravnitzky* (Heb.), letter 46 (pp. 111–12).

[35] See Yalon, 'Tsipor (tsiper) hanefesh' (Heb.), 264–5. Those familiar with rabbinical literature are amazed at Mendele's infinite acrobatics in the use of its language. I can add here to Parush and Fischler's observations on Mendele's parodic play with literal and figurative meanings (in their article '"Hybrid" or "Unity"' (Heb.), 270), that the expression used by Mendele, 'Satan came and stimulated [*girah*] me with a non-Jewish woman' is a play on the talmudic expression *gira be'eina desatana* ('an arrow in the eye of Satan'): see BT *Kidushin* 81a. For a fascinating discussion of the uses of proverbs among sages and the pomposity, defiance, and arrogance therein, which invite the powers of evil to put the user to a test, see the master's thesis

Mendele's loyalty to traditional Jewish literature, and his view of himself as the heir to that tradition, were manifest in his distaste for Zionist activists. One such was Menachem Ussishkin, later president of the Jewish National Fund, whom Mendele considered an ignoramus. The obituary of Mendele written by Zalman Epstein for *He'avar* attests to this distaste,[36] as does an anecdote in the memoirs of Hayim Tchernowitz. Tchernowitz tells a story that he heard from Mendele, who was walking home one day from the rabbinical seminary in Zhitomir with Hayim Zelig Slonimsky, another of its teachers. It was a fine summer's day, and on the way Slonimsky invited Mendele to stop at his house. No one was at home. They took off their jackets and shoes, went into the bedroom, lay down on the bed, and started a discussion. Suddenly, a Jewish woman entered, stood at the door of the room, and looked at them, half in surprise, half with amusement. They asked her, 'What is it you want, woman?' She answered, 'I have been honoured to have two fine Jews like you reclining on my bed, and you are asking me what it is I want?' It appears that, deep in conversation, they had entered someone else's house! Mendele was comparing the attitude of the intruders to the Zionist ideology of Ussishkin: 'Will he [Ussishkin] ask me about the Land of Israel? The Land of Israel is mine. I have dwelt in it all my life. I bought the Cave of the Machpelah from Efron the Hittite; with Abraham I wandered to Padan-Aram, and I quarrelled with Laban. I fought with Esau, I went down to the land of Egypt with Jacob and his sons . . . I built the Temple and I destroyed it—and now this one pushes his way into my Land of Israel, lies down on my bed, and asks me what I desire there?'[37]

by Ari Elon, 'The Symbolics of the Elements of the Plot in the Talmudic Story' (Heb.), 54–62. Cf. the story of the daughter of Rabbi Akiba (ibid. 67–73), according to which she saves herself from death by thrusting her hairpin into a crack in the wall and killing a snake destined to kill her by stabbing it in the eye. The identification of the snake with Satan is ancient, and is found in Jewish sources and early apocryphal literature. Thus it was easy for the Jewish reader to understand the transfer of the expression, 'an arrow in the eye of Satan' to the story about Rabbi Akiba's daughter. On the identification of the snake with Satan, see Ginzburg, *The Legends of the Jews*, v. 123–4 (notes to pt. 2), n. 131. On the story about Rabbi Akiba's daughter see also the sources given in Schwarzbaum, *Studies in Jewish and World Folklore*, 280.

[36]   See Epstein, 'The Great Grandfather' (Heb.), 179–80.

[37]   See Tchernowitz, *The Complete Works of Rav Tsa'ir* (Heb.), vol. i: *The Sages of Odessa*, 25–6. This is a collection of pieces previously published in serial form in the newspaper *Bitsaron*. We have personal testimony about how Mendele's image as a Jew and a nationalist influenced Simon Dubnow, who until the meeting between them in Odessa had vehemently attacked

TOPICS IN THE HISTORY OF THE BOOK THAT
DEMAND AN AUTHOR

Limitations of space prevent me from discussing such topics as the design and illustration of books as an agent of culture, a neglected field which is only now beginning to receive attention. Similarly I cannot discuss developments in the technology of Jewish printing which, according to Abraham Ber Gottlober and Shraga Feigensohn, director of the Romm printing house for decades, lagged far behind the general printing industry until the mid-nineteenth century.[38]

A further subject which cannot be addressed here is the increase in the number of Jewish public libraries during the nineteenth century. This is a fascinating social phenomenon, in which the traditional community libraries—those of the *batei midrash*—which predominated in the eighteenth century gave way partially at least to public libraries of a new kind, created by the Haskalah movement; this change needs to be studied in depth.[39]

Another absorbing subject which cannot be dealt with here is the opening up of Hebrew literature to the wonders of science. This process, which played a major role in shaping the identity of those Jews who sought knowledge of those major figures of the period who made history and changed the face of nature, has not yet found its historian. This subject is bound up with the study of itinerant scholars, chief among whom was Pinhas Elijah ben Meir Horowitz, author of *Sefer haberit* (The Book of the Covenant). The upheavals he experienced, and the search for his own path in life, left him, by his own admission within the realm of Orthodox Judaism. In general, however, his life story is similar to that of the first maskilim in eastern Europe, who were drawn to the West—men such as Isaac Satanow, Judah Ben-Ze'ev, and Shlomo

manifestations of Jewish nationalism in the Russian Jewish press. After meeting the Jewish 'sages of Odessa', headed by Mendele Mokher Seforim and their famed spokesman Ahad Ha'am, he changed his opinion completely. See Ravnitzky, *A Generation and its Authors* (Heb.), ii. 67–81, esp. pp. 68–72. On Mendele's relations with his son Meir, see ibid. 38–41.

[38] See Gottlober, *Zikhront umasa'ot*, i. 78; Feigensohn, 'On the History of the Romm Printing House', i. 270–96, esp. pp. 279–80.

[39] There are still no proper studies of the libraries of *batei midrash* or of the growth of modern Jewish public libraries. Meanwhile, see Schidorsky, *Library and Book in the Land of Israel* (Heb.), 23–33, and Gries, *Book, Scribe, and Story* (Heb.), 59–62, 131–2 and nn. 37–40. See also n. 20 above and Ch. 5 nn. 2–3.

Dubno. Horowitz's book, the first modern encyclopedia in Hebrew,[40] contains a mixture of old and new. The first part appears to deal with science,
while the second part is concerned mainly with matters of kabbalah. However,
the first part contains a blend of topics that will appear odd to the modern
reader, including astronomy, the sources of earthquakes, and a critique of
Solomon Maimon based on Kant. These are accompanied by supposedly reliable information refuting Copernicus's theory that the earth revolves around
the sun and not vice versa, and the added ornament of a section on 'birds that
grow on trees'.[41] This last, which is based entirely on fables and folk tales about
trees whose fruit is animals, is discussed seriously by rabbis, not only for the
purpose of gathering accounts of miracles and marvels but also to determine
how the laws of ritual slaughter apply to such birds.[42] Horowitz read Haskalah
works written by men like himself from eastern Europe but who went further
than he did, and he quotes them copiously, albeit with reservations. His book
was thus approved by the Jewish faithful, and served as a primary source of
information about the world for those Jews who were drawn to Haskalah.[43]

[40] On Horowitz and his book see Rosenbloom, 'The First Hebrew Encyclopedia' (Heb.),
15–65, Hebrew section. Before him, Zinberg wrote about the book at length in *A History of
Jewish Literature*, vi. 249–70, esp. pp. 260–70: before discussing Horowitz he treats the forerun-
ners of the Haskalah and science who influenced him. See also the supplement by A. M.
Haberman, in the Hebrew edition only, vol. iii. 424–5, on the positive review of the book in
Hame'asef.

[41] See Horowitz, *Sefer haberit hashalem* (Jerusalem, 1990), the first part of which deals with
all of these matters at length, and see especially the controversies with Copernicus (pp. 150–7)
and with Maimon (p. 169, and esp. pp. 360–4), and on the 'birds that grow on trees' and carniv-
orous, motile plants (pp. 492–3).

[42] See the wonderful article by Zimmels, 'Birds that Grow on Trees' (Heb.), 1–9; at p. 6 n. 10
Zimmels mentions something that Horowitz did not know: that enchanting and alarming
information was circulated about 'virgins who grow on trees'. See also Ginzberg, *The Legends of
the Jews*, v. 50–1 n. 150; Azulai, *Ma'agal tov hashalem*, 37 n. 11; and Zeidah, 'Birds that Grow on
Trees' (Heb.), 275.

[43] Kressel, *Encyclopedia of Modern Hebrew Literature* (Heb.), i. 580, entry for Pinhas
Horowitz, lists fourteen editions of *Sefer haberit* in the collection of the National and
University Library in Jerusalem, all of which were printed in the 19th century, after the first partial printing in Berlin in 1797. Kressel listed many more editions of the book than does
Friedberg in *The Library* (Heb.), i. 170, in the section for the letter *beit*, s.v. *haberit*, no. 1474. The
works of Pinhas Horowitz and the colleagues who preceded him came far earlier than new
efforts by authors such as Mendele Mokher Seforim and his fellow maskilim to disseminate
knowledge of the world and of popular science in the second half of the 19th century. This is not
the proper place to expand the discussion of that topic, just as I am unable to expand upon the

CENSORSHIP

The institution of censorship is as old as the book itself. It originated with the apprehensions of the Catholic Church in Rome that printing might be used to attack the sanctity of religion, and the fear of the monarchies of Europe that the propagation of damaging ideas might undermine their regimes. Several studies have been published on the early censorship of the Hebrew book, most of which are mentioned in the exemplary work of Amnon Raz-Krakotzkin, which is the only comprehensive treatment to date of this important topic.[44]

There is as yet, however, no comprehensive treatment of the censorship of Hebrew books under tsarist rule in imperial Russia or in Galicia under Austro-Hungarian rule at the end of the eighteenth century and during the nineteenth century. Two important studies are nonetheless worth mentioning: first, that of Saul Ginzburg, who in two articles has traced the first outlines of a history of censorship and the prohibition on or restriction of the printing of Jewish books and of their importation into tsarist Russia, and, second, the work of Raphael Mahler, who was the first to collect data on the activity of the censor in Galicia in preventing the printing of books of kabbalah and hasidism, and of books in Yiddish.[45]

prophetic-messianic model of Horowitz's book, for he was influenced, as he says in his introduction, by *Sha'arei kedushah* (The Gates of Holiness) by Hayim Vital, and, according to the general character of his writing, by the works of Abraham Abulafiah. *Sefer haberit* was an important item in the spiritual fare of Mordecai Aaron Guenzburg, author of *Aviezer*, the first autobiography in the spirit of Haskalah. See Bartal, 'Mordecai Aaron Guenzburg' (Heb.), 111.

[44] See Raz-Krakotzkin, 'The Censor, the Editor, and the Text' (Heb.), on p. 1 nn. 1–2 of which is a detailed bibliographical list on the literature dealing with the censorship of books in the Christian world. To this must be added Godman, *The Silent Masters: Latin Literature and its Censors in the High Middle Ages.*

[45] See Ginzburg, 'The Story of Printing among the Jews' (Heb.), 40–50, where he discusses the decree of 1836, calling for the censorship of all books published by Jews. He describes how memoranda written by maskilim to the authorities contributed to the closure of Jewish printing shops in small towns with licences being granted to print only in certain large cities such as Vilna, Zhitomir, and Warsaw. Ginzburg also illustrates the influence that Jewish printers and entrepreneurs had on the authorization of book imports, or conversely on the imposition of duty on books, thus establishing their contribution to the spread of Haskalah ideas among the Jews. See Mahler, *Hasidism and Haskalah* (Heb.), which devotes a chapter (pp. 133–54) to Austrian censorship in Galicia, and, on the basis of archival research reveals the struggle of the censors, who were maskilim, against kabbalah, against hasidism, and against Yiddish literature. In this context, cf. Dubnow, *History of the Jews in Russia and Poland*, iii. 227–8 (index, s.v. 'censor-

Scattered through Joseph Klausner's monumental work *The History of Modern Hebrew Literature* there is a great deal of extremely important material on the history of censorship, which exerted considerable influence on the publication of Hebrew books[46] as regards design as well as content. Klausner himself refers to an important Russian work dealing with the beginnings of censorship in Russia which has been completely forgotten.[47] Klausner provides very little biographical information regarding censors, however; we know that among them were apostates from Judaism, and maskilim,[48] but Klausner discusses only two. One of these is Naphtali Herz Homberg, who was appointed censor first in Galicia and then in Vienna. He was deeply involved in the movement for the improvement and reform of the Jewish religion and life.[49] The other, Hayim Zelig Slonimsky of Zhitomir, the editor of *Hatsefirah*, was one of the most important scientists among the maskilim; he was a mathematician and astronomer, while also a teacher in the Zhitomir rabbinical seminary.[50] As Klausner tells it, Slonimsky and Tsevi Baratz, the

ship'). See also Stanislawski, *Tsar Nicholas I and the Jews*, i, 41, and esp. p. 43, and also s.v. 'censorship' in the index (p. 239). Another matter that has so far been treated only in passing is the intervention of official rabbis appointed by the Russian authorities to serve as Jewish religious authorities in the process of censoring books. Shohet, *The Institution of the Official Rabbinate* (Heb.), II, mentions the testimony of Isaac Ber Levinsohn on this topic. See also Elbaum, 'The Official Rabbis as Censors of Books' (Heb.); on p. 185 n. 5 there is an error regarding the date of the introduction of censorship in Russia; Elbaum also fails to mention what Joseph Klausner wrote about this (see n. 46 below). See also the entry by Yehudah Slutzky in *The Jewish Encyclopedia* (Heb.), xxviii. 822–3: this survey is preliminary and much information is lacking.

[46] The censors were concerned primarily with rabbinic literature, as the main way of communicating Jewish ideas at the time, and with the newly emerging maskilic literature which they suspected as possibly harbouring revolutionary trends. Both these bodies of literature were in Hebrew. Yiddish literature was not considered of importance until the last two decades of the nineteenth century.

[47] See Klausner, *History of Modern Hebrew Literature* (Heb.), 2nd edn, vol. iv (1954), 49 n. 89. The Russian work covers the history of censorship until 1804.

[48] See in general below, and esp. n. 50.

[49] See Klausner, *History of Modern Hebrew Literature* (Heb.), 2nd edn, vol. i (1954), 211–23, and esp. pp. 216–17 on his activity in Galicia and his educational and cultural initiatives and p. 221 on his service as censor in Vienna.

[50] Ibid. 123–5. A complete biography of Hayim Zelig Slonimsky (Hazas) is still to be written; Nahum Sokolow, his colleague at *Hatsefirah*, describes him in his *Men* (Heb.), 135–62, but does not discuss Slonimsky's work as a censor. Slonimsky's letters, published by H. R. Rabinovitz in *Areshet*, 4 (1966), 447–60, are of interest; see also Ben-Menahem, 'Two More Letters by Hazas' (Heb.), 461–2.

censor in Kiev, joined in an attempt to force Eliezer Zweifel, a colleague of Slonimsky's on the teaching staff of the Zhitomir rabbinical seminary, to criticize hasidism in his book *Shalom al yisra'el* (Peace Upon Israel) as a condition for authorizing its publication.[51] Attacks on Slonimsky by his fellow maskilim for permitting the appearance of a book favourable to hasidism caused him to publish a letter of apology in *Hamelits* in which he stated that, while the censorship laws would not permit him to prevent the appearance of Zweifel's book, he and his fellow censor were of quite different opinions.[52]

[51] See Klausner, *History of Modern Hebrew Literature* (Heb.), 2nd edn, vol. vi (1959), 18–21. On Zweifel see also Gries, *Book, Scribe, and Story* (Heb.), index, s.v. 'Zweifel' (p. 157), and see further the bibliography there.

[52] See Klausner, *History of Modern Hebrew Literature* (Heb.), 2nd edn, vol. vi (1959), 20. Other censors and the various types of critics of Hebrew books are described in Zitron, *Behind the Screen* (Heb.), vol. i. The Vilna edition paints a positive picture of a philosemitic apostate, Professor Daniel Chovelsohn (see below), who began his career, after returning to St Petersburg from studies in Germany in 1850, as a member of the committee supervising Hebrew schoolbooks (*Behind the Screen*, 15). Other censors described by Zitron include the anti-Jewish Jacob Brafman, who was a censor in Vilna at the same time as Joshua Steinberg, the teller of fables, Bible scholar, and teacher in the rabbinical seminary there. Steinberg was lenient; Brafman was strict. Zitron (*Behind the Screen*, 52–3) quotes Steinberg's memoirs on the battle between Brafman and Judah Leib Gordon over pt. II of his book *Olam keminhago* (The World According to its Custom), a battle won by Gordon, who was supported by Steinberg. A lively description of a way found to pay Brafman in advance and avoid censorship is to be found in Feigensohn, 'On the History of the Romm Printing House' (Heb.), 281–3.

Brafman was succeeded in Vilna by another convert from Judaism, Nicander Vasilovitsh Zusman. Unlike his predecessor Zusman favoured Hebrew authors, and especially rabbinical scholars who wrote books of responsa. He engaged in heated polemics with them—with good intentions, according to Zitron (*Behind the Screen*, 75–7)—as an accomplished scholar who longed for his past. Zusman went on to serve as censor in St Petersburg (ibid. 74), where he was known for his strictness towards his subordinates in the provincial cities, for he suspected that their decisions were influenced by authors' bribes (ibid. 79). Zitron also mentions Zusman's ambivalent attitude towards the censor in Warsaw, Marcus Zamenhof, father of the inventor of Esperanto, Eliezer Ludwig Zamenhof (on whose career see *Jewish Encyclopaedia* (Heb.), xii. 632). Zitron (*Behind the Screen*, 82) preserves a nice anecdote about Zusman's old age, according to which, when the Jewish author Mordecai Spektor published the first volume of his *Der Hoiz Friend*, he included an article by Avraham Shalom Friedberg on the Hebrew writer Abraham Mapu, to which he appended a long note that contained interesting reminiscences on Mapu signed by 'The First Reader' of *Der Hoiz Friend*—none other than Zusman himself.

Another censor described by Zitron is Tsevi Hirsh Grinbaum, a convert from Judaism who took the name of Vladimir Vasilovitsh Fiodorov. In the early 1870s Fiodorov was appointed censor in Warsaw, where he enjoyed the company of *Hatsefirah* editor Hayim Zelig Slonimsky, his partner Nahum Sokolow, and Eliezer Zweifel. According to Zitron, although Fiodorov was

Klausner also reveals how, after 1827, the government of Nicholas I tried to restrict Hebrew printing in Russia. Publication of fifty Hebrew books was banned in 1828, and in 1831 the censor in Vilna, Zeev Tugenhold, presented the authorities with a list of hasidic books to which he took objection.[53] Tugenhold, about whom Klausner does not supply much information, was personally involved in authorizing the publication of the books of Isaac Ber Levinsohn, the well-known author of *Te'udah beyisra'el* (Mission Among the Jews).[54] Levinsohn, who was afraid of him, wrote him a flattering letter, in which he spoke ill of the hasidim, as he understood that this is what Tugenhold expected of him.[55] This, however, was of no help to Levinsohn when he wished to publish a book favourable to the message of kabbalah to which Tugenhold was vehemently opposed.[56]

Klausner highlights the nexus of connections between the censor and his friends and acquaintances, and the role of social obligations more widely in matters of censorship. He mentions three times the sense of insult felt by the poet and maskil Adam Hacohen Lebensohn, a censor known only by the surname Gniks, who was his former student, permitted publication of a pamphlet by Abraham Papirna which Lebensohn considered to slander him.[57] Klausner also reports Gniks's efforts to placate and appease his former teacher by preventing the publication of another book attacking him.[58]

Other cultural heroes discussed by Klausner include the author and publisher Samuel Fuenn and Joseph Zeiberling, both of whom became advisers to the censor in Vilna in an attempt to prevent the publication of the satirical feuilletons of Judah Leib Gordon, which militated against the ills of Jewish society and were considered by the establishment to be too radical. In a

severe as a censor, he was lenient with *Hatsefirah*. Zitron quotes (pp. 135–8) Sokolow's memoirs on the way in which Fiodorov negotiated with them: Sokolow's words suggest that the convert, who had no family, found something of the home he had abandoned in his contact with him. The censor would appease and placate Sokolow while trying, as it were, to be severe with *Hatsefirah*, and Sokolow would answer him point by point.

[53] See Klausner, *History of Modern Hebrew Literature* (Heb.), 1st edn, vol. iii (1943), 48–50.

[54] Ibid. 53.

[55] Ibid. 57–8. For a review of his elder brother's attitude towards the hasidim see Marcin Wodzinski, 'Jakob Tugenhold and the Maskilic Defense of Hasidism', *Gal-ed*, 18 (2002), 13–42. His brother Jakob was a censor in Warsaw.

[56] See Klausner, *History of Modern Hebrew Literature* (Heb.), 1st edn, vol. iii (1943), 59.

[57] Ibid. iii. 188–9, iv. 182–7 (esp. p. 186), and vi. 81, where Yehiel Mikhel Pines joins in the criticism of Papirna.   [58] Ibid. iv. 219 and n. 160.

countermove to save the situation, Gordon sought the assistance of Professor Daniel Chovelsohn,[59] who had converted to Christianity but remained sympathetic to the Jews. But in another incident, Chovelsohn joined with Zeiberling to oppose the publication of two books by Abraham Mapu, *Ayit tsavu'a* (The Speckled Bird of Prey) and *Hozei heziyonot* (Visionaries).[60]

Klausner's intention was to trace the path of modern Hebrew literature; he was not concerned with the fate of the traditional Jewish works into which the censors, guided by apostates and maskilim, sank their teeth. The balance sheet setting the damage done by the censorship against the contribution it made with regard to the main body of traditional Jewish literature has not yet been drawn up, and this needs to be addressed. The 'refining' of books—an editorial process as old as censorship itself—did not cease in the nineteenth century as maskilim and apostates from Judaism, bent on 'rooting out ignorance', denied the more traditional Jews the spiritual sustenance that they sought from rabbinic texts.

THE LITERARY RESPONSE TO EMIGRATION

I have mentioned the 'baggage' that Jewish emigrants took with them in the form of literature and reading, especially in Yiddish. To paraphrase Heine, Yiddish books in particular were the portable homeland of Jewish emigrants, accompanied by rabbinic literature in Hebrew, the holy tongue.[61] It is important to point out, however, that emigration, especially the mass migration

[59] Ibid. 322. Chovelsohn is noted for his detailed refutation of the blood libel against the Jews, and for his small but important book on Hebrew printing, in which he devoted extensive space to the role of the Jewish managing editor (*magihah*) and his work; see Chovelsohn, *The Origin of Printing among the Jews* (Heb.). On Chovelsohn and his book, see also Gries, 'On the Figure of the Jewish Managing Editor' (Heb.), 7; see also Parush, *Reading Women* (Heb.), 191–2, who notes the tendency of Katz and Zitron, whom she quotes, to place the blame for Chovelsohn's conversion to Christianity on his wife.

[60] Klausner, *History of Modern Hebrew Literature* (Heb.), 1st edn, vol. iii. (1943), 311, 316, 318, 323.

[61] Cf. the comments in Soloveitchik, 'Rupture and Reconstruction', 65–6. Heine's words are found in his *Confessions*: see 'Geständnisse', in *Werke*, xv. 43 (the Hebrew translation can be found in Heine, *And They Will Not Say Kaddish*, 175). Jacob Katz's response to Heine's words, which he read as sarcasm rather than praise, to the nation whose Torah—the expression of its spirit—was its homeland can be found in Katz, 'The Jewish Character of Israeli Society' (Heb.), 99. Shimon Federbush, by contrast, gave a positive interpretation to Heine's comments in 'Love of the Book' (Heb.), 22–3—see the section 'Kasefer ka'am' (As the Book, So the People). See also

which began in the 1880s, is not a subject that was covered or documented by the authors of the time, nor were books seen as a tool to help the Jews cope with the stresses inevitably associated with migration. One-third of the Jews in central and eastern Europe emigrated, and some 70 to 80 per cent of them were between the ages of 20 and 45. The future of the Jewish people changed continents. The young Jews who left Europe for America adopted new identities and realized new dreams. It is interesting, however, that Hebrew literature, both maskilic and traditionally religious, and indeed Yiddish literature, refrained from alluding to this.

While some expression of the people's distress is apparent in rabbinic responsa dealing with abandoned women and other unfortunates, there is no serious discussion anywhere of the problems associated with emigration. In fact, the literature of the end of the nineteenth century testifies to how the community leaders of the time—rabbis, hasidim, and maskilim alike— responded to the enormous changes taking place in Jewish life by burying their heads in the sand. The religious leadership was reluctant to attempt to stem the wave of emigration by demanding civil rights in Poland, since this would have given the Jews equal status and access to employment, and the bastion of religion would have been breached; equally, they were opposed to the idea of sending energetic young rabbis to help those who had emigrated because they feared their fate in the licentious continent of America. The maskilim were similarly unconcerned with the fate of the Jews who had left for America: their aim was to see the Jews assimilate where they were, in Poland. Both camps directed the focus of their literary attacks against Zionism, a puppy still too weak to bark.[62]

Scholem, 'The People of the Book' (Heb.), 155. Wiener, *The Jewish Religion in the Period of the Emancipation* (Heb.), 105, points out the influence of Heine's words on Samson Raphael Hirsch in his *Nineteen Letters on Judaism*, Letter XV (pp. 106–11). See also the influence of Heine's words on Jacob Bernais, as presented in Urbach, 'Jacob Bernais, his Judaism, and his Influence on Jewish Studies' (Heb.), ii. 845 n. 44. See also the marvellous phrasing of Heine's idea by Ahad Ha'am, as recorded by Bialik in 'Halakhah and Aggadah' (Heb.), end of p. 62.

[62] In this context, one should take note of a cry of distress, which went unheard. I refer to the voice of Simon Dubnow, who addressed the subject of the great exodus of Jews from Russia, particularly to the United States. See his *Letters on the Old and New Judaism* (Heb.), 105–10, 138–44. Many scholars have written about Dubnow: see esp. Eliezer Rafael Malakhi, 'Dubnow in Hebrew Literature', a bibliography, in *The Book of Simon Dubnow* (Heb.), 223–39. Since then, several studies of the man have been written, the most important being Frankel, 'S. M. Dubnov: Historian and Ideologist', 1–33.

We have seen that during the eighteenth and nineteenth centuries the book was an important agent of culture in the Jewish world, instrumental in arousing a nascent intelligentsia that eventually became integrated into modern society in central and western Europe and, via mass emigration, in the United States. In a parallel development, the awakening of Jewish nationalism at the end of the nineteenth century led to a great flourishing of Hebrew literature, as Dan Miron has shown.[63] This literature may well have influenced those idealistic individuals who dared to emigrate to the Land of Israel and dedicate themselves to preparing a home for the many they hoped would follow later.

[63] See n. 21 above and Shaked, *Books and their Audience* (Heb.), 12–36.

TEN

Book Reviews in the Hebrew Press

R EVIEWS OF JEWISH BOOKS in general and of Hebrew books in particular represent a stage in the development of Jewish journalism. Book
reviews are an important element of any study of books in the Jewish world
since they are a key way of drawing attention to works that potential readers
might otherwise not know about.

In this sense, as in many others, Hebrew periodicals shaped public consciousness and opinion, and were a key agent of culture, and some background
to put the subject in context is surely in order here. The significance of the
topic cannot be overestimated: Henri Jean Martin, a disciple of Lucien
Fèbvre, following other scholars, says that, while the eighteenth century was
the age of the book, the nineteenth century was the age of the newspaper.[1] As
an ex-ample of what the study of journalism could contribute one might cite
Richard Popkin's studies of the role of journalism as a voice for the French
Revolution and its opponents,[2] or Elizabeth Eisenstein's work showing that
journalism replaced the preacher's pulpit as a source of influence on society,
agitating vigorously for the advancement of secularization and as a focus of
opposition to Western Christianity.[3] Siegfried Henry Steinberg wrote a
detailed survey of the development of journalism in Europe in various

[1] See Martin, *The History and Power of Writing*, 414–19. See also Weill, *Le Journal*; Albert
and Terrou, *Histoire de la presse*; and Bellanger, Godechot, Guiral, and Terrou (eds), *Histoire
générale de la presse française*.

[2] See Popkin, *The Right-Wing Press in France*, and id., *Revolutionary News*.

[3] Eisenstein, *The Printing Press as an Agent of Change*, 131. See also the fascinating article by
Wittmann, 'Was There a Reading Revolution at the End of the Eighteenth Century?', 284–312,
which touches on the place of journalism among the other types of reading material.

languages in which he notes that some English newspapers of the mid-eighteenth century saw the criticism of books as their main mission, even to the detriment of their continued existence.[4] Elizabeth Eisenstein has also devoted a small book to the French cosmopolitan press from the days of Louis IV to the French Revolution in which she laments the fact that journalism, as an educator and as the first printed forum for book reviews, has been ignored by historians of the book and of culture.[5] The period she covers goes beyond that of Steinberg by more than eighty years, and she rescues from oblivion two French intellectuals, Jean Cusson and Denis de Sallo, pioneer book-reviewers, who started a newspaper, *Le Journal de Sçavans*, on 5 January 1665 with the avowed purpose of 'serving the Republic of Letters'.[6]

But let us return to the subject of Jewish periodicals. The first forerunners of Jewish periodicals began to appear in the second half of the seventeenth century, and in the eighteenth century they positively flourished. Following the fashion in Europe of the time, their main purpose was moralizing; indeed, the first Jewish periodical was entitled *Kohelet musar* (The Wisdom of Moral Instruction), a short-lived offering of the eighteenth century published in Germany in Hebrew by Moses Mendelssohn.[7]

Jewish journalism developed later than mainstream journalism, and the first Jewish journals, published during the second half of the eighteenth century, were in Hebrew. By the second half of the nineteenth century Yiddish was widely used in Jewish journalism; increasingly, the languages of the countries in which Jews were living were also used.[8] Thus, for example, we find a discussion in Russian in the Jewish newspaper *Voshod* between the Hebrew poet Judah Leib Gordon and Simon Dubnow, the young man (later a famous historian) who took his place in the book review department.[9]

All these newspapers carried announcements and reviews of Jewish books. Reviews of Jewish books in the eighteenth and nineteenth centuries, as today,

[4] Steinberg, *Five Hundred Years of Printing*, 121–6.

[5] See Eisenstein, *Grub Street Abroad*, 35.

[6] Ibid. 44–5. Eisenstein refers readers who want to know more about the meaning and history of the expression 'Republic of Letters' to Waquet, 'Qu'est-ce que la république des lettres?'.

[7] See Gilon, *Mendelssohn's Kohelet musar* (Heb.), which devotes all of ch. 2 (pp. 22–36) to a comprehensive description of moralizing weeklies in Europe.

[8] In this context, the work of Yehuda Slutzky is of great importance: see *The Jewish Russian Press in the Nineteenth Century* (Heb.).

[9] Ibid. 291–5; on Dubnow's replacement, see pp. 295–6; on Gordon's difficulties with his young replacement and heir see Stanislawski, *For Whom Do I Toil?*, 209–10.

served to publicize both those books that reviewers apparently valued and those they disliked. As has often been the case throughout the history of publishing, where the critics disliked certain books, everyone raced to read them. Conversely, some books received a flood of favourable reviews but failed to arouse even a spark of enthusiasm among the reading public.

Since the time of Joseph Klausner and his disciple Shmuel Werses,[10] attention has been paid to the criticism of Hebrew *belles lettres*. This genre reached its peak in the nineteenth century in the work of Abraham Kovner and Abraham Papirna which has been studied by the above-mentioned scholars and others, including Iris Parush and Arnah Golan.[11] To date, however, no one has carried out a general survey of the book sections of newspapers, or, as the maskilim styled it, the 'announcement of new books' section.

These book sections flourished in the Jewish press; among the learned journals *Hamazkir*, edited by Moritz Steinschneider, is particularly noteworthy. There were also such sections in the German *Monatschrift für Geschichte und Wissenschaft des Judentums*, the French *Revue des Etudes Juives*, and the English *Jewish Quarterly Review*, the latter two having been established in the last two decades of the nineteenth century. Prominent among popular newspapers was *Israelit*, published in Germany by Marcus Lehmann, who also published a substantial amount of non-Jewish literature at the end of the century. As it is not possible to deal here with all of the above, I will confine myself to a survey of the periodicals published in Hebrew from the end of the eighteenth century and the main tendencies evident in them.

Tsemah Tsamariyon has written about the history and contents of *Hame'asef*,[12] which was published in Hebrew with a German supplement as the organ of the Circle of Maskilim, founded in Berlin, whose members were disciples of Moses Mendelssohn. However, as Moshe Pelli and Shmuel Werses have noted, Tsamariyon's account of the creation of this very first book-review section in the history of Hebrew literature is somewhat rudimentary, and his description of *Hame'asef* in general is by no means comprehensive.[13] Pelli has recently published an annotated index of *Hame'asef* in a

---

[10] See the comprehensive article by Shmuel Werses, 'Criticism, Hebrew Literary', *Encyclopaedia Judaica*, v. 1114–24 and the bibliography there.

[11] Parush, 'The Culture of Criticism and the Criticism of Culture'; Golan, 'Hebrew Literary Criticism' (Heb.). On Kovner and Papirna see also Zinberg, *History of Jewish Literature*, XII. 143–71.   [12] See Tsamariyon, *Hame'asef* (Heb.), esp. pp. 154–5.

[13] Pelli, in his lecture at the World Congress of Jewish Studies (Jerusalem, 1997), and

fine, large-format publication entitled *The Gate of Haskalah*. In his detailed introduction he provides an elaborate description of literary periodicals in Europe as a background to the appearance of *Hame'asef*, and conducts a thorough examination of the influence of the *Berlinische Monatschrift* on the design and content of *Hame'asef*. There is, however, only a single paragraph on book reviews.[14]

History repeats itself, and it is evident that the inclinations of the founders of *Hame'asef* in the eighteenth century are reflected in those of their professional successors, the publishers of maskilic newspapers in the nineteenth century. These include Eliezer Silberman, in *Hamagid*, whose literary supplement was called *Hatsofeh* (The Observer), and Samuel Fuenn in *Hakarmel*, whose literary supplement was entitled *Hasharon*. The book reviews published were primarily publicity for books written by friends and colleagues; there seems to have been no attempt to survey a comprehensive selection of books published. In the case of *Hame'asef*, the book reviews were merely a showcase for the Hevrat Hinukh Hane'arim (Society for the Education of Youth), headed by Isaac Euchel, and therefore published only reviews of those books considered educationally necessary as well as notices to attract subscribers to new publishing projects.

I now turn to a practical example of how the study of book-review sections can contribute, sometimes in unexpected ways, to the study of the book in the Jewish world. *Hame'asef*'s book-review section also occasionally made mention of manuscripts available for sale, or texts seeking a publisher; there were also articles about books not yet printed. An example of this is a notice offering for sale a manuscript entitled *Shefer hatikunim* (The Beauty of Corrections), consisting of corrections and emendations on *Hayad haḥazakah* (literally 'The Strong Arm', another name for Maimonides' *Mishneh torah*).[15] In the following month, the list of manuscripts for sale included *Goralot haḥol* (Geomancy) and *Shirei avnei shoham* (Poems of Onyx) by Moses ben Gideon Abudiente.[16]

Werses, 'Tensions between Languages in and around *Hame'asef*' (Heb.), 29–69. See also Pelli, *The Generation of the Gatherers* (Heb.), on the contribution of the pioneers of *Hame'asef*, the first Hebrew periodical, to the Hebrew Enlightenment in its beginnings (1784–1815), esp. the section 'Criticism of *Hame'asef*' (pp. 14–16). It should be mentioned that Pelli does not discuss criticism of new books here. See also the review of Tsamariyon's, *Hame'asef* (Heb.) by Shmuel Feiner (*Zion*, 53 (1988), 441–6).

[14] See *The Gate of Haskalah* (Heb.), 20–4, 24–32, and 63.   [15] *Hame'asef*, 2 (1785).

[16] On Abudiente, who was a Shabatean, see Scholem, *Shabetai tsevi* (Heb.), ii. 486–90 (Heb.

Additional copies of the latter two manuscripts are extant, and photocopies can be found in the Institute of Photocopies of Manuscripts in the National and University Library in Jerusalem, but there was no known extant manuscript of the former work. Reference in the articles in *Hame'asef* to an encyclopedic scientific work, *Ahavat david* (The Love of David), by David Franco Mendes,[17] led me to the catalogue of Aaron Freimann,[18] where I discovered that it had been mentioned in *Hamagid*. From *Hamagid* I discovered that although Mendes was an active member of the Society of Maskilim in Berlin, he in fact lived in Amsterdam and had some connection with the Ets Hayim Library of the Portuguese Synagogue there. When Mendes died, his friend David Ben Raphael Montezinos wrote an article, which was serialized over several issues of *Hamagid* in 1868, on his literary legacy. In issue 34 he writes that Mendes was the owner of the manuscript with *Goralot hahol* and *Shirei avnei shoham*, and that it was he who had offered them for sale.[19] As Montezinos had written in an earlier issue,[20] the emendations of *Hayad hahazakah* in *Shefer hatikunim* were annotations made by Mendes in an edition of *Hayad hahazakah* printed by Atias in Amsterdam in 1704. Why, then, did I connect it with the library of Ets Hayim in Amsterdam? Because Gabriel Falk, who had translated Montezinos' article from Dutch, had mentioned this fact in the literary supplement of *Hakarmel* known as *Hasharon* (the reference in *Hamagid* to *Hakarmel* is incorrect!).

The first detailed book reviews in *Hame'asef* dealt with the books by maskilim. Among those reviewed were *Sefer hamidot* (The Book of Virtues) by Isaac Satanow[21] and *Tefilat yisra'el* (The Prayer of Israel), with a German

edn); in the English edition, *Sabbatai Sevi, The Mystical Messiah*, see entries in the index (p. 960).

[17] On Mendes see Michman, *David Franco Mendes*.

[18] Freimann, *Union Catalogue of Hebrew Manuscripts*, ii. 19, card no. 463.

[19] *Hamagid*, 34 (1868), 264.   [20] *Hamagid*, 14 (1865), 109.

[21] This book was brought out by a publishing house established by Hevrat Hinukh Hane'arim. An announcement of its publication appeared in *Hame'asef, Shevat 5546* [1786], 80 (the page is mistakenly numbered 81), and the review appeared in Hame'asef, Adar 2/Nisan 5546 [1786], 110–12, 124, 128, signed 'MC'. This was apparently Mordecai Berl Cohen, who is listed among the prenumeranten in Berlin on the masthead of Hame'asef in 1786. Many scholars have written about Satanow and his comrades, though much remains to be investigated, especially his attraction to kabbalah, his contribution to the writing of fraudulent approbations and works purporting to be kabbalistic, and the distribution of books on kabbalah. First to write about him was Klausner, in the *History of Modern Hebrew Literature* (Heb.), 3rd edn, vol. i

translation by David Friedländer.[22] The critic 'V— E—', whom I have been
unable to identify, opposed, in the spirit of reform, the printing of sermons
and prayer books in monolingual Hebrew editions. He describes for his readers the history of the translation of prayer books for Ashkenazi Jews, and considers it appropriate to mention in this context the talmudic injunction,
'Prayer requires intention' (JT *Berakhot* 1: 2):

For it needs no proof to those pure of mind and pure of heart, that there is no intention without understanding, and, therefore, we bless the translator (Rabbi David FL)
[David Friedländer]. . . . For although in almost every generation there arose men to
translate the prayers for the women who come to the House of God to pray—behold,
their countenance answered for them, in that they copied it without wisdom and
knowledge, because the task was regarded with contempt at that time and in the eyes
of the teachers of the people. Their hearts were too haughty to write a book to be
placed in the mouths of the masses and also in the mouths of women [according to
Deut. 31:19]. For that reason, they abandoned it to the ignorant, who incline towards
material gain, who are clumsy of tongue and speak vulgarly, to their great discredit
and shame. In the end it leads to sin, for the soul of the reader is disgusted by these
things so that prayer becomes a chore and a burden in the eyes of the daughters of
Israel, *who all know how to speak purely in the language of the nations*, but they do not
know how to speak Yiddish.[23]

The claim that all Jewish women living in German-speaking countries 'know
how to speak purely in the language of the nations' is, of course, an exaggera-
tion with regard to the time at which he was writing, the late eighteenth century.[24] Of greater importance, however, is the position he adopts towards the
legitimate spiritual need of women for a proper prayer book which, in his

(1960), 165–77. See also Werses, 'On Isaac Satanow and his Work: *The Proverbs of Asaf*' (Heb.),
and Pelli, *Genres and Issues in the Literature of the Hebrew Enlightenment* (Heb.), 101–15, in the
index under Satanow (p. 356), and in the bibliographical lists (pp. 339–40, 348) on Satanow,
Euchel, and others of the *Hame'asef* generation, and especially the works of Pelli himself listed
there. All of these references contain additional bibliography.

[22] Published in Berlin in 1786, also by Hevrat Hinukh Hane'arim. The review appeared in
Hame'asef, Iyar 5546 [1786], 138–41. On the book by Friedländer and on literature for women
written by his friends, see Shmeruk, *Yiddish Literature* (Heb.), 149–52. On David Friedländer,
see the index references to the author in Meyer, *The Origin of the Modern Jew*; Katz, *Out of the
Ghetto*; and Schorsch, *From Text to Context*. See also the more recent *Haskalah and History* by
Shmuel Feiner.   [23] *Hame'asef*, Iyar 5546 [1786], 139; emphasis added.

[24] While the intellectual salons of Mendelssohn and his friends, Jewish and non-Jewish,
opened their gates to both men and women, female socialites such as Rahel Levin Varnhagen
were an entirely marginal minority among Jewish women in general in the late 18th and early

opinion, cannot be presented in a Jewish language—he meant Yiddish—but only in what was supposedly their language of culture: German. This is simply rather transparent propaganda for the dissemination of the knowledge of German among a community which had not yet mastered it. It is similar to the approach of Mendelssohn and his friends in translating the Bible into German written in Hebrew letters, in a project known as the *Be'ur* or 'clarification'; but the use of Hebrew letters indicates that the Jewish target audience in Germany was still more familiar with reading Hebrew or Yiddish (both use the Hebrew alphabet) than German.[25]

The book section was often used to attract potential subscribers and thereby help writers and publishers alike by raising money in advance of sales. In this context it is interesting to note that the major portion of the publicity in *Hame'asef* dealing with new books was devoted to the *Be'ur*, which was announced as soon as the project was conceived in order to help finance its printing. Together with other examples cited above, this provides further evidence of the expansion of subscription projects—*prenumeranten*—in the eighteenth century. The technique was not always successful. The promoters of *Hame'asef* failed, for example, in their efforts to finance publication of the second part of *Imrei binah* (Sayings of Wisdom) by their friend Isaac Satanow, the first part of which had been published in Berlin in 1784, even though they announced that the manuscript was ready for printing as soon as he had finished it. That is to say, they sought to reassure potential buyers that the work was not simply a figment of the author's imagination and that they would therefore not be risking their money in subscribing to it.[26]

Another promotion that failed, which was also part of the effort to encourage Jews to read German, was for a translation of Abraham Jagel's *Lekaḥ tov* (Good Lesson). The translation in question was by Moses ben Uri Feivelman Segal of Braunschweig; it followed three earlier translations of the book into

19th centuries. On this unusual intellectual, who stood out from her female co-religionists, and from German women in general, see Arendt, *Rahel Varnhagen: The Life of a Jewess.*

[25] See *Hame'asef*, Tevet 5544 [1784], 78–80; Adar 5544 [1784], 92–6; Tevet 5548 [1788], 111–12; and Nisan 5548 [1788], 239–40. On the German translation of the Bible, see Sandler, *The Explanation of the Torah by Moses Mendelssohn* (Heb.). Study of Mendelssohn's translation reveals the great tension between propaganda for the German language and culture and the demonstration of loyalty to traditional commentary, ignoring the documentary criticism of the time, as, for example, in the commentary on Genesis. On documentary criticism, see Cassuto, *The Documentary Method* (Heb.).   [26] See *Hame'asef*, Nisan 5548 [1788], 236–9.

German, and does not appear to depend on them. An announcement of its preparation appeared in *Hame'asef* in 1785.[27] A comparison of the sample translation printed there with the Hebrew–German bilingual edition of the book published by the convert Karl Anton (whose name prior to his conversion had been Moses Gershon Hacohen), makes it clear why the public was not particularly enthusiastic about buying yet another edition.[28]

The history of book reviews in Hebrew during the nineteenth century is mostly a history of criticism in the periodicals of the Haskalah. This is too big a subject to treat exhaustively here, and I have therefore chosen to focus on three rather more unusual examples of the genre.

BIKURIM

The first book reviews appeared in *Bikurim* (First Fruits), published for only two years (1864/5 and 1865/6) and edited by Naftali Keller, who died while still in his prime and before the printing of the second volume had been completed. This highly talented man, who has virtually disappeared from literary history, subdivided the review section in the first volume by subject; the categories included the Bible, rabbinic literature, grammar books, books of rhetoric and poetry, studies on various topics, and periodicals.[29] In the survey of rabbinic literature, Keller laments the absence of a translation of Jewish legends with an extensive commentary, along the lines of the edition of Mendelssohn's *Be'ur*.[30] He then praises Isaac Hirsch Weiss for publishing *Sifra devei rav*, a halakhic midrash on Leviticus, with the commentary of Abraham ben David (Rabad), following the Oxford manuscript, with notes

[27] See ibid. Marheshvan 5545 [1785], 28–31. This was a bilingual edition. The translator of the Hebrew original explains its importance to his future readers, and gives an example of his translation into German with Hebrew characters.

[28] The edition of Karl Anton was printed in Braunschweig in 1756. Before converting to Christianity, Anton was a student of Jonathan Eibeschütz. Remarkably, following his conversion, when his former rabbi was accused of Shabateanism, Anton wrote a book in the defence of his beloved teacher. See Dotan, 'Rabbi Jacob Emden and his Generation', Hebrew section, p. 110. On the many translations of *Lekah tov*, see the fine article by my friend Morris Faierstein, 'Abraham Jagel, *Lekah tov* and its History', 319–50. A book by Jagel, *Gai ḥizayon* [A Valley of Vision] has been published in a critical edition by David Ruderman, with translations into English and Hebrew and an introduction on the man and his work.

[29] 'Casting an Eye on New Books Published this Year', *Bikurim*, 1 (1864–5), 189–206.

[30] Ibid. 192.

and references.[31] In the section on 'studies on various topics', Keller complains that in *Zikhron tsadikim* (A Memorial to Tsadikim) by Naftali Hertz, a *magid meisharim* (preacher) in Lemberg, in 1863, the subject of the work—the tombs of famous men buried in Lemberg—has not been properly researched. He points out, for example, that Hertz has plagiarized word for word what was written about the Hakham Tsevi (Tsevi the Sage), the father of Jacob Emden, in *Hame'asef* in 1810 without mentioning its source, and even without noticing that he had also copied the phrase 'to be continued in following issues'. Keller also expresses his astonishment that those rabbis of Lemberg who had written approbations for the book had not noticed its flaws.[32]

In the second volume of *Bikurim*, the survey appeared without mention of subjects, but with the same headings as the first volume.[33] A major part of the survey was devoted to a review of periodicals. Most of it comprised a critique of Moritz Steinschneider and an article he had published in the *Jahrbuch für Israeliten* in which he strongly criticized the Hebrew press.[34] Steinschneider's view was that it was controlled by dilettantes who, instead of encouraging Jews to learn the local language (especially in Slavic countries), were trying to revive Hebrew by using it as the medium for conveying news of the outside world. Steinschneider's views were an expression of his fervent belief that, following the emancipation of the Jews, Hebrew was becoming a dead language except for the purpose of religious ceremonies and customs and as a tool for scholars who would use it to erect a splendid monument to Jewish culture and literature. Keller attacked Steinschneider vigorously, saying that he—and other maskilim such as Solomon Judah Rapoport—was prepared, like non-Jewish scholars, to present popular information about the Jews and Judaism in the local vernacular, thereby accepting what was self-evident to non-Jews, namely that popular journalism was an important medium through which to educate the nation. But despite the fact that, unlike Latin in the wider society, Hebrew was still very much alive among the Jews, Steinschneider and others did not support the use of Hebrew for this purpose. In Keller's view, those who used the holy tongue were not 'gathering dry bones', but were acting 'for love of the language'. The intention of those who wrote in Hebrew had always been 'to arouse and stimulate a love of the Hebrew language and to ensure

[31] Vienna, 1863.   [32] *Bikurim*, 1 (1864–5), 194–200.   [33] *Bikurim*, 2 (1865–6), 175–97.
[34] See *Jahrbuch für Israeliten* of Leopold Wertheimer and Joseph Ritter Von Kompert (eds), vol. 24 (Vienna, 1865), 84 ff.

thereby its continued use by the people'. With barely veiled sarcasm he asks Steinschneider how many educated Jews in his own country were, even on his estimation, capable of reading the Bible in Hebrew.[35] Keller's words imply that neglect of Hebrew as a living language, in both sacred and secular contexts, would lead to its disappearance, and that Steinschneider and his colleagues were responsible for that neglect in German-speaking countries. What was possible for an individual with a divided soul like Steinschneider was not possible for the entire nation, which could not continue to foster the culture which the language conveyed to them and their children by imprisoning it and limiting it to being a vehicle for religious studies.

Keller's words anticipated the literary and journalistic expressions of the national awakening, but that is not their main significance. Rather, here was a young man who staunchly opposed Steinschneider's inclination to hold an impressive funeral for historical Judaism, long before Gershom Scholem did so in his famous article 'Reflections on Wissenschaft des Judentums'.[36]

HAPISGAH

The Jewish newspapers and periodicals of nineteenth-century Europe mainly represented the views of maskilim and their fellow-travellers, most of whom lived in central and western Europe and were keen to take advantage of the opportunities becoming available to them and therefore more eager to abandon the world of Torah. The Jews of eastern Europe tended to be more faithful to the tradition. The practice of critical book-reviewing developed so strongly in the newspapers of the maskilim, chiefly *Hamagid* and *Hakarmel*, that in the late 1870s, Joseph Brill wrote a satire entitled 'The Doctrine of Critics'.[37]

---

[35] *Bikurim*, 2 (1865–6), 195.

[36] See esp. pp. 386–93. On Keller see also Klausner, *History of Modern Hebrew Literature* (Heb.), 3rd edn, vol. ii (1960), 40–3. Ungerfeld, 'Between Letteris and Smolenskin' (Heb.), 250, writes that Keller was the editor of a newspaper named *Bikurei ha'itim hahadashim*. In the same volume of *Moznayim* as Ungerfeld's article appears, Getzel Kressel corrects this error. See 'For the Sake of Precision' (Heb.), 428, which correctly states that Keller did not edit a newspaper of that name. Rather, an annual named *Bikurei ha'etim hahadashim* appeared years before Keller published his *Bikurim*. That annual was edited by Yitzhak Isidore Bush and Yitzhak Shemuel Reggio (Yashar).

[37] On Brill, see Kressel, *Encyclopedia of Modern Hebrew Literature* (Heb.), i. 346–7 and the additional bibliography there.

The establishment of groups that regarded themselves as representatives of Orthodox Judaism began in Germany long before it did in eastern Europe. Hence, there was a place in Germany for a popular newspaper such as the *Israelit*, edited by Marcus Lehmann, as mentioned above. It was only in the 1870s that a similar development occurred in eastern Europe with the establishment of Mahzikei Hadat (The Adherents of Religion) and its publication of the same name. *Maḥzikei hadat* did not publish book reviews, and until the end of the century there were in fact hardly any Orthodox publications in Hebrew—newspapers, periodicals, or annuals—which had a section devoted to reviewing books. *Hapisgah* (The Summit), published in Vilna, was an exception.

Hapisgah was edited by Rabbi Hillel David Cohen of the Trivash family. Cohen, known as Ravin, was the head of the religious court of Wylkowyszky in the Kovno (Kaunas) district, and a prolific writer, being the author of volumes of responsa entitled *Venigash hakohen* (And the Priest Approached), *Avodat hakohen* (The Service of the Priest), and *Eden ganim* (The Eden of Gardens). It was only with the second volume of *Hapisgah*, published in 1896, that a section called 'Collection of New Books' appeared, written by Cohen himself.[38] Not surprisingly it reviewed only books faithful to the Jewish tradition, among which the scholarship of Samuel Abba Horodetsky on the life of Rabbi Samuel Edeles (the Maharsha) in a book called *Shem mishmuel* (A Name from Samuel), won special praise.[39] Cohen wrote that Horodetsky had been chosen by Providence to represent those faithful to Judaism.[40] Further praise of Horodetsky appeared in later issues, first when he published *Kerem shelomoh* (The Vineyard of Solomon), on the life of Solomon Luria, then in a review of *Hagoren* (The Threshing Floor), which Horodetsky edited.[41] Israel Levner, who wrote primarily for young people, receives similar praise. He was well known for his anthology *Kol agadot yisra'el* (All the Legends of Israel), which he wrote—following the maskilic style—not in the rabbinic Hebrew in which they had been preserved for generations but in the biblical Hebrew that was now considered superior; as such his work could compete with the works of maskilim, and was a bestseller as a gift for generations of barmitzvah boys.

---

[38] *Hapisgah*, 2 (1896), 62–4.

[39] Drogobych, 1895.   [40] *Hapisgah*, 4/2 (1897), 71.

[41] Ibid. 4/2 (1897), 64, on *Kerem shelomoh* (Drogobych, 1897); 5/1 (1899), 71–3, on *Hagoren*.

Thus, his *Children's Companion* was praised for 'implant[ing] in children the foundations of faith and the main tenets of the religion'.[42]

A careful reading of *Hapisgah* shows that its writers were attentive followers of the Haskalah journals *Hatsefirah*, edited by Hayim Zelig Slonimsky (and, after him, by Nahum Sokolow) and *Hamelits*, edited by Alexander Zederbaum, for its columns were full of bitter attacks on them.[43] There was likewise harsh criticism of a novel by Reuven Asher Brodes, *Hadat vehahayim* (Religion and Life) in an article entitled 'Visits of the Spring' by Shmaryahu Appelbaum, on the grounds that it misrepresented a Talmudic passage.[44] The review claims that Brodes has not understood the simple sense of the Talmud in *Hulin 47b*; according to Brodes the passage says that the lung is kosher, whereas in fact it says the opposite. It never occurred to the Orthodox reviewer that Brodes might have misquoted the passage intentionally, in order to present his protagonist in an ironic light.

The publisher and contributors of *Hapisgah* reacted strongly to the publication in 1897 of *Hashiloah* as a prestigious journal for maskilim and Zionists. Their ire was drawn in particular by a series of articles by Rav Tsa'ir (Hayim Tchernowitz).[45] One issue of *Hapisgah* in fact contained an entire section entitled 'The Field of Criticism' that consisted mainly of attacks on him.[46] The battle lines were drawn.

HASHILOAH

Hashiloah, my third example of a publication containing exceptional book reviews, was inaugurated in the year of the First Zionist Congress in Basle in

[42] On Levner, see Kressel, *Encyclopedia of Modern Hebrew Literature* (Heb.), ii. 170–1 and the additional bibliography there. On Levner's *Re'a hayeladim* [Children's Companion] (Warsaw, 1892), and on *Haristomatiyah* [Chrestomathy] (Vilna, 1908), readings for children, which he wrote with Y. Steinberg, see Ofek, *Children's Literature in Hebrew: The Beginning* (Heb.), 202–5. The review of the *Companion* appeared in *Hapisgah*, 4/2 (1896), 72.

[43] See *Hapisgah*, 3/1 (1897), 24–8 and 23–4.

[44] Ibid. 4/2 (1897), 24–7. On scholarship on Brodes today, see Werses, 'On Scholarship in Haskalah Literature Today' (Heb.), 32–3.

[45] See Tchernowitz, 'On the History of the *Shulhan arukh* and its Diffusion' (Heb.).

[46] The section appeared in *Hapisgah*, 7/1 (1901), and contained three articles: 'An Answer with Love (What I Told My Son Regarding Rav Tsa'ir)' by Moses Shalom Kazarnow (pp. 17–27); 'Arise and We Shall Arise' by Matityahu Morgenstern, a rabbi from Bolgrad in *Bessarabia* (pp. 27–30), and 'To Remove a Deceitful Cataract' by the publisher (pp. 31–5).

1897 with Asher Ginzberg, who wrote under the pen-name Ahad Ha'am ('one of the people'), as its editor. Ginzberg wrote a special introductory article to the first issue entitled 'Missions of *Hashiloah*', in which he stated that

> the word 'criticism' is mainly used by us in its restricted sense: judgement of new books. Our aim, however, is to expand that concept to its true boundary: the judgement of the human spirit and the fruit of man's work in relation to truth (rational criticism), good (moral criticism), and beauty (aesthetic criticism). In this sense, not only books, but all ideas and actions both new and old, which have made, are making, or will make an impression on the life of the people and its spirit are subject to criticism. . . . Books, however, are especially susceptible to criticism, in that one usually credits them with the ability to bring many ideas and actions to judgement and to show the connections between them and their common foundations. We will accept critical articles of that kind with pleasure if—and it is unfortunate that here, too, we must add something that ought to be self-evident—their virtue lies not only in stinging and mocking, but also in researching the true depths of the subject and shedding light on it in general, in all its details, with knowledge, good taste, and in a worthy style for every matter, according to its intrinsic or historical character and value.[47]

These words smack of pretension and a promise which it is difficult to say that *Hashiloah* managed to fulfil. The newspaper was not seen as a landmark in the formulation of a broad critical doctrine which could be applied to all the creations of the Hebrew man of spirit, combining 'philosophical, ethical, and aesthetic criticism'. A representative sample of the critical material from its first year shows that of all the promises Ginzberg made, only a modest number bore fruit. However, this contribution was still substantial.

In point of fact, the first volume of *Hashiloah* contains three sections that touch directly on book reviews, and comments on books also appear elsewhere in the volume. Thus we find a critical article by Simon Bernfeld on Moritz Güdemann's *Hatorah vehahayim be'artsot hama'arav* (The Torah and Life in the Lands of the West).[48] The article expresses both praise and reservations regarding the translation of the German original, *Geschichte des Erziehungswesens und der Kultur der abend-ländischen Juden während des Mittelalters*. The translator, Abraham Shalom Friedberg, responded to this criticism in a short article, 'On the Purity of Language'.[49] Another critique by Bernfeld, entitled 'Old and New [Criticism]', appears at the end of the vol-

[47] *Hashiloah*, 1 (1897), 4–5.

[48] Published by Ahiasaf (Warsaw, 1897); the review appears in *Hashiloah*, 1 (1897), 182–8.

[49] *Hashiloah*, 1 (1897), 487–8.

ume and deals with two books: *Yalkut shelomo* (Solomon's Compendium) by Solomon Rubin, which contains a discussion of faith and opinion among the Jews, the Persians, and the Indians, and also treats the subject of Elisha ben Avuyah (the second-century sage who abandoned Judaism); and *Netsaḥ yisra'el* (The Eternal One of Israel), by Zeev ben Tuviyah Schur, on the eternal nature of the Torah and of the Jewish people, and in support of Herzl and Zionism.[50]

David Neumark's article 'Jewish Existence' is also essentially a book review. Neumark criticizes Solomon Schiller's *Byt narodowy Żydów: Traktat historiczno-polityczny* (The National Existence of the Jews: A Historical-Political Tract) on the grounds that in his desire to arouse the Jewish people to nationalism, he has forgotten the fundamental elements of faith and religion.[51] Today, Schiller has been rescued from oblivion by Shraga Bar-Sela, a scholar who wrote a doctoral thesis on him after having defended him against Neumark and translated his words into Hebrew.[52]

Two issues of *Hashiloaḥ* contained sections by the scholar Hayim Brody entitled 'The Year's Harvest', with short surveys of book on Jewish subjects published in 1896 in vernacular languages. All of these were concerned essentially with Bible study: commentaries and translations of the Bible; an instruction manual for Bible study, looking at how the Bible is composed; scientists and the Bible; faith and criticism in relation to the Bible; beliefs and opinions in the Bible; Jewish history in the biblical period; the Land of Israel; and Hebrew language and grammar.[53]

Ginzberg started a section called 'About Everything (People—Events—Books—Periodicals)';[54] in keeping with the heading, various subjects were discussed, but the prime topic was books. He himself (as Ahad Ha'am) wrote a section which he called 'A Small Compendium', where he discussed various matters concerned with national life such as the distribution of charity in the Land of Israel, which continued as it had always done, in line with the description in *Megilat sefer* (Scroll of the Book), the autobiography of the prominent eighteenth-century sage Jacob Emden.[55] Under the title 'Shem and Japhet',

[50] *Yalkut shelomo*, published by the author (Cracow, 1896); *Netsaḥ yisra'el* published by the author (Chicago, 1897); Bernfeld's article appears in *Hashiloaḥ*, 1 (1897), 568–75.

[51] (Lemberg, 1896); the article appears in *Hashiloaḥ*, 1 (1897), 372–8.

[52] See Bar-Sela, *Builder of Bridges* (Heb.). Bar-Sela's Hebrew translation of Schiller's article appeared in *Meḥkarei yerushalayim bemaḥshevet yisra'el*, 4 (1984), 143–79.

[53] *Hashiloaḥ*, 1 (1897), 188–92, 473–6.   [54] Ibid. 385–92, 478–88.   [55] See ibid. 390–1.

Simon Bernfeld defended Israel Hayim Tawiow from the criticism of those who dismissed his books *Eden hayeladim* (The Eden of Children) and *Moreh hayeladim* (The Teacher of Children) because of mistakes in them.[56] Under the title, 'The Lost', Mikha Joseph Berdyczewski wrote briefly in praise of Yiddish stories by David Pinski which had been published by the Zeitgeist publishing house.[57] A 'Books and Authors' section, signed by 'M. Balshan' (the pen-name of Judah Leib Kantor, a Russian-born maskil who founded the first Hebrew-language newspaper), appeared once in the volume, and here we find a critique of the fifth volume of *Otsar hasifrut* (Jaroslaw, 1897), which contained a collection of essays and literary works.

It is of course difficult to expect the press, then or now, to supply deep analysis of or current information on the world of the Jewish book and its readers, the sensibilities of various reading publics and their literary tastes, or the relative popularity of particular types of book. As we have seen, most Jewish journalism, both popular and scholarly and including periodicals and annuals, was written by and for the community of maskilim, but they were a minority within the reading public; most of the Jews in eastern Europe had no secular education and were not interested in reading anything other than the traditional Jewish religious literature in Hebrew and Yiddish. The importance of that literature and its relevance for the reading public was not reflected in the journalism of that generation.

As we have seen, those who regarded themselves as the faithful guardians of Judaism rarely published book reviews and surveys of books. Evidence of the literary tastes and sensibilities of those who maintained a religious way of life is easier to find in the memoirs of those who abandoned the tradition. Such is true of Mordecai Guenzburg, whose autobiographical *Aviezer* served as a model for the memoirs and autobiographies of his friends, maskilim such as Judah Leib Levin, Abraham Ber Gottlober, Moses Leib Lilienblum, Judah Leib Katznelson (known as Buki ben Yogli), and others.

Surveys and reviews of books will not provide information on the revolution that occurred in Jewish literature and the effect this had on its readers

---

[56] *Hashiloah*, 391. On Tawiow see Kressel, *Encyclopedia of Modern Hebrew Literature* (Heb.), ii. 2–3, and the additional bibliography there. On *Eden hayeladim*, see Ofek, *Children's Literature in Hebrew: The Beginning* (Heb.), iii. 18; on Tawiow as a writer of feuilletons, see Karniel, *The Hebrew Feuilleton* (Heb.), 205–46.   [57] *Hashiloah*, i (1897), 391–2; 'B. Pinski' is printed in error.

from the 1880s onwards, when secular literature in Yiddish (some of which was called 'cheap' even by those who wrote it) began to thrive. Nor will they tell us of the sudden awakening of that sleeping beauty, Hebrew literature, at the end of the century, under the influence especially, of Ben-Avigdor (Abraham Leib Shalkovich), the founder and owner of the Tushiyah publishing house which specialized in publishing foreign works in Hebrew translation.

What, then, can be learned from this survey of book reviews and book reviewing? Certainly that newspapers and periodicals were used for the purposes of publicity and propaganda, particularly for literature that the maskilim wished to promote, and for the sale of manuscripts and the advancement of their publication. It provides some insight into the beginnings of pertinent criticism of the contents of books and their manner of production, and preliminary information on books in vernacular languages dealing with Judaism and the Jews (centred primarily on Bible studies). It is not an adequate picture, or even a partial one, of the world of the Jewish book. But it is a reflection of a specific reading public, and it is doubtful whether it represents the average Jewish reader during the period surveyed. Then, as now, most of the information about the books that really engaged people was communicated by word of mouth—by enthusiastic or disappointed readers speaking to others who trusted their taste and discernment.

ELEVEN

The Bibliographer and Librarian as an Agent of Culture

The Contribution of Abraham Ya'ari to the Study of Jewish Publishing in Eastern Europe

A S I HAVE REPEATEDLY ACKNOWLEDGED in this book, Jewish bibliographers and librarians have played an immensely important role in the creation of a solid basis for the study of Jewish culture in an era of national rebirth. The significance of their work in collecting data on the history of the books published for the Jewish reading public in the eighteenth and nineteenth centuries and for an understanding of what that history implies is exemplified in the labours of Abraham Ya'ari, to whom this chapter is devoted.

I did not know Abraham Ya'ari. He died in 1967, shortly before I entered the Hebrew University in Jerusalem in 1968. I began my studies of Jewish philosophy, kabbalah, and Hebrew literature while still a member of a kibbutz in the Jordan Valley—a small partner in one of the great enterprises of Zionism that today's journalists and scholars often see, from the vantage point of fashionable cafés, as no more than a real estate development project. At that time, I met Abraham Shapira (otherwise known as Patchi), who was then, as today, a member of Kibbutz Yizra'el; and like Abraham Ya'ari, he was an important promoter of Hebrew culture.

One evening Shapira persuaded me to join him in a visit to the home of Yehudah Ya'ari, Abraham's brother. Like Abraham, Yehudah had studied

This chapter is an expanded version of a lecture given at a conference in honour of the hundredth anniversary of Abraham Ya'ari's birth. The conference, 'Abraham Ya'ari: Bibliographer and Scholar of the Land of Israel', was held in Jerusalem on 14 March 2001 under the sponsorship of the National and University Library and the Hebrew University.

library science, but devoted most of his life to creative writing. He sat us down in his large and impressive library. I am, of course, an insatiable bookworm, and he noticed that while Patchi was exchanging pleasantries with him, I was eyeing his books with curiosity. He asked if I was a student. I told him that I was. 'In which department?' 'Jewish philosophy and kabbalah.' Judah smiled and said: 'Ha! Gershom Scholem's department! Well, I have a story for you about him and a book of mine. One day he came here, and like you, he was running his eyes over my books. His eyes lit up when he saw a particular book, which he removed from the shelf, saying to me: "From the six days of Creation, that book was meant to be in my library. How did it get to you? It seems that the First Cause has brought me here so that I can take it from you on permanent loan." And he did.' From the tone of his voice I got the impression that Judah Ya'ari was pleased that the great scholar of kabbalah, Gershom Scholem, should have found in his library a book that he had been looking for. (Scholem later actually published a list of the books he lacked in his library, and then complained that this had caused them to increase in price.[1])

Although I had never met Abraham Ya'ari, in March 2001 I was asked by Abraham David, a researcher at the Microfilm institute of the National and University Library in Jerusalem, to join a distinguished group invited to mark the hundredth anniversary of Ya'ari's birth and to speak about his many contributions to Hebrew and Jewish culture. In consequence of this, I turned once again to *Kiryat sefer*, a staple part of my reading as an undergraduate at the Hebrew University, because Ya'ari, as an employee of the National and University Library, was a major contributor to its pages. On re-reading that journal I lamented its demise; it was unquestionably the most important Jewish bibliographical publication of the twentieth century. Some had believed that the many small trees which grew around it would bear similar fruit, and that cutting it down would remove a shadow which hung over the heads of the younger journals. Regrettably, the small trees withered, and nothing has replaced the splendid tree that was felled.[2]

[1] See Scholem, *Ascend to Scholem* (Heb.). Scholem began his career in Jerusalem as a librarian and remained a bibliophile and an enthusiastic collector of books all his life. However, he abandoned the librarian's profession, while Ya'ari continued to specialize in it and in his research into books all his life. Here I should mention Karl Schottenloher, a non-Jewish counterpart of Ya'ari's, whose scholarship in the history of the European book as a cultural resource won him lasting fame. See his *Books and the Western World: A Cultural History*.

[2] The last issue of *Kiryat sefer* with articles on Jewish bibliography was published in

During the 1930s, *Kiryat sefer* functioned as a vital correspondence club—a virtual literary meeting-place for bibliophiles and scholars of the Jewish book throughout the Jewish diaspora, and Abraham Ya'ari was a respected member of this circle. Largely through letters rather than articles, its members passed information and scholarship between them on the pages of each new issue like skilled basketball players who keep the ball constantly in play: Abraham Ya'ari (from Jerusalem), Yeshayahu Sonne (from Florence and Rhodes), Isaac Rivkind (from New York), Hayim Lieberman (from Otwock, Warsaw, and Brooklyn), and Pinhas Kohn (from Vilna). The information they communicated may appear to the ordinary reader to have been merely bibliographical, but for them God was present in the infinitely small details, to paraphrase the well-known aphorism of Aby Warburg. Contributions from other librarians, such as Michael Wilenski (from Cincinatti) and Dov Ber Wachstein (from Vienna), were also printed from time to time, as were notes from other bibliophiles who were regular subscribers. These last included the book collector Hayim Shimon Neuhausen from Baltimore and the district judge Tsidkiyahu Harkabi (from Tel Aviv). (Harkabi's father, Meir Harkabi, a ritual slaughterer from Yavne'el, thought his son had gone off the rails when he chose to study law at the American University of Beirut. His grandson, Tsidkiyahu's son Yehoshofat, likewise disappointed him; following a brilliant military and scholarly career as an orientalist, he became a preacher at the gates on the lessons to be learned from the Bar Kokhba rebellion.)[3]

In acting as a correspondence club for bibliophiles, *Kiryat sefer* was in the tradition of Haskalah periodicals of the nineteenth century such as *Kerem ḥemed* (Charming Vineyard), *Otsar neḥmad* (Lovely Treasure), *Kokhevei yitsḥak* (The Stars of Isaac), and the like, where Jewish scholars had exchanged

1993. From 1994 on it consisted of a listing of the new books acquired by the Jewish National and University Library, sometimes with very short book reviews. This was a compromise solution as the original intention was to cease publication completely.

[3] See Tsidkiyahu Harkabi's 'What We Have Not Seen Is Not Proof' (Heb.), 279. Among the faithful correspondents to *Kiryat sefer* was the great historian Simon Dubnow, whose last letter from Riga, before he was murdered by the Nazis, was sent to Joseph Meisel, who published it in *Kiryat sefer*, 20 (1943–4), 177–9. Dubnow expresses concern for the fate of his archive, and regrets that he can no longer receive issues of *Kiryat sefer*. Getzel Kressel has published a short and incomplete survey of Jewish bibliographical journals entitled 'Our Bibliographical Press', in his *Mysteries of Books and Authors* (Heb.), 60–4, where he also writes about fifty years of *Kiryat sefer* (pp. 65–72).

letters and ideas. These and similar publications are listed in Menuhah Gilboa's *Lexicon of Hebrew Journalism in the Eighteenth and Nineteenth Centuries*.

These heroes of culture, among whom Abraham Ya'ari was a shining star, regarded their writing in *Kiryat sefer* as a contribution to the national revival, part of the garnering of knowledge on the cultural assets of the Jewish people. This information is of paramount importance for every scholar of the book and of Hebrew culture, and indeed, for anyone who wishes to contribute to the great flow of Jewish cultural history. Sadly, however, now that *Kiryat sefer* is no more, its treasures no longer figure in the bibliographical lists of a great majority of the new generation of scholars. From their youth they have spurned the drudgery of reading the bibliographical material insisted upon by teachers of the older generation. Thus new work is published almost daily on the Ba'al Shem Tov and the spirit of hasidism—and, of course, on women and gender—which imbibes material from the chalice of modern scholarship but regrettably abandons the 'old wine' stored on the shelves of the library, available and accessible to all.

Abraham Ya'ari's enormous contribution to the creation of a solid basis for Jewish studies is too vast to be dealt with here. Two bibliographies of his writings have been compiled, one by Uri Ben-Horin for Ya'ari's fiftieth birthday and the other by Naftali Ben-Menahem as part of a posthumously published Festschrift entitled *In the Tents of the Book*, which also contains eulogies of which the most important are those of Shmuel Werses.[4] The difference

---

[4] See Ben-Horin, *The Works of Abraham Ya'ari* (Heb.); *In the Tents of the Book* (Heb.), where, on pp. 11–16, headed by appropriate tributes, is a list of Ya'ari's works compiled by Ben-Menahem, which extends Ben-Horin's list to cover the period 1949–66. The editors also included an article from Ya'ari's literary estate on Hebrew printing in Mezhirov (pp. 17–27). This complements a series of his articles on small Jewish presses in Poland and Russia (see below). Additional eulogies were published in *Yerushalayim*, 2 (1967), by Gedalyah Alkoshi (pp. 396–7) and Shemuel Ashkenazi ('Scribal Errors: From a Reader's Notebook' (Heb.), pp. 379–95). Here, among other errors great and small, Ashkenazi mentions a slip of Ya'ari's pen in his understanding of a verse from the book of Daniel. When the volume was in press and Ashkenazi learned, as he told me personally, that Ya'ari had died, he added a letter from Ya'ari, acknowledging his error, and presented his words as a memorial. For further praise of Ya'ari, see Haberman, 'Abraham Ya'ari, the Author and Bibliographer' (Heb.); Kressel, 'Two Who Passed Away' (Heb.), on Nathan Michael Gelbar and Abraham Ya'ari, which describes Ya'ari as 'the greatest bibliographer of our day' (p. 64; there is a longer version of this piece in Kressel's *Mysteries of Books and Authors*, pp. 123–8); and Bergmann, 'The Young Abraham Ya'ari' (Heb.),

between the two bibliographies is that whereas Ben-Horin took the trouble to list some of the series of articles that Ya'ari had published in the weekend and holiday literary supplements of Hebrew-language newspapers (primarily in *Davar* under the heading 'In the Folds of a Book'), Ben-Menahem did not. These unlisted pearls may be lost for ever, for Ya'ari never collected them. Ben-Menahem did, however, take the trouble to collect his own articles about books during his lifetime, which he published first in the literary supplements to *Hatsofeh* under the heading 'Scribal Decorations', a somewhat overblown title for a collection of newspaper articles.[5]

It is true that Ya'ari collected and revised some of the articles he published in weeklies and periodicals in works such as *In the Tents of the Book* and *Studies of the Book*. He also published monographs such as *Emblems of the Hebrew Printers*, *Jewish Printing in the Lands of the East*, and *Hebrew Printing in Constantinople*.[6] As fate would have it, however, his great contribution to the study of Hebrew and Yiddish printing in eastern Europe remains, for the most part, dispersed through other publications: in his articles in *Kiryat sefer*; in small pamphlets that he compiled from his writings and published under the title 'Bibliographical Gleanings'; and in his newspaper articles. There is one exception. Ya'ari published a monograph on *Hemdat yamim* (Delight of Days), a major work of homiletics and ethics published anonymously in the eighteenth century. In this monograph, which he entitled *Ta'alumat sefer* (Mystery of a Book), he devoted a special chapter to *Hemdat yamim*'s circulation in eastern Europe, and particularly its influence on the disciples of Israel Ba'al Shem Tov, and also dealt with the identity of the author of this work, which had long been considered to be of Shabatean origin. Ya'ari's identification of the author as Benjamin Halevi, a kabbalist of seventeenth-century Safed, provoked a swift response from Gershom Scholem in *Behinot*, a journal

whose remarks are full of fondness and nostalgia: when Bergmann was a new immigrant, Ya'ari was his Hebrew teacher and inspired him with his enthusiasm for the renewal of the nation and of the Hebrew language. I am grateful to my friend Abraham Shapira for providing me with a photocopy of this fine article, which is printed below as an appendix.

[5] Ben-Menahem republished these *Hatsofeh* articles in a single volume entitled *In the Gates of the Book* (Heb.).

[6] On *Emblems of the Hebrew Printers*, see also his 'Supplements to the Emblems of Hebrew Printers' (Heb.), and new additions in Yitshak Yudlov, *Printers' Emblems* (Heb.).; on *Hebrew Printing in Constantinople*, see the supplements and corrections in Hacker, 'Printers of Constantinople in the Sixteenth Century' (Heb.).

edited by the bibliophile agronomist Solomon Zemach.[7] This led to a series of articles in response by Scholem's student, Isaiah Tishby.[8]

Scholem and Tishby contributed a great deal to scholarship on the identification of *Ḥemdat yamim* and its sources. They did not, however, add to Ya'ari's important remarks, which remain the basis for scholarship on the influence of the book in eastern Europe at the time of the Ba'al Shem Tov and later through the work of Alexander Susskind, author of *Yesod veshoresh ha'avodah* (The Basis and Root of Worship), who recommended that *Ḥemdat yamim* should be studied daily, like the Zohar. (Susskind's relative Joseph Klausner called him 'a hasid among mitnagedim' because he lived in Grodno which was certainly not a centre of hasidism at the time.) Many editions of Susskind's book were printed, as Ya'ari documents, including some which tried to downplay the importance of *Ḥemdat yamim* because of its alleged Shabatean connections.[9] While Ya'ari showed that *Ḥemdat yamim* was originally popular among the disciples of the Besht, he demonstrated that by the time of *Shivḥei habesht* the attitude to it was quite negative because it had since become tainted by association with Shabateanism.[10]

Ya'ari was also interested in scholarship dealing with the Land of Israel. As Shmuel Werses has noted, this interest grew after Ya'ari's son Gur was killed in the War of Independence.[11] In contrast, most of Ya'ari's work on the history of Hebrew and Yiddish publishing in eastern Europe was carried out before this tragedy befell his family, though he continued his interest in this area even after his son was killed and, as will be shown below, produced important works at a later stage too. His initial contribution to the study of Hebrew and Yiddish publishing in eastern Europe was his review of the first of a series of

[7] See Scholem, 'And the Mystery Remains Intact' (Heb.). Ya'ari responded in *Beḥinot*, 9 (1955), 71–80, and Scholem replied to Ya'ari in the same issue (pp. 80–4). Both Scholem's critique and his response were reprinted in his *Researches in Shabateanism* (Heb.), 250–87, with an appended bibliography prepared by the editor, Yehuda Liebes (pp. 287–8).

[8] See the list of Tishby's works in the bibliographical supplement prepared by Liebes mentioned in n. 7 above. These were reprinted in a collection of Tishby's work, *Studies in Kabbalah and its Offshoots* (Heb.), ii. 339–416. This volume does not include some of Tishby's material mentioned by Liebes that remains in manuscript.

[9] For detail see Ya'ari, *Mystery of a Book* (Heb.), 124–7 and the reference to Klausner there.

[10] On the attitude of the Ba'al Shem Tov and his disciples towards *Ḥemdat yamim* see ibid. 134–41; see also Ya'ari's later article, 'Two Basic Editions of *Shivḥei habesht*' (Heb.), 252.

[11] See Werses, 'A Bibliographer of our Literature', in Ya'ari's *In the Tents of the Book*, 8–10; this volume also includes praise from Nathan Rotenstreich (p. 5) and Yissakhar Yoel (pp. 6–7).

important articles by Israel Halpern on the Council of the Four Lands and
the Hebrew book, which was published in *Kiryat sefer*.[12] He went on to write
a review of Hayim Dov Friedberg's *History of Hebrew Printing in Poland*.[13] In
these articles he surveys the work of other historians who, like Friedberg,
made use of bibliography as part of their attempt to create a new Jewish history. He thus draws readers' attention to the works of Meir Balaban and Jacob
Shatzky, whom he considers fine historians of eastern European Jewry. Ya'ari's
critiques are pertinent rather than petty, providing a basis for understanding
the social and cultural history of east European Jewry.

Ya'ari's critique of Halpern's work includes a reassessment of a regulation
of the Jaroslaw fair of 1686 pertaining to printing which Halpern interpreted
as a general prohibition on the printing of books but which Ya'ari understands
as relating only to the printing of books of sermons. Ya'ari's argument is based
on the fact that Halpern had reconstructed the regulation, the text of which is
no longer extant. According to Ya'ari, it is inconceivable that the rabbis of the
Council of the Four Lands, in whose jurisdiction Jaroslaw was located, would
have prohibited the printing of the Talmud or commentaries on it, since these
are the essence of study for Jews everywhere, and no Jewish life is possible
without them. Moreover, he found that the regulation is not mentioned at all
in approbations of ordinary books such as that granted at the fair of Jaroslaw
in 1692 for an edition of *Midrash rabah* published in Frankfurt an der Oder in
1693, or that granted in Jaroslaw in 1693 for *She'elot uteshuvot beit ya'akov* (The
Responsa of the House of Jacob) by Jacob ben Samuel, head of the rabbinical
court of Zusmir, which was printed in Frankfurt an der Oder in 1693. Ya'ari
does not stop there, but goes on to show that the approbation by Naftali
Cohen Katz of Poznan for Hayim Krochmal's *Mekor ḥayim* (The Source of
Life) (Fuerth, 1697) states explicitly that this regulation was 'not to give an
approbation *to collections of sermons*', and he makes a similar statement in his
approbation to *Berit mateh mosheh* (The Covenant of the Staff of Moses),
printed in Berlin in 1701: 'Although there are regulations of the lands not to

[12] See Halpern, 'The Council of Four Lands and the Hebrew Book' (Heb.), 366–78. Articles
by Halpern in later issues include 'The Approbations of the Council of Four Lands' (Heb.),
105–11, 252–64, and 'More on the Councils of Poland and Lithuania and their Relation to the
Book' (Heb.), 250–3. Ya'ari's review appeared in *Kiryat sefer*, 9 (1932–3), 393–4.

[13] This appeared in *Kiryat sefer*, 9 (1932–3), 432–9. See also Rivkind, 'History of Hebrew
Printing in Poland', an article in *Kiryat sefer* offering a significant contribution to Ya'ari's work.
Friedberg published a revised edition of his book in Tel Aviv in 1950.

print *any book of sermons*, the aforementioned regulations do not refer to this.'
Ya'ari's ardour did not cool until he had presented further proof from the tes-
timony of Gabriel ben Judah of Cracow, who was himself at the Jaroslaw fair.
In his approbation to *Yad avi shalom* (Hand of the Father of Shalom) by
Joseph Shalom, the chief rabbinical judge of Piszczac, which was printed in
Offenbach in 1720, he writes that he gave an approbation even though he cus-
tomarily refrained from endorsing books, especially books of sermons, for 'I
was with those appointed in the decrees of the angels with the Sages of the
Four Lands in the states of Poland and in Jaroslaw in 1688 not to print such
books'.[14] Ya'ari here adds information to that presented by Halpern by showing that the approbation was issued by the Council of the Four Lands in 1688.

What lessons can we learn from this? Certainly that approbations contain
precious gems for the study of Jewish history, and that they are ignored today
just as they were then, in the early 1930s, when Ya'ari began his work. After
Loewenstein had prepared his index of approbations (*Index Approbationum*),
Ya'ari and his colleagues added a great deal of invaluable information, much of
which is contained in their articles, and the essence of which is to be found in
the index cards of the Hebrew bibliographical project of the National and
University Library in Jerusalem. Sadly, scarcely any use is made of that information today. For over thirty years I have been following in the footsteps of
Ya'ari and his colleagues, and have accumulated a treasure trove consisting of
hundreds of approbations issued by that nineteenth-century genius, Joseph
Saul Halevi Nathansohn, the rabbi of Lemberg whose contemporaries styled
him 'the minister of approbations'.[15] I regret to say, however, that for the present these remain unpublished. They are of interest because Nathansohn,
unlike many other scholars, took the trouble to read almost every book he was
asked to endorse. He corrected and reprimanded the authors both of kabbalistic works and halakhic works. Some authors took offence at this approach
and proceeded to excise the criticism from Nathanson's approbation, claiming
that they had dealt with all his comments and corrections in the body of their
book.

---

[14] The phrase 'in the decrees of angels' ('bigezerat irin') is to be found in approbations to
traditional Jewish books through the ages. It is a warning from the rabbis who signed the
approbation to respect the copyright of the printer who was the publisher and distributor of the
book.
[15] See my remarks on Nathansohn and his approbations in Chapter 9 above, near n. 7.

8. One of the printers' marks used by Aaron ben Yonah, the first
Hebrew printer in Ostrog (Ostraha), in the press he owned there from
1793 to 1828. The text says '*Gedruckt bei r. aharon, madpis*
(Printed by R. Aaron, printer)'
This mark was used in a number of books he printed and is reproduced here
from a Passover Haggadah published in Ostrog in 1819

Ya'ari's work on marvellous literature of approbations began to reveal its potential as a mirror of Jewish spiritual life, but it has since sunk once more into oblivion. The pioneering work of Ya'ari and Israel Halpern are milestones on a road that has not yet been paved—a road that would enable scholars to assess the involvement of the great rabbis of the past in the circulation of Jewish books and to identify those who were engaged in this work. Such scholarship would also enable us to reappraise the information on books, authors, and readers which is hidden in these approbations. In his later writings Ya'ari meticulously recorded each person who gave approbations: even the men who approved the printing of books in the small printing shops of villages in Russia and Poland. If the information concerning the approbations would have been available decades earlier it would have enabled historians to uncover some of the information that Shaul Stampfer discovered only much later: namely, that Levi Isaac of Berdichev, the disciple and apparently also the scribe of the Magid, Dov Ber of Mezhirech, was not persecuted as a hasid, but was accepted as an important rabbinic authority He was sought out by the printers in his home town of Berdichev—men such as Samuel ben Yissakhar Ber Segal, the greatest Jewish printer in Russia and Poland in the late eighteenth and early nineteenth centuries, who was active in both Berdichev and other cities and towns. Similarly, printers from other cities such as Minkovtsy also sought approbations from him. As Stampfer has shown, the tsadik Levi Isaac of Berdichev and the arch-mitnaged Hayim of Volozhin, the disciple of the Vilna Gaon, both wrote approbations for the same books.[16] I myself have shown that Levi Isaac and his contemporary and friend Israel ben Shabetai of Kozienice, a disciple of the Magid of Mezhirech and an important scholar and community leader, also signed approbations for the same books as great non-hasidic rabbis of Poland and Russia.[17]

Ya'ari's review of the first edition of Friedberg's *History of Hebrew Printing in Poland*[18] states correctly that Friedberg fails to mention printing shops in

---

[16] See Stampfer, 'Rabbi Hayim of Volozhin and his Approbations' (Heb.), 165–7.

[17] See Gries, 'Rabbi Israel ben Shabetai of Kozienice' (Heb.), 128–9 and n. 2. On the approbations given by Levi Isaac of Berdichev to the printers of Minkovtsy, see Ya'ari, 'Bibliographical Gleanings 42' (Heb.), 267–76. The list of books on pp. 270–3 includes approbations for books 1, 2, 5, 7, 9, and 14: these include books of sermons, kabbalah, and midrash. What can be learned from the approbations of Levi Isaac is well described in Liberman, 'Bibliographical Notes' (Yid.), 92–3. See also Liberman's additional remarks in his *Rachel's Tent* (Heb.), i. 66–8.

[18] See *Kiryat sefer*, 9 (1932–3), 432–9; see also another detailed review: Rivkind, 'History of

Poland at the end of the nineteenth century. It also points out that Friedberg's book lacks an index of the names of books or a map indicating the locations of the printing shops, and that he has failed to indicate books whose title pages appear to have been falsified. The falsification of title pages, a topic that fascinated Ya'ari (and which has been treated by several scholars, as discussed below), received splendid treatment from him later in his career, in his excellent article about the printing house belonging to *rebetsin* Judith Rosanis (that is, the wife of Rabbi Rosanis), as we shall see below.

Ya'ari mentions books that Friedberg had missed, as well as printers and presses in cities he had not dealt with (such as Ostrog), and derives from them important material regarding the history of printing and the fate of the book which is missing from Friedberg's account.[19] He likewise mentions scholarship published after Friedberg's book, such as an article by Saul Ginzburg in the Yiddish periodical *Tsukunft* on the history of Jewish printing in Russia,[20] and articles that had been forgotten, such as that of Aaron Freimann in *Hatsofeh leḥokhmat yisra'el* on the lot of a Jewish printer in Lublin.[21]

Ya'ari's supposed pettiness and rummagings did, however, result in a splendid discovery. While examining a list of the books printed in the city of Sarmusel (Novy Dvor) in Romania, where an enterprising non-Jewish printer named Johann Anton Krieger was active,[22] Ya'ari noticed that Krieger numbered the titles that he published in running order. This information resulted in another article by Ya'ari in *Kiryat sefer*, a short while after his review of Friedberg was published.[23] What prompted this second article was that Ya'ari had subsequently found a calendar for 5547 (1787) on whose last page there was a list of all the forty-five books that Krieger had published up to the end of 5546 (1786). While Friedberg had mentioned 15 of these books, and Ya'ari had added another 6 in his review of Friedberg, this extremely important list now enabled him to add 24 more books, including prayer books, whose existence had previously been unknown to us. These are, in the main, *tikunim* (mid-

Hebrew Printing in Poland' (Heb.), 95–104, 384–95, and the comment by Liberman in 'Bibliographical Notes' (Yid.), 94.

[19] See *Kiryat sefer*, 9 (1932–3), 433–4.

[20] Ginzburg, 'On the History of Jewish Printing Produced in Russia', 589–94; mentioned by Ya'ari on p. 435 of his *Kiryat sefer* review.

[21] See Freimann, 'The First Hebrew Printer in Lublin' (Heb.), 282–95, mentioned by Ya'ari on p. 436.   [22] See Ringelblum, 'Johann Anton Krieger' (Yid.).

[23] 'Bibliographical Gleanings 1' (Heb.), 371–2.

night prayer and study services) and *seliḥot* (penitential prayers). In the 1780s a significant number of these bore evidence of the influence of kabbalah and its adepts. This information supplements our knowledge regarding the intensive printing of books of kabbalah and *tikunim* of kabbalistic origin in eastern Europe from the 1870s on. At that time the centre of this activity for the entire Jewish world was Zolkiew.[24]

Only one tractate of the Talmud appears in the aforementioned list of books printed in Sarmusel, namely *Bava metsia*. Furthermore, Ya'ari's articles dealing with small presses in Russia and Poland, which are discussed below, lead to the interesting conclusion that they did not print tractates of the Talmud used for study in the regular curriculum. We know that until the nineteenth century, rabbis generally commissioned the printing of individual tractates of the Talmud according to need rather than purchasing full sets. It is surprising, therefore, that those tractates needed for study in small towns and cities were not supplied by local printers; it seems that marketing considerations dictated that these should be supplied by the larger printing houses. It may be asked, on the other hand, why the major printers seemingly ignored considerations of commerce and profit in respect of the large market for daily and festival prayer books, a market parallel to that for the Talmud, as revealed by the list of prayer books published in Sarmusel. Here, perhaps, the local need for specific prayer books with the addition of one or other kabbalistic variation gave rise to the editions printed in Sarmusel as they appear on the list.

The next stage in Ya'ari's writing provides a valuable and basic contribution to the history of the circulation of Yiddish literature, bilingual Yiddish–Hebrew works, and literature translated from Hebrew into Yiddish.

Since Ya'ari began to gather his data, never hesitating to present the conclusions deriving from his research, a great deal more scholarship has been undertaken. He was preceded by outstanding scholars such as Max Erik Weinreich, and Zalman Rejzen, but it was Chone Shmeruk who constructed a complete description of Yiddish literature (on the basis, it has to be said, of the groundwork laid by Ya'ari) and recounted it wonderfully in *Yiddish Literature: Chapters in its History* during the 1970s.[25] Ya'ari's research revealed

---

[24] See Gries, 'The Copying and Printing of Books on Kabbalah' (Heb.), 208, 210. For a revised and annotated version see above, pp. 77–8.

[25] See also Shmeruk, *Yiddish Literature in Poland* (Heb.). Shmeruk and Turniansky (eds), *Yiddish Literature in the Nineteenth Century* (Yid.), contains sixteen papers by the best scholars

previously unknown translations of books such as *Ben hamelekh vehanazir* (The Prince and the Monk),[26] whose stories had enormous influence on Jewish writers of the late Middle Ages and the early modern period.[27] Two other Yiddish translations discovered by Ya'ari were of *Hovot halevavot*[28] and *Igeret ba'alei hayim* (The Epistle of the Animals).[29] In characteristic style, Ya'ari uncovered the story of an educated woman who had turned to publishing a translation of *Igeret ba'alei hayim*. This was Rivkah, the daughter of Joseph, the scribe of the city of Brody, who was unaware of the earlier translation of the book published by *rebetsin* Rosanis in Lemberg.[30] Echoing and adding to this, another bibliophile, Hayim Lieberman, immediately sent a note to *Kiryat sefer* mentioning another unknown translation of this work, whose author was identified only by the initials A.G.[31] While Ya'ari was bringing this heroine of culture to our attention he was simultaneously refuting Gustav Karpeles' statement in his *Geschichte der Jüdishen Literatur* that *Hovot halevavot* had been translated into Yiddish by Rivkah Tiktiner, the author of *Meneket rivkah* (The Wet Nurse of Rebecca), a translation printed in 1604. In the same article he also reprimanded Zalman Rejzen for repeating Karpeles' words in his *Leksikon fun der Yidisher literature, prese un filologye* (Vilna 1926–9) without first checking their accuracy.[32]

Perhaps encouraged by Ya'ari's words, Pinhas Kohn of Vilna soon sent a short article on Jewish midwives as authors of books to the next volume of *Kiryat sefer*. As a coda to Ya'ari's remarks, Kohn mentioned the Yiddish works

of 19th-century Yiddish literature, who produced their work in parallel with Ya'ari during the 1920s and 1930s in the Soviet Union. For a review of this volume see Werses, 'A Monument for Yiddish Literature' (Yid.).

[26] See Ya'ari, 'Bibliographical Gleanings 3', 376–8, which adds the information in Prilutski, 'Bibliographical Notes' (Yid.). See also Liberman, *Rachel's Tent* (Heb.), i. 300–2.

[27] See Schirman, *The History of Hebrew Poetry in Christian Spain and Southern France*, 256–73. For more on its frequent editions during the 18th century and its influence on the disciples of the Besht, see Gries, 'The Historical Figure of the Besht', 432–3 and n. 68.

[28] 'Bibliographical Gleanings 19' (Heb.), 398–410.

[29] 'Bibliographical Gleanings 18' (Heb.), 394–8.   [30] Ibid. 395–6.

[31] See Liberman, 'On Translations of *Igeret ba'alei hayim* into Yiddish' (Heb.), 272.

[32] See Ya'ari, 'Bibliographical Gleanings 19' (Heb.). The third edition of Karpeles' book was published in Berlin, 1920–1. On Tiktiner's book see Shmeruk, 'The First Jewish Woman Author in Poland' (Heb.), 13–23, repr. in id., *Yiddish Literature in Poland* (Heb.), where he adds a description of her book as an appendix under the heading 'Bibliographical List of Printers in Poland in Yiddish before the Persecutions of 1648–9' (see pp. 101–2, no. 44).

of two midwives, and the fact that they had been authorized to work in this profession in the early nineteenth century after completing an official course sponsored by the authorities in Vilna.[33] While this exchange of information is impressive, it is particularly surprising that there is no mention of it in Iris Parush's important book, *Reading Women: The Benefit of Marginality*, which also fails to mention women publishers in the wake of Ya'ari's work, and also *Daybreak* by Mordecai Zalkin, on the Haskalah in Russia during the nineteenth century, which devotes special attention to education and culture in general and to the place of women in particular.[34]

Even if ethical literature in Yiddish included stories as a way of offering good advice and spreading knowledge of customs and halakhah, it still provided spiritual nourishment for the masses and made them aware of the legitimacy of Yiddish as an important and recognized means of expression, in manuscript and print. Great contributions were made by Eliezer Pavir, Isaac Meir Dik, Menahem Mendel Lefin, and others in adapting into modern Yiddish the old Yiddish of ethical literature in general and of the stories in particular, creating a basis for entirely new popular uses of the Yiddish language.

In the series 'Bibliographical Gleanings' that Ya'ari wrote for *Kiryat sefer* early in his career, he highlighted the literary contribution of Isaac Meir Dik, who played a major role in laying the foundations for the popularization of Yiddish language and literature.[35] This research preceded Ya'ari's important work in identifying and analysing highly influential examples of Yiddish literature easily assimilated by the masses. This ranged from Yiddish editions of *Shivḥei habesht* to the work of Eliezer Pavir, who adapted the sixteenth-century central European Yiddish of the *Ma'aseh bukh* to eighteenth-century east European Yiddish. Ya'ari also studied the work of various printers in this field, as discussed below.

He proved that Pinhas Kohn was in error in his Yiddish article in *Yivo*

---

[33] See Kohn, 'Midwives as the Authors of Books' (Heb.), 118–21.

[34] *Daybreak* (Heb.) is an important reworking of a master's thesis subsequently expanded and developed into a doctoral dissertation. See pp. 101–2 n. 66, 126, 145, 167, 172, 202 and esp. pp. 208–12 ('The Education of Girls'). See also the important comments in Feiner, 'The Modern Jewish Woman'.

[35] See Ya'ari, 'Bibliographical Gleanings 8' (Heb.), 515–20. See also Liberman, 'On the Bibliography of I. M. Dik' (Yid.), 171–4. For more on Dik and his work see Zinberg, *History of Jewish Literature*, xiii. 78–90, and below at nn. 41–2.

bleter when he identified an anonymous story, *Ma'aseh avinadav* (The Story
of Avinadav), printed in Vilna in 1848, as Dik's first work.[36] Ya'ari discovered
that the story had been reprinted in Warsaw in 1855, an edition unknown to
Kohn, and refuted the attribution to Dik, since he was also able to prove that
the book had first been printed before Dik's birth, in Frankfurt an der Oder in
1791 as *Ma'aseh aminadav*, as a bilingual edition in Yiddish and Hebrew.
Ya'ari's investigation showed that this first Frankfurt an der Oder edition was
merely a translation of a German treatise by Johan Jakob Dush, originally
called *Moralische Briefe*.[37] After publishing these comments, Ya'ari discovered
that Noah Prilutski had written earlier about another edition of *Ma'aseh
aminadav*, printed in Vilna in 1851, but without revealing the source of the
book or denying its attribution to Dik.[38]

Ya'ari was not satisfied with mere bibliographical correction, however. For
the benefit of his readers, he added an account of Dik's positive attitude
towards Yiddish as a language of literature and written culture,[39] and he concluded his article with a list of six previously unknown stories by Dik.
Although Dik's name does not appear as their author, they are signed with the
pseudonym of the supposed copyist, A. Shapira, whom Ya'ari identifies as
Dik.[40] Ya'ari's erudition and breadth of knowledge provide important additional information for lovers of literature among his readers, namely, that the
subject of Dik's story *Der Yored* (He Who Goes Down), which was published
in Warsaw in 1855, was the same as that of S. Y. Agnon's *Vehayah he'akov lemishor* (And the Crooked Shall Be Made Straight). Ya'ari suggests that Dik
and Agnon drew on the same source.[41] He also provides information on the

[36] Kohn, *Dik's Unknown Writings in Yiddish and Hebrew* (Yid.), 325–34; see Ya'ari,
'Bibliographical Gleanings 8' (Heb.), 516.

[37] 'Bibliographical Gleanings 8', 517–18. For some reason, Zinberg's doubts regarding the
attribution of *Ma'aseh aminadav* to Dik were rejected in an addition to his notes (see Zinberg,
History of Jewish Literature, xiii. 80–1 n. 28). The addition, written by M. Astor, was printed
without Astor's name, which appears in the Hebrew edition of the book, in an appendix to the
same chapter, n. 40.

[38] See Prilutski, *The Yiddish Consonant* (Yid.), 211; Ya'ari, 'Supplements to Earlier Chapters
[of the Bibliographical Gleanings]' (Heb.), 534.

[39] 'Bibliographical Gleanings 8', 518. [40] Ibid. 519.

[41] Ibid. 520. See also Ya'ari, 'From a Folk Tale to an Artistic Story' (Heb.). For more on
Agnon's sources for 'Vehayah ha'akuv lemishor', see Nigal, 'Hasidic Elements in one of Agnon's
Works' (Heb.). Additional information can be found in Nigal's 'S. Y. Agnon and his Hasidic
Sources' (Heb.), in his *East and West Studies*, 251–5, where we also find a reference to another
interesting article on the subject by Yehoshua Mondshine.

sources for Dik's books. Twenty-two years later, Ya'ari published a comprehensive article which contains an introduction to Dik's work and his contribution to Jewish culture, with a full annotated bibliography and a list of works by Dik in the collection of the National and University Library in Jerusalem.[42]

Early in Ya'ari's career he had devoted considerable attention to Yiddish versions of *Shivḥei habesht*,[43] and towards the end of his life he returned to that subject in a long article.[44] It had commonly been assumed that both the Hebrew edition of *Shivḥei habesht*, first printed in Kopys in 1814, and the early Yiddish edition, printed in Ostrog or Korets in 1815, had a Hebrew version as their source.[45] Ya'ari's article showed that the differences between the editions were not merely the result of chance changes in wording and scribal or typographical errors; rather, he suggested that these variants had to be taken into account in all subsequent scholarship in order to understand the attitudes of the editors towards the material. These concerns were echoed by Shmeruk.[46] Ya'ari states that the 1814 Kopys edition—according to which the Besht knocked a copy of *Ḥemdat yamim* off a table in disgust when he saw it lying there—is apocryphal; the earliest printed Yiddish version completely lacks the story. He thus concludes that its inclusion was an anachronistic effort, at

[42]   See Ya'ari, 'The Books by Isaac Meir Dik that are in Jerusalem' (Heb.), 76–92, 211–29. See also Liberman, *Rachel's Tent* (Heb.), i. 489–501. Shmuel Werses proposes another point of view on Dik's work in 'Erter's "Transmigration of the Soul" in the Yiddish Version of Isaac Meir Dik' (Heb.), 29–49. See also id., 'The Right Hand Pushes Away, the Left Brings Close' (Heb.), 27–32. Parush, *Reading Women* (Heb.), makes good use of Dik's contribution to the popularization of Yiddish literature: see references to him in the index (p. 337), and text (esp. pp. 136–73). Of the items listed in Parush's bibliography, Roskies, 'Aizik Meyer Dik and the Rise of Yiddish Popular Literature', and id., *A Bridge of Longing* (see esp. pp. 56–98), are particularly worth noting, offering an account of Yiddish literature that stresses its relative lack of influence and importance before Dik. The literature of stories and the literature of ethics and history in Yiddish translation—as well as ethical literature in Yiddish such as the many works, frequently reprinted, of Yehiel Mikhel Epstein—all go entirely unmentioned by Roskies. In this context, see my comments in Ch. 4 n. 11.

[43]   See 'Bibliographical Gleanings 10' (Heb.), 129–31, and the comments in Liberman, 'Bibliographical Notes' (Yid.), 93–4.

[44]   'Two Basic Editions of *Shivḥei habesht*' (Heb.), 249–72, 394–407, 552–62.

[45]   See Shmeruk, *Yiddish Literature: Chapters in its History* (Heb.), 213–14.

[46]   In this context, see Shmeruk's strong criticism (ibid. 219 n. 35) of Dan, *The Hasidic Story* (Heb.), for ignoring the need to compare the Hebrew and Yiddish versions of *Shivḥei habesht*.

9. The printers' mark used by Joseph Rosman of Brin (Brünn; now Brno)
in the press he owned there from 1797 to 1803. The ribbon in the eagle's mouth bears
Rosman's name in Yiddish and the plaque by the pillar bears his initials in
Latin characters. This mark is reproduced here in an edition of the Rashba's
Ḥidushei halakhot on the talmudic tractate *Gitin* which was published in 1799.
According to Abraham Ya'ari, a similar device was used by the
printer Israel Jaffe when he published *Shivḥei habesht* in Kopys in 1814

the time of the 1814 printing, to shape the text in such a way as to heighten the Besht's campaign against Shabateanism and to spare his reputation from being stained by his liking for the book.[47]

Long after Ya'ari and Shmeruk had published their work, Yehoshua Mondshine and Moshe Rosman showed in detailed research that most of the changes between the editions of *Shivḥei habesht* in Hebrew and Yiddish can be explained by the transition from an oral to a written literary culture. They were made by the editors in order to simplify the tale for the readers' benefit. Most of these changes are thus not to be explained by positing the existence of different unbroken narrative traditions, whose narrators or editors had fundamentally different outlooks from one another.[48]

Ya'ari did not limit himself to gathering data on books printed in small presses in the minor cities and towns of Russia and Poland. Found among his papers was the start of a pioneering work on the translation of plays on biblical themes from Hebrew into Yiddish at the end of the eighteenth century and during the nineteenth century. Chone Shmeruk devoted a thorough study to the origin of this genre, and Shmuel Werses has returned to it.[49]

In his description of the printers of Laszczów,[50] Ya'ari dwelt on the Yiddish translation of the play *Milḥamah beshalom* (War on Peace) that was published there in 1814. The original Hebrew version was printed anonymously in Shklov in 1796 but was in fact by Hayim Abraham b. Arieh Leib Hacohen, a rabbi in Moghilev. In 1801 it was translated into Yiddish by Eliezer Pavir, a *sofer* (scribe of religious documents and texts) in Zolkiew, and

---

[47] 'Two Basic Editions of *Shivḥei habesht*', 252 and compare the text at n. 10 above.

[48] See Mondshine, *Shivḥei habesht: A Manuscript* (Heb.), 22–47; Rosman, 'On the History of a Historical Source' (Heb.), 180–3.

[49] See Shmeruk (ed.), *Biblical Plays in Yiddish* (Heb.), introduction and appendices (pp. 12–152); Werses, 'From Changes of Language to Changes of Meaning' (Heb.), 55–78.

[50] 'Bibliographical Gleanings II' (Heb.), 238–47. Here Ya'ari was highly critical of the list of the printers of Laszczów and the information that emerges from the list in Friedberg, *History of Hebrew Printing in Poland* (Heb.). He did not stop there but also attacked the article by Jacob Shatzky, 'On the History of Jewish Printing Shops in Poland' (Yid.), 178–82. Since Shatzky preached to bibliographers and instructed them on how to proceed, Ya'ari showed that he had not checked the earlier works from which he copied, and that all the things he found fault with in Friedberg were equally faulty in his own work. Ya'ari demonstrates this by showing a misreading of the Polish on the title page of one of the books: the source of the misreading was in Friedberg, and Shatzky simply copied it. As a result, an imaginary settlement was created near Laszczów.

published there under the title *Gedulat yosef* (The Greatness of Joseph) since it deals with the life of the biblical Joseph and his brothers. The work was then reprinted in Laszczów in 1814. Ya'ari's account mentions earlier scholars who had noted this, such as Isaac Rivkind, as well as those who failed to do so, such as Hayim Dov Friedberg and Jacob Shatzky.[51] Ya'ari identified 54 editions of this book, whereas Shatzky listed 40 and Friedberg only 12. In discussing the large number of Yiddish editions Ya'ari concludes that studying differences in spelling and style in the various editions could provide important information on changes in the writing of Yiddish in the nineteenth century. On this subject, Shmuel Werses has suggested to me that, since there was no standard Yiddish orthography during the nineteenth century, the variants, rather than indicating a development towards the creation of a standard spelling, in fact reflect the lack of such a development.

Ya'ari roundly attacked Shatzky, but I still note with regret that this eminent historian of the Haskalah in nineteenth-century Russia and Poland in general, and in Lithuania in particular, has almost been forgotten. It is no coincidence that his extensive works—including his pioneering study of the Haskalah in Lithuania[52]—are hardly cited now. In the spirit of the days when it appeared, it was severely criticized by Barukh Shohetman for precisely those things for which scholars of today would praise it.[53] Shohetman complained that Shatzky ignored literary criticism and the literary value of the works, and chose instead to focus on details such as the number of copies printed in the various editions, the authors' royalties, and the like. Shatzky's monumental work on Warsaw has been similarly ignored.[54] In his later scholarship, however, Shmeruk expresses great appreciation for Shatzky's work.[55]

The note on the translation of *Milḥamah beshalom* led Ya'ari to write a special article on another biblical play, *Gedulat david umelukhat shaul* (The Greatness of David and the Kingdom of Saul), by Joseph Ha'efrati, which originally appeared in Hebrew under the title *Melukhat shaul* (The Kingdom

[51] Rivkind, 'History of Hebrew Printing in Poland' (Heb.), 389; Shatzky, 'The Yiddish Editions of the Play *War on Peace*' (Yid.), 151–8.

[52] Shatzky, *A Cultural History of the Enlightenment in Lithuania* (Yid.).

[53] See his review in *Kiryat sefer*, 28 (1952–3), 353–4.

[54] See Shatzky, *History of the Jews of Warsaw*.

[55] See Shmeruk, *Yiddish Literature: Chapters in its History*, index s.v. 'Shatzky' (p. 338); see also Shmeruk, *Yiddish Literature in Poland*, index s.v. 'Shatzky' (p. 291).

[56] 'Bibliographical Gleanings 13' (Heb.), 384–8.

of Saul).[56] Ya'ari was not satisfied with describing the translation as 'free writing in Yiddish': he compared it to the original, pointing out what had been omitted and what had been added. Shmuel Werses later wrote at length on the vicissitudes of this translation and the changes in it, including changes to the title page and to the names of the characters.[57]

Of more importance, the listing of Yiddish books printed in Laszczów uncovered an edition of a translation of the *Ma'aseh Bukh*—the important collection of stories of Hasidei Ashkenaz, of which no Hebrew edition exists—which was an updated version in the Yiddish of the time, done by Eliezer Pavir.[58] Pavir called his book *Sipurei hapelaot* (Stories of Marvels); it grew to be much loved, and Ya'ari found twenty-one editions of it, the most recent of which is entitled *Niflaot r. yehudah hehasid* (The Marvels of Rabbi Judah the Hasid).[59] Many years later, Ya'ari's interest in Pavir's book gave rise to a detailed article on his literary career.[60] This article was itself the foundation stone for research into the ways in which Yiddish was transformed from a spoken to a written language in the nineteenth century, beginning with new translations of the Bible and continuing with adaptations of biblical plays and hagiographies. This finally gave rise to secular literature in general and fiction in particular from the 1880s onwards.

At the very end of his life Ya'ari published two more articles containing important contributions to research in Yiddish language and literature. The first of these surveyed the history of scholarship dealing with the presence of Hebrew elements in the Yiddish language. It had originally been published by Lipa Karpel for the Second Zionist Congress, which took place in Basle, since hundreds of Hebrew expressions were included in this work.[61] In the second

[57] See Werses, 'From Changes of Language to Changes of Meaning'.

[58] See *Ma'aseh Book*, trans. M. Gaster; on this work, see Shmeruk, *Yiddish Literature: Chapters in its History*, 87 n. 24, and references there to other studies. The latest comprehensive survey of Yiddish narrative is Zfatman-Biler, 'Narrative in Yiddish' (Heb.), which places the *Ma'aseh bukh* alongside other collections of stories and other forms of stories in Yiddish. See also her article, '*Ma'aseh Bukh*, Outlines for a Picture of a Genre in Old Yiddish Literature' (Heb.), 126–52.   [59] See Ya'ari, 'R. Eliezer Pavir and his Literary Work' (Heb.), 517–20.

[60] See ibid. 499–520; see also Liberman, 'A Note on the Article "R. Eliezer Pavir and his Literary Work"' (Heb.), 272. To these we must add the important insights into the work of Eliezer Pavir in Zfatman-Biler, '*Ma'aseh Bukh*, Outlines for a Picture of a Genre in Old Yiddish Literature', 143–4.

[61] See Ya'ari, 'A Story to Prove the Plethora of Hebrew Elements in the Yiddish Language' (Heb.), 288–92.

article Ya'ari once again demonstrated his erudition, as well as his determination to uncover the metamorphoses of a work in Yiddish, in this case, a poem about the Ten Commandments.[62]

As indicated above, Ya'ari's companions in the correspondence club for lovers of Hebrew and Yiddish books never sat back in silence. Hayim Liberman discovered yet another Yiddish adaptation of the story of Judah the Hasid, printed in 1817 in Laszczów and entitled *Berakh avraham* (He Blessed Abraham).[63] Before this he had added books to Ya'ari's list such as a bilingual Hebrew–Yiddish edition of the Song of Songs (Laszczów, 1810), and a bilingual Grace after Meals in Hebrew and Yiddish with a Passover Haggadah (Laszczów, 1814). He also corrected Ya'ari's listing of *Gedulat yosef*.[64] Ya'ari himself added books that had been printed in Laszczów and which had reached the National and University Library in Jerusalem. Among them was a prayer in Yiddish by the *rebetsin* Mamele bat Tsevi Hirsch, the wife of Rabbi Isaac, head of the rabbinical court in Belz.[65]

It would be going too far to conclude, from the printing of a few books in Yiddish, that Laszczów was the centre of a literary revolution. We would, however, do well to follow in Ya'ari's footsteps and take note of what the printing houses of that town contributed to the vast majority of the Jewish community, whose native language was Yiddish; a contribution implying recognition of their spiritual needs, and of the Yiddish spoken at the time. At the same time, the printers of Laszczów also satisfied the popular demand for *Tsena urena*, the familiar translation of the Pentateuch into Yiddish combined with legends and stories.[66]

---

[62] See Ya'ari, 'The Metamorphosis of a Yiddish Poem' (Heb.), 397–410. The book was first printed in Prague in 1685 and not printed in Poland until the fourth edition, when it was printed by a woman, Yente bat Isaac (see ibid. 397–9). Another edition of this version, but corrupted and without indication of place or date, was printed by Noah Prilutski. See Prilutski, 'The Unknown Old Yiddish Poet Yente bat Yitzhak' (Yid.), and also Ya'ari's 'Metamorphosis', 399–402.   [63] See Liberman, 'Another Book Printed in Laszczów' (Heb.), 140.

[64] Id., 'On the History of Hebrew Printing in Laszczów' (Heb.), 553–4.

[65] See Ya'ari, 'Supplements to the Bibliography of Printing in Poland–Russia' (Heb.), 298, which mentions *Kuntres: teḥinah, teshuvah, tefilah, utsedakah* [Pamphlet: Supplication, Repentence, Prayer, and Charity] (Laszczów, 1816), which he had acquired for the National and University Library in Jerusalem, and which he did not find mentioned in the bibliographical lists in his possession.

[66] There were many printings of *Tsena urena*: sixty-four before 1785 and another 110 editions between 1785 and 1910. See Shmeruk's concise remarks in *Yiddish Literature: Chapters in its*

As I have shown, Ya'ari made an important contribution to the study of Yiddish literature and heightened our understanding of the role played by those who printed and promoted it at the end of the eighteenth century and during the nineteenth century, a period in which the Jewish world experienced great changes. I shall conclude my discussion of this topic by noting that his sharp eye caught a primary source of rules for spelling Yiddish, printed in 1819. These rules are the only ones known at that time but, according to Shmuel Werses, their publication influenced no one. They appeared in *Magid atidot* (The Herald of Future Things; 1819) by Isaac Ze'ev, *shohet uvodek* (i.e. a ritual slaughterer), the son of Joseph Apter.[67] This was a book of dream interpretation similar to a well-known book by Solomon Almoli.[68] At the end of *Magid atidot*, Uvodek has added 'marvellous rules' for performing multiplication with one's fingers, as well as rules for writing 'the language of Ashkenaz', which Ya'ari defines as the first effort to set rules for writing Yiddish.

Ya'ari's 'Bibliographical Gleanings' on small printers in Poland and Russia not only provided the basis for my analysis, presented above, of the data on Yiddish books printed in Laszczów, but are a blessing in their own right. They deserve to be collected and printed in a separate volume for easy reference, since they provide new information on books and printers, as well as on rabbis giving approbations who were previously unknown to us. They also offer an extensive account of the typographical career of the greatest of the Jewish printers in Poland and Russia at the end of the eighteenth and in the early nineteenth centuries: Samuel ben Yissakhar Ber Segal.[69] We find a wonderful account of the world of the Jewish book in Shklov[70] as a mirror reflecting, as

History (Heb.), 115–16, which are based on his comprehensive article, 'The Eastern European Versions of *Tsena urena*' (Yid.), 195–211. See also Turniansky, 'The *Tsena urena* of Herz Homberg' (Heb.) and her article, 'A Maskilic Version of *Tsena urena*' (Heb.), 835–41.

[67] See 'Bibliographical Gleanings 12' (Heb.), 248–9.

[68] On Almoli and his works see Yalon, 'Chapters from *The Gatherer from all the Camps*' (Heb.), 96–108. For more on the genre and the man, see Yudlov, 'On the Interpretation of Dreams by Rabbi Hai Gaon' (Heb.), 107–20, esp. p. 111. Similarly, see Grinbaum, 'The Interpretation of Dreams, History and Sources' (Heb.), 180–201.

[69] 'Bibliographical Gleanings 52' (Heb.), 100–1. On this, see my *Literature of Customs* (Heb.), appendix VI—the location and year of the printing of *Kuntres kishutei kalah* (Pamphlet on the Ornaments of the Bride) (pp. 361–4).

[70] See Ya'ari, 'Hebrew Printing in Shklov' (Heb.), 49–72, 135–60, and the additions in Liberman, *Rachel's Tent* (Heb.), i. 149–93.

Ya'ari says, a combination of wisdom, enlightenment, and knowledge. Many years passed before scholars of Jewish history reached that world.[71]

In the spirit of the times, I shall conclude with some remarks on books, printing, and women. Ya'ari's attention was drawn to a pamphlet on women and the printing trade published by Abraham Meir Haberman.[72] Following the custom of that circle, Ya'ari added to Haberman's list, and Isaac Rivkind added to Ya'ari's additions; ultimately, Ya'ari combined all the lists in a long and exhaustive article in his *Studies of the Book*.[73] These combined lists lead us to the interesting conclusion that most of the Jewish women involved in the book trade during the eighteenth century lived in the German-speaking lands. Indeed, in the eighteenth century most of the major Jewish printers were in Amsterdam, though some were in other German-speaking cities.[74] When the centre of Jewish printing moved to eastern Europe during the nineteenth century, however, and the status of women improved there as part of the first stirrings of the Haskalah and emancipation, we find that, of 24 women who were active in the printing trade during that century, 17 were in eastern Europe.[75] Most of them operated small printing houses and carried on their husband's business after becoming widowed. Prominent among these women printers was *rebetsin* Rosanis.[76] Ya'ari points out that bibliographers such as Meir Balaban, Hayim Dov Friedberg, and Abraham Meir Haberman all mention her. Before him, however, no one had written a comprehensive article on this active woman, the books she printed, and, no less important, on the books printed long after her death whose title-pages were falsified to appear as though she had printed them during her lifetime.

[71] See Fishman, *Russia's First Modern Jews*. Fishman refers to the majority of the studies that preceded his own, including those of Ya'ari. On the broad background and environment, see Etkes, 'On the Question of Harbingers of Haskalah in Eastern Europe' (Heb.), 95–114, and the discussion of Shklov against the background of Haskalah in Russia during the 19th century in Zalkin, *Daybreak* (index, p. 352).

[72] See Haberman, *Jewish Women as Printers, Typesetters, Publishers* (Heb.).

[73] See pp. 252–302.   [74] See Ch. 2 above at n. 32.

[75] This information has been gathered from Ya'ari's lists in *Studies of the Book*: for the 18th century, see pp. 260–70, nos. 5, 6, 17 (Yehudit Rosanis), 18, 20, 22, 25; for the 19th century, see pp. 270–4, nos. 26, 28, 29, 30, 32, 33, 35 (Devorah Romm of Vilna), 37, 38, 40, 41, 44, 46, 47, 48, 49.

[76] See 'Bibliographical Gleanings 36' (Heb.), 95–108. Ya'ari also published 'Supplement to the Bibliography of Printing Houses in Poland–Russia 3' (Heb.), 298—301, where he added a list of genuine and forged editions by Yehudit Rosanis.

Yehudit Rosanis came from a family of printers. Her great-grandfather, R. Uri Feibish Halevi of Amsterdam, transferred the family printing house to Zolkiew in 1695, and Yehudit Rosanis was the daughter of his grandson, Aaron ben Hayim. She married David ben Menahem, who joined R. Uri's grandsons in running the family printing house; after the death of her husband she appeared on the title pages of books as the partner of her relatives. In 1782, when the Austrian authorities decided to concentrate the Jewish printers in that part of Galicia (the capital of which was Lemberg) under their jurisdiction, the printing shop was transferred from Zolkiew to Lemberg and remained there even after the governmental decree was rescinded. Some of the printers of Zolkiew who had moved to Lemberg then moved back to their native city. Yehudit, however, who was by now a widow, married Tsevi Hirsh Rosanis, head of the rabbinical court of Lemberg, and in 1788 began to print Hebrew books under her own name with the help of Naphtali Herz Grossman, the son of her first marriage.[77] Ya'ari compiled a list of the 24 printing press workers named in her books. Among these, 8 were from Zolkiew, 7 from Lemberg, and 5 from other cities; a further 4 are mentioned without the name of their city, although they may have been residents of Lemberg. At the time of writing, the lists compiled by Ya'ari and his colleagues have not been used to collate the names of printing press workers, and their places of work have not been mapped and compared to their places of origin. Were this to be done, it would provide information on the degree of mobility among these workers, as well as additional biographical and professional information which would constitute a very interesting index of the status of the printing profession in Jewish society.

Yehudit Rosanis's second husband died in 1805, and from that date her printing activities ceased. Ya'ari conjectures that she, too, might have died around the same time. In addition to her administrative and entrepreneurial functions, she also took the trouble to attract readers by writing her own introduction, in Yiddish, to *Igeret ba'alei ḥayim*, the various Yiddish translations of which were noted by Ya'ari, as mentioned above.[78]

The cessation of her press in 1805 notwithstanding, several books that were in fact published between 1830 and 1845 appear to have been printed there.

[77] According to Ya'ari, who used information that Meir Balaban found in the archive and published. See Ya'ari, 'Bibliographical Gleanings 36' (Heb.).

[78] Ibid. 105–6 no. 36; see also above at n. 29.

This was apparently an effort on the part of an enterprising press to avoid both the censor and the duty charged on books: they simply falsified the name and location of the press and gave the date of printing as 1802 or 1804. Samuel Weiner was the first bibliographer to take note of Jewish books published with such falsified title pages. When sorting the books he used in his *Congregation of Moses* he found a contradiction between the Gregorian date and the Hebrew date in *Hakdamah vederekh ets ḥayim* (Introduction and Path of the Tree of Life) by Tsevi Hirsh Eichenstein of Zhidachov. Using the typeface as a guide, he found four more books with similarly falsified title-pages.[79] Ya'ari found ten more books published by Yehudit Rosanis, and two years later, following further investigation of these books, he published a supplement to the bibliography of printing in Poland and Russia. In this, he describes a Yiddish book, *Ein sheineh historiya*, containing tall tales and penitential prayers with a Yiddish translation, printed by Yehudit Rosanis in Lemberg between 1788 and 1793. No less importantly, Ya'ari found and listed five more books with similarly falsified publication details.[80]

Both Ya'ari's method for proving that title pages were falsified and his research methods in general demonstrate clearly the meticulous nature of his approach. For example, *Ahavat shalom* (The Love of Peace) by Menahem Mendel of Kosov was ostensibly printed by Yehudit Rosanis in Lemberg in 1804. Ya'ari, however, discovered that the true date could be derived from the end of the introduction. Here, the numerical value of letters of the author's Hebrew name that were underlined to mark their inclusion in a chonogram indicates that the year of printing was actually 1833.[81]

In *Eldad hadani*, which was ostensibly printed in Lemberg in 1804, Ya'ari found that the approbation by Tsevi Hirsh ben Shimon Meiseles, the chief

---

[79] Ya'ari refers to Weiner's *Congregation of Moses*, 381 no. 3220. Ya'ari used Weiner's notes from a catalogue that he printed of an exhibition on printing in Poland and Russia in St Petersburg in 1894. He proved that the fact that Gershom Scholem had not seen a book did not constitute proof that it had never existed. See Ya'ari, 'Note on the List of Wunderbar' (Heb.), 84. This comment contains a response to part of an article by Scholem, 'On the Problem of the Book' (Heb.), 293–5, where he attacks the Wunderbar list and lists the suspect books as mere inventions. Ya'ari himself added seven books to the list of those with falsified title pages, in which the place of printing was purportedly Mogilev. See Ya'ari, 'The Hebrew Press in Mogilev' (Heb.), 312–13.   [80] See n. 76 above.

[81] In Ya'ari's 'Bibliographical Gleanings 36' (Heb.), in the list of books, the ones with falsified title pages are nos. 41–51.

religious judge of Zolkiew, was certainly falsified, since this rabbi died on 18 Kislev 5561 (1801), and it was unlikely that a small book of this kind would have been presented for approval three years before it was printed.[82]

Ya'ari observed that *Birkat david* (The Blessing of David), a commentary on the Pentateuch by Abraham David, the rabbi of S. Y. Agnon's home city, Buczacz, was printed, according to its German-language title page, by Yehudit Rosanis in 1800, whereas the Hebrew date on the title page is 5565 (1815). Ya'ari showed that both dates are false. The editor's introduction states that the book was printed after its author's death, and it is known that Abraham David of Buczacz died on 29 Tishrei 5601 (1841).[83] Ya'ari found evidence for the true date of printing in the epilogue by the production editor which started with the phrase 'A prayer to the God of David' printed in oversize letters. The numerical value of the Hebrew letters in the phrase is 605—an allusion to the date 5605 (1845).

One book on Ya'ari's list (no. 46) with a falsified title page, *Sipur haḥalomot* (The Story of Dreams) is not, as Ya'ari copied from its title page, a simple anthology taken from *Tsitsat novel tsevi* (The Fading Flower of Beauty, a title derived from Isaiah 28: 4) by Jacob Sasportas. Instead, it is a clumsy effort to write a kind of early maskilic novel on Shabateanism, a work better known under the title *Me'oraot tsevi* (The Adventures of Tsevi). There are highly significant variants among the editions, which I will not describe here as I have discussed them at length elsewhere.[84]

In conclusion, I must mention the important list of works by *badḥanim*, or Jewish wedding jesters, that Ya'ari compiled. While he modestly says that several scholars had preceded him in collecting the names of such works and of those who wrote the history of the genre,[85] Ya'ari more than quadrupled the list. He apparently felt that he was perpetuating a Jewish world that had been lost as a result of the Holocaust. His brief words on the nature of the Jewish jester are a starting point for important research on these entertainers who on the surface appear to provide only light amusement, but without whom it is

---

[82] Ya'ari also refers to Shlomo Buber, *Kiryah nisgevah* (Exalted City), sect. 238.

[83] Ya'ari also refers to Shmerler, *Toledot rabad*, 68.

[84] See Gries, 'Definition of Shabatean Hagiographical Literature', 358–9 nn. 24–5, where there is also additional bibliography.

[85] He mentions Yehezkel Lifschitz, Baer Slutzky, Isi Charik, Ya'akov Shatsky, Zalman Rejzen, and Zalman Silberzweig.

difficult to live anywhere, at any time.[86] This was the lesson learned by Ben-Broka from Elijah the prophet, as told in tractate *Ta'anit* of the Talmud: when Elijah shows him who will receive honour in the world to come, they include two jesters, who (to use the talmudic phrase), 'made people happy when they were sad'.[87]

I have given here just a glimpse of the riches contained in Ya'ari's many works in order to demonstrate that his scholarship is an object lesson in method and content for scholars of Jewish literature, Jewish thought, and Jewish history. It is to be hoped that those of his articles which have not yet been collected will find someone to gather them and review them in the name of scholarship and in his honour.

May his memory be blessed.

[86] See Ya'ari, 'Books of Jesters' (Heb.), 109–26, and id., 'Supplements to Books of Jesters' (Heb.), 264–72. Strangely, in a doctoral dissertation on the Jewish jester written for Bar-Ilan University by Arielah Krasney, under the direction of Professor Yosef Bar-El, which was later published, many earlier scholars are mentioned, from Shatzky and Schiffer to Rivkind and Shmeruk. Ya'ari and his scholarship, however, are not mentioned at all, although the author certainly made use of the latter. See, for example, the sources mentioned in Krasney, *The Jester* (Heb.), 218–19 n. 94, and compare them to Ya'ari's work. A work of entirely different quality is Baumgarten, 'L'Art des badhanim dans la société hassidique', and it is no surprise that at the beginning of this article Baumgarten refers to Ya'ari's work. Baumgarten's Israeli colleague in research on hasidic jesters, Ya'akov Mazor (Ya'ari's son-in-law), also published a study on them. See Mazor, 'The Jester and Hasidic Society' (Heb.), 41–80. For a revised English version see Ya'akov Mazor, 'The Badkhn in Contemporary Hasidic Society'.

[87] See BT *Ta'anit* 22a. The story about the jesters was a particular favourite of the Besht. See my remarks in *The Literature of Customs* (Heb.), 343 n. 7. The jester's importance and virtue are emphasized in the Zohar, where King David is called 'the king's jester'. See Zohar 2: 107a and compare what is written there to 1: 148a on David and on the court jesters. That is to say, even the Holy One, blessed be he, needs a jester. This being the case, we humans need them even more.

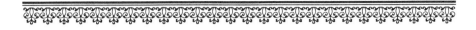

The Revolution in the World of Hebrew Books at the Start of the Twentieth Century

IN RUSSIA, 1905 was the year of a failed revolution. In the world of Hebrew books, however, it merely marked the continuation of a successful revolutionary process that had been going on for some years. The pivotal figure of the revolution was Abraham Leib Shalkovich, a writer and publisher whose colourful career terminated with his sudden death at the age of 55 in 1921. Shalkovich was better known by his pen-name of Ben-Avigdor, the name he adopted when he published his first short stories.[1]

The revolution in Hebrew publishing, known as *hamahalakh heḥadash* ('the New Move'), involved writers such as Mikha Josef Berdyczewski, originally of Medzibezh; Isaac Leib Peretz, originally of Zamosc; and David Frischmann, originally from near Lodz, as well as literary critics such as Reuben Brainin, originally from Lyady. Perhaps most noteworthy of the young and vibrant figures was Asher Ginzberg of Odessa, better known as Ahad Ha'am, who campaigned vigorously to strengthen the cultural basis for Zionism and the return of the Jews to their homeland in Erets Yisra'el as a prerequisite for political activism. This task, which he considered of colossal importance, was to be achieved through the written word: the challenge was to appeal to the sensitivities and expectations of young, modernizing Jews and provide them with a

This Afterword is based on a lecture delivered at a conference held at the Goren-Goldstein Centre for Jewish Studies at the University of Milan in June 2005 on 'Judaism and Western Culture at the Beginning of the Twentieth Century'.

[1] See Chapter 9.

solid intellectual basis for going in pursuit of a Jewish renaissance in the ancient cradle of Judaism.[2]

To achieve these noble aims, Ahad Ha'am and the elitist circle that developed around him in Odessa wanted to establish a publishing house that would produce the necessary literature.[3] In this they followed the trail blazed by the circle of students and admirers of Moses Mendelssohn who, almost a century earlier, had established a publishing house for a similar purpose;[4] perhaps for this reason they called themselves Benei Moshe, the sons of Moses. Their ambition was achieved in 1893: Ben-Avigdor was appointed secretary of Benei Moshe in Warsaw, and in this capacity he set up the Ahiasaf publishing house, working at first with Elazar Kaplan and afterwards also with Zalman Gluskin and Matityahu Cohen.[5] But he soon became unhappy with the publishing policy dictated by Ahad Ha'am and his faithful followers in Odessa, and after three and a half years in office he resigned. Shortly afterwards, in the summer of 1897, Ahad Ha'am published a series of articles in *Hamelits*, the first Hebrew-language newspaper to be published in Russia (founded 1860), setting out his proposal. He envisioned the creation of a treasure-house of knowledge for the modern Jew, a project that he entitled *Otsar hayahadut* (The Treasure of Judaism), which was supported by Benei Moshe and which the Ahiasaf publishing house was meant to serve. The idea was to publish what he conceived as a Jewish compendium, which at the time was a very novel idea; the subsequent appearance of *The Jewish Encyclopedia* in America later forced Benei Moshe to clearly articulate the differences between their project and the American one.

In 1904 Dr David Neumark, an eminent historian of Jewish philosophy who had been appointed director of the office of Otsar Hayahadut in Berlin, published a programmatic essay entitled 'The Literary Value and the Historical Place of Otsar Hayahadut' in *Hashiloah*, a periodical whose first

[2] The two best biographies of Ahad Ha'am are Zipperstein, *Elusive Prophet*, and Yosef Goldstein, *Ahad Ha'am: Biography* (Heb.).

[3] See Salmon, 'Ahad Ha'am and Benei Moshe' (Heb.), 291–301, and the additional bibliography there.

[4] See Feiner, 'Itzik Euchel' (Heb.), 427–69. See also id., 'Educational Programmes and Social Ideals' (Heb.), 393–424.

[5] The best description of Ben-Avigdor's publishing career, albeit only partial, is Shulamit Shalhav, 'From Intentions to Deeds' (Heb.), see esp. p. 12. See also her article on Ben Avigdor's early literary and commercial activity, 'Ben-Avigdor and Penny Books' (Heb.), 281–300.

editor, Ahad Ha'am, had resigned in 1902 after editing ten volumes and was succeeded by Dr Joseph Klausner.[6] In the same edition, in an article addressed to 'lovers of Hebrew literature', Benei Moshe set out the goals of their project. The article was signed by David Neumark and Dr Joseph Klausner, director of the organization's Warsaw office.[7] (Klausner also went on to become a prominent figure in the development of the Hebrew University of Jerusalem as the first chair of the Department of Hebrew Literature.)

It took Benei Moshe another two years to produce the first publication in the series, a booklet entitled *Otsar hayahadut in Hebrew: Its Nature, Purpose and Essence. A Sample Issue*, which was published by Ahiasaf in Warsaw in 1906. Klausner's prefatory remarks explained that the project initiated by Benei Moshe was aimed at saving the Jewish nation from cultural annihilation, and that as an ongoing project it would have an element of vitality that was missing from the *Jewish Encyclopedia* project mentioned above. The publication also contained Ahad Ha'am's programme as originally published in *Hamelits*, Neumark's article from *Hashiloah*, and four sample entries from *Otsar hayahadut*: 'Ikarim' (Roots), by David Neumark (pp. 1–74); 'Amos', on the prophet, by Tsevi Perets Hayot (pp. 75–84); 'Perushim' (Pharisees), by Ismar Elbogen (pp. 85–94); and 'Sefarim ḥitsoniyim' (Apocrypha), by Joseph Klausner (pp. 95–120). Reading these entries today it is hard to see how they could have nurtured a thirst for knowledge, however. If we compare these sample entries to those on halakhah and aggadah written by Louis Ginzberg for *The Jewish Encyclopedia*, it is clear that the claims of Benei Moshe to clarity and liveliness were highly exaggerated.[8]

Otsar hayahadut failed miserably, but the historical irony is that a series of *Otsarot* later published in America over a forty-year period for an east European Jewish readership was a great success. The man behind this colossal publishing activity was Judah David Eisenstein (1854–1956), a Jew originally from Mezhirech in Poland who had emigrated to America at the age of 18 and who became not only a successful clothing manufacturer but also the founder of the first Hebrew society in the United States. He began his publishing activity with a ten-volume encyclopedia in Hebrew entitled *Otsar yisra'el* (New York, 1907–13), and continued with many other titles, all of which began

[6] See *Hashiloah*, 13 (1904), 13–20.   [7] Ibid. 402–4.

[8] For a detailed list of Ginzberg's contribution to *The Jewish Encyclopedia* see Boaz Cohen, *Bibliography of the Writings of Professor Louis Ginzberg*.

with the word *Otsar*. Throughout his life Eisenstein supported his family as a producer of women's lingerie in New York, using his spare time and money for his publishing. His titles included *Otsar midrashim* (1915), on Midrash; *Otsar dinim uminhagim* (1917), on laws and customs; *Otsar derushim nivharim* (1918), on rabbinic homilies; *Otsar derashot* (1919), on sermons; *Otsar peirushim vetsiyurim al hagadah shel pesah* (1920), on the Haggadah; *Otsar ma'amarei hazal'* (1922), on the sayings of the Sages; *Otsar ma'amarei tanakh* (1925), a concordance of biblical sayings; *Otsar masa'ot* (1926), an anthology of Jewish travelogues; *Otsar vikuhim* (1928), on disputations; and *Otsar musar umidot* (1941), on ethics and morals. His compendia attempted to present the best of Jewish literature in the various genres. Among his many publications, only one lacks the word *Otsar* from its title. This is *Derekh hayim* (1930), which is a collection of laws, customs, and prayers for the sick, the terminally ill, and the dead.

Another early twentieth-century project that aimed at collecting the best of Jewish writings through the ages was initiated by Hayim Nahman Bialik of Odessa, who was to become a great Hebrew writer and Israel's national poet. He first proposed the project, which he called 'Kinus', at a lecture in Vienna in 1913 entitled 'The Hebrew Book', but the idea took wing only after the First World War when the Moriyah publishing house he established moved to Berlin. (It later changed its name to Devir, relocated to Tel Aviv, and to this day remains a major Israeli publishing house.[9])

But let us return to Ben-Avigdor. After resigning from Ahiasaf he distanced himself from Benei Moshe and opened his own independent publishing house, Tushiyah. This was in 1897, around the time that Ahad Ha'am published his article about his Otsar Hayahadut programme. In his first decade at Tushiyah, Ben-Avigdor produced hundreds of new titles and booklets, as well as the first Hebrew-language children's magazine, *Olam katan* (Small World), published in Warsaw and Krakow from 1901 to 1905, and later a monthly for Jewish adolescents, *Hane'urim* (The Youth), likewise published in Warsaw and Cracow (1904–5). He also published a monthly in Cracow for educators and parents, *Pedagog*, but it was rather short-lived (1903–4).

Ben-Avigdor tried to bring Jewish readers the best of world literature in lively modern Hebrew translation as well as the best of new Hebrew writing. He did so through a major new initiative he called 'Biblioteka' ('library' in Russian), with separate series, all with *Biblioteka* in the title, for adults, for

---

[9] See Ofek, *Children's Literature in Hebrew: 1900–1948* (Heb.), i. 77–93.

adolescents, and for young children. Unlike the elitist programmes of Ahad Ha'am and the Benei Moshe group, the Biblioteka series aimed at bringing the messages of the new world to a wide Jewish readership in a lively, modern Hebrew. It was an enormous success, and the hundreds of new titles that it produced drastically changed readers' expectations of Hebrew literature.[10]

Thanks to Ben-Avigdor, Hebrew became a language of daily life for the first time since the Roman empire, a secular language that gave Jews access to the modern world like everyone else. We may assume that his publishing activity reflected a response to that of Yiddish writers and publishers at the time: Ben-Avigdor wanted Hebrew to win the fight for the soul of the Jew in the modern world and to be a lingua franca for Jews whose vernacular was Yiddish, Ladino, or Arabic. He did not scorn the achievements of high Jewish literature but wanted to adapt it for the modern Jew. Unlike Ahad Ha'am and Benei Moshe, who were concerned only with the thin new layer of Jewish intellectuals, Ben-Avigdor's Tushiyah aimed to reach the Jewish masses.

Tushiyah's output was extraordinary in every way, and in volume far exceeded that of Ahiasaf and other Hebrew publishing houses in the first decade of the twentieth century. Ahiasaf made some effort to publish booklets of what they perceived as popular writings (namely, works that members of their circle had previously published in *Hashilo'ah*), but the number of publications was small. The same was true of Moriyah, the publishing house established by Hayim Nahman Bialik.

Looking at all this publishing activity, one might well ask where were the people to read all these Hebrew books at the beginning of the twentieth century, especially those aimed at children and young people. In fact the only real demand at this time was in Europe. In Erets Yisra'el the number of Jewish children remained very small until the second major wave of emigration (the so-called 'Second Aliyah') began to establish itself and raise a generation of Hebrew-speaking children. Because this coincided with the First World War, local publishing initiatives were needed to meet the demand for books for schooling and recreation.[11] Demand in America was also low at this time: the

---

[10] See Ofek, '*Tushiyah* for the Children of Israel' (Heb.), 421–8; id., *Children's Literature in Hebrew: 1940–1948* (Heb.), i. 19–26. At the end of the second volume (ii. 624–721), Ofek supplies a detailed list of books published between 1908 and 1948, subdivided into (*a*) books for pleasure; (*b*) collections and readings; and (*c*) periodicals for adolescents. It also includes some books published earlier but lacks the publishers' names.

millions of Jewish newcomers were doing their best to gain proficiency in English language, so access to literature in Hebrew was very much a secondary concern. The eventual transfer of the centres of Hebrew literary creativity from eastern Europe to Germany and later to Erets Yisra'el, as well as the growth of publishing in Erets Yisra'el, is beyond the scope of this Afterword. However, let me at least mention that it was primarily a response to the Communist revolution in Russia, which suppressed the Jews and other minorities, as well as to the growing fascism in Poland between the two world wars.[12]

To a large extent the authors writing for Tushiyah, Ahiasaf, and Moriyah were the same. However, Tushiyah far exceeded its rivals in the number of titles and the variety of genres published. As a case study, let us consider the *Bikurim* (First Fruit) series, just one of the series that Ben-Avigdor created at Tushiyah. Two hundred titles were published in this series over a short period, mostly during 1907, as individual booklets; they were later bound for subscribers in two volumes with a total of four parts. Meant for children and young people, the series was wide-ranging in both style and content. For example, there were works written originally in Hebrew; short stories, novels, poems, and biographies translated from other languages; excerpts from new Hebrew plays; and Bible stories retold for popular consumption. There were plays by the Yiddish dramatist Peretz Hirschbein from eastern Poland and a history of Japan adapted and translated from Russian by Yehudah Goor (Grasowski), originally from Pohost in Belorussia, who also translated Charles Dickens's *A Tale of Two Cities*.[13]

Among the writers and translators contributing to *Bikurim*, a significant number started their literary careers in eastern Europe and then moved to Erets Yisra'el where they made their living in the new Jewish educational and literary frameworks. These included Zalman Epstein, originally from Luban in Belorussia (whose younger brother Yitshak had emigrated to Erets Yisra'el

[11] See Ofek, *Children's Literature in Hebrew: 1900–1948* (Heb.), i. 122–66. For statistical information on the growth of children's literature in Palestine during the First World War and particularly the 1920s, when publishing houses from abroad moved in and new publishing houses were established in Palestine, see Esther Kandelshein, 'Printed Publications in the Hebrew Alphabet' (Heb.), 200–28.

[12] See Shavit, 'The Rise and Fall of the Literary Centres in Europe' (Heb.), 423–39.

[13] A full list of these publications is to be found in the catalogue of the National and University Library Jerusalem, under Wilkomitz, Simhah Hayim.

in 1886 and was one of the founding fathers of Hebrew education there); the educator Simhah Hayim Wilkomitz, originally from Nesvizh in Belorussia,[14] who became Yitshak Epstein's successor in the schools of Metulah and Rosh Pinah;[15] Shmuel Leib Gordon from Lithuania, who was Ben-Avigdor's brother-in-law and a prolific writer for this and other series;[16] and Moshe Ben-Eliezer,[17] who went to America in 1906, stayed four years, and then returned to eastern Europe and edited periodicals in Yiddish and Hebrew, including periodicals for children. In 1925 he was appointed editor of *Ben-artzi* (Fellow Countryman), the first magazine for children to be published in Tel Aviv, and moved to Erets Yisra'el.

Members of the Zionist group Hovevei Tsion (Lovers of Zion) who contributed to *Bikurim* and continued to do so after emigrating to Erets Yisra'el included Alter Moshe Gunzer,[18] Asher Erlich,[19] Mosheh Barukh Lazebnik,[20] and the prominent writer and public figure Alexander Siskind Rabinovitz,[21] who published over a hundred books and booklets and pioneered the writing of Hebrew short stories with social content. Rabinovitz moved to Tel Aviv in 1906, and served as a teacher and as a librarian of Sha'ar Zion, the largest public library in Tel Aviv and later the main municipal public library.

Among the Lovers of Zion we might also note Simhah Ben-Zion Gutman,[22] a famous editor and writer who had taught with Bialik in Odessa, who came to Tel Aviv in 1905, and whose son Nahum was to become one of Israel's most popular painters and writers for children, following the style of Rudyard Kipling's 'Just So' stories.[23]

Yehudah Goor (Grasowski) emigrated to Erets Yisra'el in 1887 but supported himself by writing books for publication in the centres of Hebrew publishing in eastern Europe. He was a very successful author of books for the

---

[14] See Getzel Kressel, *Encyclopedia of Modern Hebrew Literature* (Heb.), i. 654.

[15] Ibid. 139–40.

[16] Ibid. 453–4. He made several attempts to settle and work in Palestine, where he taught and tried to complete his voluminous modern commentary on the Bible. He did not quite accomplish his mission—the commentaries on Daniel, Ezra, Nehemiah, and Chronicles had to be written by other scholars—but the entire work was edited and revised by a group of scholars and published in several very popular editions in the 1960s and 1970s.

[17] Ibid. 263–4.   [18] Ibid. 437–8.

[19] Ibid. 151. His fame was due to his expertise in astronomy, and particularly to his invention of an astronomic globe.   [20] Ibid. ii. 241.

[21] Ibid. 814–15.   [22] Ibid. i. 293–4.   [23] See p. 93.

new Hebrew schools, including grammar books, dictionaries, adaptations of biblical stories, and books on geography. However, even though his books were successful (his Hebrew dictionary, for example, went into many editions), in 1911 his desire for a steadier cashflow led him to take a job with a bank in Tel Aviv which he held until 1929.[24]

Other contributors to *Bikurim* included bilingual Yiddish and Hebrew speakers such as Abraham Rejzen,[25] who went to America (the brother of Zalman Rejzen, famous author of the Yiddish lexicon), and Shalom Asch,[26] a prominent author who moved between countries in Europe and America and whose fate finally brought him to Israel in 1954 after at least ten former visits. (Asch died that same year while visiting his daughter in London.) There were also famous Hebrew writers who remained in Europe. One such was Israel Benjamin Levner,[27] best known for his book *Kol agadot yisra'el* (All the Legends of Israel), which was the last maskilic attempt to recast the rabbinic language of Aggadah into the more biblical style that the maskilim considered superior. It was first published in the mid-1890s, and was reissued numerous times. Another famous story-teller was Judah Steinberg,[28] originally of Lipkany in Bessarabia, whose contribution to *Bikurim* and to the new Hebrew children's literature led Uriel Ofek to call him 'the Hebrew Andersen'. One might also mention Yosef Meyuhas, a Sephardi educator and native resident of Jerusalem,[29] and Kadish Silman, an Ashkenazi educator from near Vilna who arrived in Erets Yisra'el in 1907 at the age of 27 and whose mastery of Hebrew made people think that he too was a native resident of Jerusalem.[30]

The great enterprise that Ben-Avigdor initiated involved people as diverse as the Polish Jew Aaron Luboshitzki,[31] who was among the first to publish poems with accompanying musical notation, and the Vilna-born Professor Nahum Slouschz, who was raised and educated in Odessa, and later in Geneva and Paris,[32] who was one of the founders of Hahevrah Lehakirat Erets Yisra'el (The Society for the Research of the Land of Israel), and the first to excavate on its behalf in Palestine. Slouschz was also a renowned

[24] See Kressel, *Encyclopedia of Modern Hebrew Literature* (Heb.), i. 439–40.
[25] Ibid. ii. 860–1.   [26] Ibid. i. 158–60.   [27] See p. 148.
[28] See Ofek, *Hebrew Children's Literature: 1940–1948* (Heb.), i. 26–30.
[29] See Kressel, *Encyclopedia of Modern Hebrew Literature*, ii. 341 2.
[30] See ibid. 495–6.   [31] See ibid. i. 174–5.   [32] See ibid. ii 510–12.

philologist, and his doctoral dissertation on the history of modern Hebrew literature was the first critical academic attempt in that area. His *A History of the New Hebrew Literature* was published in Hebrew in three volumes by Tushiyah (Warsaw, 1906), as well as in French, English, and other languages. He further contributed to the realization of Ben-Avigdor's dream by translating the works of such famous French authors as Guy de Maupassant and Émile Zola, adding his own introductions so as to give readers a fuller understanding of the French context.

Anyone looking for new editions of the classics of Jewish thought at this time will be disappointed: neither Ben-Avigdor nor his rivals in Benei Moshe were interested in such projects. Only in the 1920s, with the emergence of new publishers in Germany, did these works begin to be published. But even they did not publish critical editions of Aggadah and Midrash. Editions of these books were published by scholars such as Solomon Buber in Lemberg, and Meir Friedman (Ish Shalom) and Abraham Weiss in Vienna, through regular publishing houses rather than through presses committed to the revival of Hebrew culture.

Ben-Avigdor's reputation in America earned him an invitation to visit New York, where he provided his audience with a sharply critical description of modern Hebrew literature while praising Judah Leib Kantor, founder of *Hayom* (the first Hebrew-language daily newspaper) in 1886, for bringing everyday secular language to his readers. In fact, Ben-Avigdor's Hebrew was no less lively than that in Kantor's daily paper:[33]

He [Kantor] removed the sanctity of the language and made it a simple language of everyday life ... by bringing the 'only surviving beautiful language' down to the level of a market, he imbued it with power and life. Language is not a toy, a kind of spectator-sport with which to amuse audiences through miraculous acts like dancing on a tightrope; it is a vital commodity with which to express things that are needed, things that are of interest to the people, and to discuss all the new questions and needs. We are not writing 'the holy tongue'; rather, we are modern writers speaking to our readers in the language of our writing and literature about everything that is going on in the world in general and the Jewish world in particular. The language is a completely secular tool by which Hebrew readers can be informed of telegrams concerning international affairs and news of the world of science, literature, art, and theatre. Even news about actresses like Sarah Bernhardt, or Rachel [The stage name of Elisa Felix], and rates of exchange and commodity prices, can and must be communicated in Hebrew.

[33] See Ben-Avigdor, *The New Hebrew Literature* (Heb.), 18–19.

Ben-Avigdor went on to praise Kantor's newspaper as the first that people did not worry about tearing, or dirtying with cheese or butter; for Ben-Avigdor, this was a sign that Kantor had succeeded in transforming a sacred language into a secular one. In Ben-Avigdor's view, this gave new life not only to the language but even more so to its users.

After returning from his trip to America, Ben-Avigdor published another booklet[34] critical of modern Hebrew literature in which he accused Dr Klausner of having accepted so completely Ahad Ha'am's vision of the task facing Jewish intellectuals being to create a spiritual focus for Jewish life that he had come to see Ahad Ha'am himself as that spiritual focus. He ended by saying that following the course of Dr Klausner's thinking, we may assume that if he (Klausner) had been engaged in cosmography he would have placed Ahad Ha'am at the centre of creation.[35]

Ben-Avigdor was not alone in his attitude to Klausner; Nobel Prize winner Shmuel Yosef Agnon could not stand him either. Agnon was deeply distressed when, following Klausner's death, the Jerusalem city council decided that the street on which they both lived should be renamed in Klausner's honour.[36] Thereafter, every letter Agnon wrote or received included the annoying address 'Shmuel Yosef Agnon . . . Klausner Street, Jerusalem'—an indignity that Ben-Avigdor, who died earlier, did not have to suffer.

[34]   See Ben-Avigdor, *The Young Hebrew Literature* (Heb.).   [35]   Ibid.
[36]   See Amos Oz, *A Tale of Love and Darkness* (Heb.) 48–9.

The Young Abraham Ya'ari

S. H. BERGMAN

OTHERS better qualified than I will write about the bibliographer, about the scholar. I should like to write here about the young Abraham Ya'ari, the gentle, lyrical man, who was not widely known.

I met Abraham Ya'ari in Jerusalem within a few weeks of my emigration to Palestine in 1920. At the time he was a young student in the teachers' seminary directed by David Yellin. This seminary was in the centre of town, not far from Ethiopia Street, the first home of the National Library, of which I was the director. Abraham often visited us to read and borrow books. He was a true pioneer, totally imbued with the concept that building the land signalled a new beginning in the life of the Jewish people. He took the Hebrew sur-name Ya'ari in place of his former family name, Wald (which means forest in German, as does Ya'ari in Hebrew). The psychoanalyst and graphologist David Feigenbaum, who lived in Jerusalem, pointed out an interesting graphological fact to me. When Abraham Ya'ari wrote in European languages using the Roman alphabet and came to a word beginning with the letter 'w', he drew a line from the end of the letter right through it, as if he wished to erase it. 'Don't you see', Feigenbaum said, 'this man writes the first letter of his original name as though he wished to erase the entire name—to erase his diaspora past!'

What attracted me so much to Abraham in those early years was his enthusiasm. His brother, my friend the author Judah Ya'ari, was then a mem-ber of Kibbutz Beit Alfa in the Hashomer Hatsa'ir movement. I made my first visit to this kibbutz with Abraham (I suppose this was before my friends from Czechoslovakia settled in Heftsibah, a neighbouring kibbutz), and before we

This article was first published in *Davar*, 18 November 1966.

passed through its gates he said to me: 'Remove the shoes from your feet, for the place on which you are standing is holy ground.' The kibbutz was holy ground in Abraham's eyes!

During my initial years in the country I was not fluent in the language, and the student Abraham was always prepared to act as an amanuensis for me. I would read a letter to him in bad Hebrew, and he would rewrite it in good Hebrew (there were as yet no typewriters in the National Library).

When a Workers' Seminary was established in Jerusalem at Dov Rabin's initiative, and I was called on to teach philosophy in Hebrew, Abraham would sit in on the class and record my mistakes. After the lecture, he would come to me and discuss my many sins.

Abraham participated actively in every 'progressive' educational movement. In 1921, when Deborah Kelen, an American Jew, established a private school in Jerusalem based on modern American methods, she was not accepted with enthusiasm at first, and only a small circle of parents supported her. Abraham became her Hebrew teacher, and in 1923, when she held the first exhibition of drawings by her students in the Lemel School—drawing was central to her curriculum—Abraham helped her and was excited about the exhibition.

In the winter of 1923 the Jerusalem Workers' Council decided to hold a ceremony in memory of Karl Liebknecht and Rosa Luxemburg. I was asked to give a lecture, and Abraham was asked to read passages from their letters. The memorial was held on 14 January 1923. I did not talk about the pair's leftist politics but about the marvellous humanism revealed in their letters, especially in those of Luxemburg.

I believed then—and I still believe today—that those two representatives of the extreme left wing of the workers could become the property of all humanity, in the same way as A. D. Gordon, from the 'right' wing had. The hopes of mankind are embodied in individuals such as these. Our rivals at that time, however, the members of Mapam, did not agree. A few moments before the ceremony was due to begin, a long letter was handed to me, written in good German. That letter—a terrible document of internecine hatred—is still in my possession. There were three pages of personal invective, of defamation of Hapo'el Hatsa'ir and Zionism. The letter concluded with the words: 'Withdraw your hands, your filthy hands, from *our* Karl Liebknecht, from *our* Rosa Luxemburg.' The letter was signed 'A. Weintraub'.

I showed the letter to Abraham, and he declared that the signature was forged. I wrote in my journal at that time: 'The letter shocked me, not with respect to its contents, for it is right on several points . . . but what can I think about someone who is so base as to sign such a letter with a false name? When Abraham Ya'ari told me, this fact made me sadder than did the entire contents of the letter.'

Today I must add that, in the climate of those times, it is quite possible that the writer of the letter might have thought that I was liable to hand it in to the British police. This episode underlines the importance of direct dialogue, in Buber's understanding of the word. If, at the time, the writer of the letter had come to me and Ya'ari, and we had *conversed*—held a real dialogue—who knows? Perhaps such a dialogue would have had a revolutionary effect on the lives of all three of us. The anonymity of the letter, however, deprived the writer from the outset of any relationship with us, providing him only with the opportunity of satisfying the passionate hatred in his heart against the society in which he lived.

A few years later, Abraham joined the staff of the National Library as a librarian. One major question preoccupied him: how could we bring books to readers? This consideration led him to write his first book, *Belles Lettres in Hebrew*, published in 1927. Dedicated to the memory of Joseph Hazanovitz, it is based on the bibliographical material collected by Professor Ben-Zion Dinur over many years. It is appropriate to quote from the introduction:

In the Land of Israel, a generation has grown up and been educated on Hebrew litera-ture. The tribulations of that generation are many. Modern Hebrew literature is still scant. The character of the nation, which has absorbed all of the cultures of the world within itself, has not yet found full and comprehensive expression in literature. The boundaries of modern Hebrew literature are still narrow. It has, nonetheless, served as a faithful expression not only of all of our national and social aspirations over the past two hundred years, but also for the inner world of the individual, which remains the area of the influence for the national culture. It is rich and varied, if only we knew how to mine its wealth. With this list we wish, therefore, to help the Hebrew reader, and especially the reader in the Land of Israel, to use our literature and to extract all that is within it. The meagreness of Hebrew creativity in recent years will be less burdensome to our development, and it will be easier for us to pass through the transitional years in our literature, if we know it better, if we are not content with reading new books, but if we also seek books published years ago. The distant past has become classical for us, and it is the flesh of our flesh. The recent past, however, the past which this book is intended to encompass, is still forgotten. We want to help save it from oblivion.

During this period Ya'ari worked not only as a librarian and bibliographer but also as a translator; he translated two important books from German for the Philosophical Masterpieces series published by the Hebrew University of Jerusalem: *The Vocation of Man* by Fichte, and the *Prolegomena* by Kant.

I began by saying that others better qualified than I would speak about Abraham Ya'ari as a bibliographer (and let them not forget the bibliography of the states of the Mandate[1] that was published by the American University of Beirut in 1933). I wished only to uncover the psychological roots of his bibliographical work, the delicacy of his young soul, which was perhaps veiled for years by his scholarship. Sometimes it appeared to me that, in later years, the open heart of his youth had disappeared. Life, with its trials and tribulations, can impose deep suffering on an individual. Recently, however, I had the impression that he had become young again, and the cordiality of his speech and smile had returned. At our last meeting, in the hospital, he told me with real joy about his recent discoveries in the history of hasidism. He said nothing about his illness.

A close friend of his later years, E. I. J. Poznansky, said to me: 'It isn't enough for a person to know how to live with honour. Abraham knew how to die with honour.'

[1] Bergman was evidently relying on his memory here. The publication to which he was referring was the Hebrew-language section of *A Post-War Bibliography of the Near Eastern Mandates*, a publication under the general editorship of Stuart Dodd that comprised a preliminary survey of the publications in the social sciences dealing with Iraq, Palestine and Trans-Jordan, and the Syrian states from 11 November 1918 to 31 December 1929.—Z.G.

Bibliography

ABOAB, ISAAC, *Menorat hama'or* [The Lamp of the Light], (Constantinople, 1514).

AGNON, SHMUEL YOSEF, *From Me To Myself* [Mi'atsmi el atsmi] (Jerusalem, 1976).

——'The Praise of Noah' [Shivḥo shel no'aḥ], repr. by A. M. Haberman in *Hed hadefus*, 12 (1959), 33.

ALBERT, PIERRE, and FERNARD TERROU, *Histoire de la presse*, 5th edn (Paris, 1986).

ALGAZI, SOLOMON BEN ABRAHAM, *Shema shelomo* [The Fame of Solomon] (Amsterdam, 1710).

ALKOSHI, GEDALYAH, 'On Abraham Ya'ari' [Al avraham ya'ari], *Yerushalayim*, 2 (1967), 396–7.

AL-NAKAWA, ISRAEL, *Menorat hama'or* [The Lamp of the Light], ed. H. G. Henelau (New York, 1929–32).

AMARILIO, ABRAHAM, *Berit avraham* [The Covenant of Abraham] (Salonika, 1796–1802).

ANDERSON, BENEDICT, *Imagined Communities*, 2nd revised edn (London, 1991).

ARENDT, HANNAH, *Rahel Varnhagen: The Life of a Jewess* (London, 1957).

ASHKENAZI, S., 'Scribal Errors: From a Reader's Notebook' [Ta'uyot soferim: mipinkaso shel kore], *Yerushalayim*, 2 (1967), 379–95.

ASSAF, SIMCHA, *Sources for the History of Jewish Education* [Mekorot letoledot haḥinukh beyisra'el], 4 vols (Tel Aviv and Jerusalem, 1922–43).

AYASH, JUDAH, *Leḥem yehudah* [The Bread of Judah] (Leghorn, 1748).

AZULAI, HAYIM JOSEPH DAVID, *Ma'agal tov hashalem* [The Complete Cycle of Good], ed. A. Freimann, 2nd edn (Jerusalem, 1983).

——*Shem hagedolim* [The Name of the Great] (Leghorn, 1774; 2nd edn Leghorn, 1786).

BAHUR, ELIYAHU, *Pariz un' vienna: A Critical Edition* [Pariz un' vienna: mahadurah bikortit], ed. Chone Shmeruk, in collaboration with Erika Timm (Jerusalem, 1996).

BAHYA BEN ASHER, *Be'ur al hatorah* [Commentary on the Pentateuch] (Amsterdam, 1726).

BAKON, ISAAC, *Mendele Sholem Aleikhem: A New Examination* [Mendele sholem aleikhem, beḥinah meḥudeshet: a nayer araynblik] (Tel Aviv, 1995).

BAR-DAYAN [BORODIANSKY], HAYIM, *The Jewry of Lithuania* [Yahadut lita], 2 vols (Tel Aviv, 1960).

BAR-ILAN, MEIR, 'The Wonders of R. Judah Yudl Rozenberg' [Niflaot r. yehudah yudl rozenberg], Alei Sefer, 19 (2001), 173–84.

BAR-LEVAV, AVRIEL, '"When I was alive": Jewish Ethical Wills as Egodocuments', in R. Dekker (ed.), *Egodocuments and History: Autobiographical Writing in its Social Context Since the Middle Ages* (Rotterdam, 2002), 45–59.

—— 'On the Concept of Death in *Sefer haḥayim* by Rabbi Simon Frankfurt' [Tefisat hamavet besefer haḥayim lerabi shimon frankfurt] (doctoral dissertation, Hebrew University of Jerusalem, 1997).

—— 'Rabbi Aaron Berakhyah of Modena and Rabbi Naphtali Hacohen Katz, the First Authors of Books on the Sick and the Dead' [Rav aharon berakhyah mimodena verav naftali hacohen kats, avot hameḥabrim sifrei ḥolim umetim], *Asufot*, 9 (1995), 189–234.

BAR-SELA, SHRAGA, *Builder of Bridges: The National Doctrine of Solomon Schiller* [Boneh hagesharim: mishnato hale'umit shel shelomo schiller] (Tivon, 1990).

—— 'Hakiyum ha-le'umi shel hayehudim: masah historit medinit' [Hebrew translation of Schiller, *Byt narodowy Żydów*], *Meḥkarei yerushalayim bemaḥshevet yisra'el*, 4 (1984), 145–79.

BARTAL, ISRAEL, 'Mordecai Aaron Guenzburg: A Lithuanian Maskil in the Face of Modernity' [Mordekhai aharon ginzburg: maskil lita'i mul hamodernah], in Immanuel Etkes (ed.), *Religion and Life: The Jewish Haskalah Movement in Eastern Europe* [Hadat vehaḥayim: tenuat hahaskalah hayehudit bemizraḥ eiropah] (Jerusalem, 1993), 109–25.

BARUCHSON, SHIFRA, *Books and Readers: The Culture of Reading of the Jews of Italy in the Late Renaissance* [Sefarim vekore'im: tarbut hakeriyah shel yehudei italiyah beshalhei harenesans] (Jerusalem, 1997).

BARZILAI BEN BARUKH YA'AVETS, *Leshon arumim* [The Language of the Cunning] (Izmir, 1747).

BAUMGARTEN, JEAN, 'L'Art des badhanim dans la société hassidique: Pensée religieuse, rites matrimoniaux et traditions orales en langue Yiddish', in J. Baumgarten and D. Bunis (eds), *Le Yiddish, culture et société* (Paris, 1999), 97–135.

BEIT-ARIÉ, MALACHI, 'The Relationship Between Early Hebrew Printing and Handwritten Books: Attachment or Detachment?', *Scripta Hierosolymitana*, 29 (1989), 1–26.

BELLANGER, CLAUDE, JACQUES GODECHOT, PIERRE GUIRAL, and FERNARD TERROU (eds), *Histoire générale de la presse française*, 5 vols (Paris, 1969–76).

BEN-ARI, NITSA, *Romance with the Past: The Judaeo-German Historical Novel of the Nineteenth Century and the Creation of a National Literature* [Roman im he'avar: haroman hahistori hayehudi-germani min hame'ah hatesha-esreh veyetsiratah shel sifrut leumit] (Tel Aviv, 1997).

BEN-AVIGDOR [ABRAHAM LEIB SHALKOVICH], *The New Hebrew Literature and Its Future* [Hasifrut ha'ivrit haḥadashah ve'atidoteiha] (New York, 1908).

—— *The Young Hebrew Literature* [Hasifrut ha'ivrit hatse'irah] (Vilna, 1910).

BEN-GURION, DAVID, *Yoman d. ben-gurion* [Journal of D. Ben-Gurion], IDF Archive, Givatayim.

BEN-HORIN, URI, *The Works of Abraham Ya'ari* [Ḥiburei avraham ya'ari] (Jerusalem, 1949).

BEN-MENAHEM, NAFTALI, 'Commentators on Ibn Ezra on the Bible' [Mefarshei ibn ezra al hamikra], in id., *Topics on Ibn Ezra* [Inyanei ibn ezra] (Jerusalem, 1988), 149–81.

—— *In the Gates of the Book* [Besha'arei sefer] (Jerusalem, 1967).

—— 'Two More Letters by Hazas' [Shenei igerot nosafot shel hazas], *Areshet*, 4 (1966), 461–2.

BEN-SASSON, HAYIM HILLEL, *Ideas and Leadership: The Social Views of the Jews of Poland in the Late Middle Ages* [Hagut vehanhagah: hashkafoteihem haḥevratiyot shel yehudei polin beshalhei yemei habeinayim] (Jerusalem, 1960).

BENAYAHU, MEIR, 'The Transfer of the Centre of Printing from Venice to Amsterdam and the Competition between them and Printing in Constantinople' [Ha'atakat merkaz hadefus mivenetsia le'amsterdam vehataḥarut beineihen levein hadefus bekushta], *Meḥkarim al toledot yehudei holland*, 1 (1975), 41–67.

BERGMANN, SAMUEL HUGO, 'The Young Abraham Ya'ari' [Avraham ya'ari hatsa'ir], *Davar* (18 Nov. 1966).

BERLIN, ISAIAH, *The Roots of Romanticism* (Princeton, NJ, 1999).

BERLINER, ABRAHAM, *Selected Writings* [Katavim nivḥarim] (Jerusalem, 1969).

BERNFELD, SIMON, *Generation of Upheavals* [Dor tahapukhot], 2 vols (Warsaw 1898).

BIALIK, HAYIM NAHMAN, *Ariyeh ba'al guf* [Arieh the Strong Man], in *Sipurim* (Tel Aviv, 1965).

—— 'Halakhah and Aggadah' [Halakhah ve'agadah], in id., *Complete Works* [Kol kitvei h. n. bialik], 4 vols, vol. ii, *Literary Fragments* [Divrei sifrut] (Tel Aviv, 1965) 56–70.

—— '*Hamelits*, *Hatsefirah*, and the Colour of Paper' [Hamelits, hatsefirah, vetseva haneyar], in id., *Complete Works* [Kol kitvei h. n. bialik], 4 vols, vol. ii: *Literary Fragments* [Divrei sifrut] (Tel Aviv, 1965), 133–9.

—— 'On Nation and Language' [Al umah velashon], in id., *Oral Sayings* [Devarim shebe'al peh], 2 vols (Tel Aviv, 1935), i. 15–20.

BLOCH, GEORGE T. (comp. and trans.), *Mesmerism*, introd. E. H. Hilgard (Los Altos, Calif., 1980).

BONFIL, ROBERT, 'Reading in the Jewish Communities of Western Europe in the Middle Ages', in Guglielmo Cavallo and Roger Chartier (eds), *A History of Reading in the West* (Amherst, Mass., 1999), 149–78.

BRAININ, REUVEN, 'On the Life of Professor Tsevi Schapira' [Letoledot haprofesor tsevi shapira], *Hashiloaḥ*, 4 (1898), 181–9.

BRENNER, JOSEPH HAYIM, *The Collected Writings of Joseph Hayim Brenner* [Kol kitvei yosef hayim brener], 3 vols (Tel Aviv, 1967).

BREUER, MORDECAI, 'The Rise of *Pilpul* and *Hilukim* in German Yeshivot' [Aliyat hapilpul vehahilukim beyeshivot ashkenaz], in E. Hildesheimer and K. Kahana (eds), *A Memorial to Rav Yehiel Jacob Weinberg* [Sefer hazikaron lerav yehiel ya'akov weinberg] (Jerusalem, 1969), 341–55.

BRILL, JOSEPH, 'Doctrine of Critics or Treatise of Critiques' [Mishnat mevakrim o masekhet bikurim], *Hashahar*, 8/7 (1877), 317–24.

BUBER, SOLOMON, *Kiryah nisgevah* [Exalted City] (Cracow, 1899–1903).

BURGIL, NATAN BEN ABRAHAM, *Hok natan* [The Law of Nathan] (Leghorn, 1776).

CASSUTO, MOSHEH DAVID (UMBERTO), *The Documentary Method and the Order of the Books of the Torah* [Torat hate'udot vesiduram shel sifrei hatorah], 2nd edn (Jerusalem, 1953).

CAVALLO, GUGLIELMO, and ROGER CHARTIER (eds), *Storia della lettura nel mondo occidentale* (Rome, 1995); trans. into French as *Histoire de la lecture dans le monde occidental* (Paris, 1997); trans. into English as *A History of Reading in the West* (Amherst, Mass., 1999).

CHARTIER, ROGER, 'The Bibliothèque Bleue and Popular Reading', in id. (ed.), *The Cultural Uses of Print*, 240–63.

—— *The Order of Books* (Stanford, Calif., 1994).

—— 'Urban Reading Practices 1660–1780', in id. (ed.), *The Cultural Uses of Print*, 183–239.

—— (ed.), *The Cultural Uses of Print in Early Modern France* (Princeton, NJ, 1987).

CHOVELSOHN, D., *The Origin of Printing among the Jews* [Reshit ma'aseh hadefus beyisra'el] (Warsaw, 1897).

CHRISMAN, MIRIAM USHER, *Bibliography of Strasbourg Imprints* (New Haven and London, 1982).

—— *Lay Culture, Learned Culture: Books and Social Change in Strasbourg 1480–1599* (New Haven and London, 1982).

COHEN, BERL, *Hebrew Subscription List* [Sefer haprenumeranten: wegwiser zu prenumerirte hebraishe sforim un zeire khotmim fon 8767 kehilos in eirope un zfon afrike = A Tour Guide to Pre-Subscribed Hebrew Books and their Subscribers in 8,767 Communities in Europe and North Africa] (New York, 1975).

COHEN, BOAZ, *Bibliography of the Writings of Professor Louis Ginzberg* (New York, 1933).

COHEN, HAGIT, 'In the Bookseller's Shop: Jewish Bookstores in Eastern Europe in the Second Half of the Nineteenth Century' [Behanuto shel mokher hasefarim: hanuyot sefarim yehudiyot bemizrah eiropah bamahatsit hasheniyah shel hame'ah hatesha-esreh] (Master's thesis, Bar-Ilan University, 2001).

COHEN, ISAAC JOSEPH, *The Sages of Transylvania* [Hakhmei trancilvaniyah] (Jerusalem, 1997).

CORBIN, ALAIN, 'Backstage', in Michelle Perrot (ed.), *A History of Private Life*, 5 vols (Cambridge, Mass., 1990), iv. 535–9.

DAN, JOSEPH, *The Hasidic Story* [Hasipur haḥasidi] (Jerusalem, 1975).

—— *The Hebrew Story in the Middle Ages: Studies in its History* [Hasipur ha'ivri biyemei habeinayim: iyunim betoledotav] (Jerusalem, 1974).

——and ISAIAH TISHBY, *Selected Ethical Literature* [Mivḥar sifrut hamusar] (Jerusalem, 1970).

DARNTON, ROBERT, 'History of Reading', in P. Burke (ed.), *New Perspectives on Historical Writing* (University Park, Pa., 1992), 140–67.

—— *The Kiss of Lamourette: Reflections in Cultural History* (New York, 1990).

—— *Mesmerism and the End of the Enlightenment in France* (Cambridge, Mass., 1968).

DAVID, ABRAHAM, 'The Round Trip of Rabbi Petahyah of Regensburg in a New Version' [Sibuvo shel r. petaḥyah miregenshburg benusaḥ ḥadash], *Kovets al yad*, NS 13/23 (1996), 235–69.

DIMITROVSKY, HAYIM ZALMAN, 'On the Method of Pilpul' [Al derekh hapilpul], in Saul Lieberman and Arthur Hyman (eds), *Jubilee Book in Honour of Shalom Baron* [Sefer hayoval likhvod shalom baron] (Jerusalem, 1975), 111–81.

DINUR, BEN-ZION, *Historical Writings* [Dorot vereshumot], 4 vols (Jerusalem, 1978).

—— *The Jews in Exile* [Yisra'el bagolah], 10 vols, 2nd edn (Jerusalem, 1973).

DORMAN, MENAHEM, *Menasseh ben Israel* [Menasheh ben yisra'el] (Tel Aviv, 1989).

DOTAN, SAMUEL, 'Rabbi Jacob Emden, 1697–1776, and his Generation' [Rabi ya'akov emden vedoro 1697–1776], *Hebrew Union College Annual*, 4 (1976), Heb. section, 104–24.

DUBNOW, SIMON, *The Book of Life* [Sefer haḥayim] (Tel Aviv, 1936).

—— *History of the Jews in Russia and Poland: From the Earliest Times Until the Present Day*, 3 vols (Philadelphia, 1916–20).

—— Letter from Riga, *Kiryat sefer*, 20 (1943–4), 177–9.

—— *Letters on the Old and New Judaism* [Mikhtavim al hayahadut hayeshanah vehaḥadashah] (Tel Aviv, 1936).

EDWARDS, MARK U., Jr., *Printing, Propaganda and Martin Luther* (Berkeley, Calif., 1994).

EISENBACH, ARTHUR, *The Emancipation of the Jews of Poland 1180–1870* (Oxford, 1991).

EISENSTEIN, ELIZABETH, *Grub Street Abroad: Aspects of the French Cosmopolitan Press from the Age of Louis XIV to the French Revolution* (Oxford, 1992).

—— *The Printing Press as an Agent of Change: Communications and Cultural Transformation in Early Modern Europe*, 4th edn (Cambridge, 1985).

EISENSTEIN, JUDAH DAVID, *Derekh ḥayim* [A collection of laws, customs and prayers for the sick, the terminally ill, and the dead] (New York, 1930).

EISENSTEIN, JUDAH DAVID, *Otsar derashot* [A Treasury of Sermons] (New York, 1919).

—— *Otsar derushim nivḥarim* [A Treasury of Rabbinic Homilies] (New York, 1918).

—— *Otsar dinim uminhagim* [A Treasury of Laws and Customs] (New York, 1917).

—— *Otsar ma'amarei ḥazal* [A Treasury of Sayings of the Sages] (New York, 1922).

—— *Otsar ma'amarei tanakh* [A Treasury of Biblical Sayings] (New York, 1925).

—— *Otsar masa'ot* [A Treasury of Travelogues] (New York, 1926).

—— *Otsar midrashim* [A Treasury of Midrash] (New York, 1915).

—— *Otsar musar umidot* [A Treasury of Ethics and Morals] (New York, 1941).

—— *Otsar peirushim vetsiyurim al hagadah shel pesaḥ* [A Treasury of Commentaries on the Passover Haggadah] (New York, 1920).

—— *Otsar vikuḥim* [A Treasury of Disputations] (New York, 1928).

—— *Otsar yisra'el*, 10 vols (New York, 1907–13).

ELBAUM, ELHANAN, 'The Official Rabbis as Censors of Books' [Harabanim mita'am kemetsanzerei sefarim], *Alei sefer*, 19 (2001), 185–94.

ELBAUM, JACOB, *Openness and Insularity: Late Sixteenth-Century Literature in Poland and Ashkenaz* [Petiḥut vehistagrut: hayetsirah haruḥahnit-sifrutit bepolin uve'artsot ashkenaz beshalhei hame'ah hashesh-esreh] (Jerusalem, 1990).

ELON, ARI, 'The Symbolics of the Elements of the Plot in the Talmudic Story' [Hasimbolikah shel markivei ha'alilah basipur hatalmudi] (Master's thesis, Hebrew University of Jerusalem, 1983).

EMDEN, JACOB, *Megilat sefer* [The Scroll of the Book], ed. A. Bik (Shauli) (Jerusalem, 1979).

Encyclopaedia Judaica, 1st edn (Jerusalem, 1972).

EPSTEIN, ZALMAN, 'The Great Grandfather' [Hasaba hagadol], *He'avar*, 1 (1918), 179–80.

ERIK, MAX, *The History of Yiddish Literature* [Di geshikhte fun der yidishe literatur] (Warsaw, 1928).

ETKES, IMMANUEL, *Master of the Name: The Besht. Magic, Mysticism, and Leadership* [Ba'al hashem: habesht. Magyah, mistikah, hanhagah] (Jerusalem, 2000).

—— 'On the Question of Harbingers of Haskalah in Eastern Europe' [Leshe'alat mevasrei hahaskalah bemizraḥ eiropah], *Tarbiz*, 57 (1989), 95–114; repr. in id. (ed.), *Religion and Life: The Jewish Haskalah Movement in Eastern Europe* [Hadat vehaḥayim: tenu'at hahaskalah hayehudit bemizraḥ eiropah] (Jerusalem, 1993), 25–44.

—— 'The Place of Magic and "Masters of the Name" in Ashkenazi Society at the Turn of the Seventeenth Century' [Mekomam shel hamagyah uva'alei hashem baḥevrah ha'ashkenazit bemifneh hame'ah ha-17–18], *Zion*, 60 (1995), 69–104.

ETSTAH, JOSEPH, *The Life of Joseph* [Ḥayei yosef] (Tel Aviv, 1988).

FAIERSTEIN, MORRIS M., 'Abraham Jagel, *Lekaḥ tov*, and its History', *Jewish Quarterly Review*, 89 (1999), 319–50.

FEDERBUSH, SIMON, 'Love of the Book' [Ḥibat hasefer] in id., *Studies in Judaism* [ḥikrei yahadut] (Jerusalem, 1965), 7–57.

FEIGENSOHN, SHRAGA [SHAFAN HASOFER], 'On the History of the Romm Printing House' [Letoledot defus rom], *Yahadut lita*, 2 vols (Tel Aviv, 1960), i. 270–96.

FEINER, SHMUEL, *Haskalah and History: The Emergence of a Modern Jewish Historical Consciousness* (London, 2002)

——'The Modern Jewish Woman: A Test Case in the Relationship between the Haskalah and Modernity' [Ha'ishah hayehudit hamodernit: mikreh boḥan beyaḥasei hahaskalah vehamodernah], *Zion*, 58 (1993), 453–99.

——Review of Tsamariyon, *Hame'asef: The First Modern Periodical in Hebrew, Zion*, 53 (1988), 441–6.

——'Educational Programmes and Social Ideals: The "Ḥinukh Ha-Nearim" School in Berlin 1778–1820' [Programot hinukhiyot ve'ide'alim ḥevratiyim: Beit hasefer 'Ḥinukh Hane'arim', Berlin 1778–1820], *Zion*, 60 (1995), 393–424.

——'Itzik Euchel: The Initiator of the Enlightenment Movement' [Itzik euchel: hayazam shel tenuat hahaskalah begermaniyah], *Zion*, 52 (1987), 427–69.

FEINGOLD, BEN-AMI, '*Kotzo shel yod*: The Anatomy of a Satire' ['Kotso shel yod': anatomiyah shel satirah], *Meḥkarei yerushalayim besifrut ivrit*, 2 (1983), 73–103.

FISHMAN, DAVID E., *Russia's First Modern Jews: The Jews of Shklov* (New York, 1995).

FRANKEL, JONATHAN, 'S. M. Dubnov: Historian and Ideologist', in Sofia Dubnov-Erlich (ed.), *The Life and Work of S. M. Dubnov: Diaspora, Nationalism and Jewish History* (Bloomington, 1991), 1–33.

FRANKFURT, MOSES, *Kehilot mosheh* (Amsterdam, 1724).

FREIMANN, AARON, 'The First Hebrew Printer in Lublin' [Hadefus ha'ivri harishon belublin], *Hatsofeh leḥokhmat yisra'el*, 10 (1926), 282–95.

——*Union Catalogue of Hebrew Manuscripts and their Location*, 2 vols (New York, 1968).

FRIEDBERG, HAYIM DOV, *History of Hebrew Printing in Poland* [Toledot hadefus ha'ivri bepolaniyah] (Antwerp, 1932; 2nd edn Tel Aviv, 1950).

——*The Library* [Beit eked sefarim] (Tel Aviv, 1950; 2nd edn 1953).

GARLAND, HENRY B., *Storm and Stress* (London, 1952).

GELBER, NATHAN MICHAEL, 'On the History of Jewish Doctors in Poland in the Eighteenth Century' [Letoledot harofe'im hayehudim bepolin bame'ah hayod-ḥet], *Harofe ha'ivri*, 21/1 (1948), 61–9.

GILBOA, MENUHAH, *Lexicon of Hebrew Journals in the Eighteenth and Nineteenth Centuries* [Leksikon ha'itonut ha'ivrit bame'ot hashemoneh-esreh vehatesha-esreh] (Jerusalem, 1992).

GILON, MEIR, *Mendelssohn's Kohelet musar in the Context of its Period* [Kohelet musar lemendelsohn al reka tekufato] (Jerusalem, 1979).

GINZBERG, LOUIS, *The Legends of the Jews*, 7 vols (Philadelphia, 1928).

GINZBURG, CARLO, *The Cheese and the Worms: The Cosmos of a Sixteenth-Century Miller*, 6th edn (Harrisonburg, Va., 1986).

GINZBURG, SAUL, 'On the History of Jewish Printing Produced in Russia' [Tsu der geshikhte fun yidishen druk: vezen in rusland], *Tsukunft* (Oct. 1932), 589–94.

—— 'The Story of Printing among the Jews' [Ma'aseh hadefus beyisra'el], in id., *Historical Writings* [Ketavim historiyim] (Tel Aviv, 1944), 40–50.

GODMAN, PETER, *The Silent Masters: Latin Literature and its Censors in the High Middle Ages* (Princeton, NJ, 2000).

GOITEIN, SOLOMON DOV, 'Jewish History and Arab History: A Comment on the Differences Between Them' [Toledot yisra'el vetoledot ha'aravim: he'arah al hahevdelim beineihem], *Zion*, 3 (1938), 107–10.

—— 'The *Makamah* and the *Maḥberet*: A Chapter in the History of Literature and Society in the Orient' [Hamakamah vehamaḥberet: perek betoledot hasifrut vehaḥevrah bamizraḥ], *Maḥbarot lasifrut*, 5/1 (1951–4), 32–7.

GOLAN, ARNAH, 'Hebrew Literary Criticism: Its Development and Manifestations, 1897–1905' [Bikoret hasifrut hayafah ha'ivrit: hitpatḥutah vegiluleiha bashanim 1897–1905] (doctoral dissertation, Hebrew University of Jerusalem, 1976).

GOLDENBERG, SOLOMON, 'Are There Hebrew Readers?' [Hayesh kore'im ivriyim?] *Hashiloaḥ*, 17 (1917–18), 417–22.

GOLDMANN, NAHUM, *The Autobiography of Nahum Goldmann: Sixty Years of Jewish Life* (New York, 1969).

GOLDSTEIN, YOSEF, *Ahad Ha'am: Biography* [Aḥad ha'am: biografiyah] (Jerusalem, 1992).

GOODY, JACK, *The Interface Between the Written and the Oral* (Cambridge, 1987).

—— *The Logic of Writing and the Organization of Society* (Cambridge, 1986).

GORDON, JUDAH LEIB, *The Writings of Judah Leib Gordon* [Kitvei yehudah leib gordon] (Tel Aviv, 1950).

GOTTLOBER, ABRAHAM BER, *Zikhronot umasa'ot* [Memoirs and Journeys], 2 vols, ed. R. Goldberg (Jerusalem, 1976).

GRAFF, HARVEY J., *The Legacies of Literacy: Continuities and Contradictions in Western Culture and Society* (Bloomington and Indianopolis, 1991).

GRAFTON, ANTHONY, APRIL SHELFORD, and NANCY SIRAISI, *New Worlds, Ancient Texts: The Power of Tradition and the Shock of Discovery* (Cambridge, Mass., 1992).

GRIES, ZEEV, 'Between History and Literature: The Case of Jewish Preaching', *Journal of Jewish Thought and Philosophy*, 4 (1994), 113–22.

—— 'Between Literature and History: Introductory Remarks for Examination and Discussion of *Shivḥei habesht*' [Bein sifrut lehistoriyah: hakdamot lediyun ve'iyun beshivḥei habesht], *Tura*, 3 (1994), 153–81.

—— 'A Bibliographer and Librarian as an Agent of Culture: The Contribution of

Abraham Ya'ari to the Study of Jewish Printing in Eastern Europe' [Bibliograf vesafran kesokhen tarbut, terumato shel avraham ya'ari leḥeker hadefus hayehudi bemizraḥ eiropah], *Mada'aei hayahadut*, 41 (2001–2), 109–30.

—— *Book, Scribe, and Story in Early Hasidism: From the Besht to Menahem Mendel of Kotsk* [Sefer sofer vesipur bereshit haḥasidut: min habesht ve'ad menaḥem mendel mikotsk] (Tel Aviv, 1992).

—— 'The Copying and Printing of Books of Kabbalah as a Source for its Study' [Ha'atakat vehadpasat sifrei kabalah kemakor lelimudah], *Maḥanayim*, 6 (1994), 204–11.

—— 'Definition of Shabatean Hagiographical Literature' [Hagdarat sifrut hashe-vaḥim hashabeta'it], *Meḥkarei yerushalayim bemaḥshevet yisra'el*, 17 (2001), 353–64; also published in Rachel Elior (ed.), *The Dream and its Breaking. The Shabatean Movement and its Branches: Messianism, Shabateanism, and Frankism* [Haḥalom veshivro. Hatenuah hashabeta'it usheluḥoteiha: meshiḥiyut sha-beta'ut ufrankizm], 2 vols (Jerusalem, 2001), ii. 353–64.

—— *The Early Kabbalah* [Hakabalah hakedumah] (Kiryat Tivon, 1979).

—— 'From Myth to Ethos: Outline of a Portrait of Rabbi Abraham of Kalisk' [Mimitos le'etos: kavim lidemuto shel r. avraham mikalisk], in Shmuel Ettinger (ed.), *A People and its History* [Umah vetoledoteiha], 2 vols (Jerusalem, 1984), ii. 117–46.

—— 'Hasidic Stories of Prayer as a Source for a Concept of the World and of Man' [Sipurei tefilah ḥasidim kemakor letefisat olam ve'adam], in Zeev Gries, H. Kreisel, and B. Huss (eds), *Abundance of Dew* [Shefa tal]: *Studies in Jewish Thought and Culture Presented to Beracha Sack* (Jerusalem, 2004), 219–35.

—— 'Heresy', in Arthur A. Cohen and Paul Mendes-Flohr (eds), *Contemporary Jewish Religious Thought* (New York, 1986), 339–52.

—— 'The Historical Figure of the Besht: Between the Historian's Scalpel and the Literary Scholar's Paintbrush' [Demuto hahistorit shel habesht: bein sakin hamenatḥim shel hahistoriyon lemikhḥolo shel ḥoker hasifrut], *Kabalah*, 5 (2000), 411–46.

—— 'Is It True That the Best Part of a Story Is Its Falsehood? The Place of Hagiographic Literature in the History of Hasidism' [Ha'omnam meitav hasipur kezavo? Mekom sifrut hashevaḥim betoledot haḥasidut], *Da'at*, 44 (Winter 2000), 85–94.

—— 'Kabbalah and Halakhah' [Kabalah vehalakhah], *Mada'ei hayahadut*, 40 (2000), 187–97.

—— *The Literature of Customs: Its History and Place in the Life of the Followers of the Besht* [Sifrut hahanhagot: toledoteiha umekomah beḥayei ḥasidei habesht] (Jerusalem, 1990).

—— 'On the Figure of the Jewish Managing Editor in the Late Middle Ages' [Ledemuto shel hamevi ledefus hayehudi beshalhei yemei habeinayim], *Igeret ha'akademiyah hale'umit hayisra'elit lemada'aim*, 11 (July 1992), 7–11.

GRIES, ZEEV, 'Printing as a Means of Communication among Jewish Communities Shortly after the Expulsion from Spain: Introductory Remarks for Examination and Discussion' [Hadefus ke'emtsai kesher bein kehilot yisra'el batekufah hasemukhah legerush sefarad: hakdamot le'iyun vediyun], *Da'at*, 28 (Winter 1992), 5–17.

——'Rabbi Israel ben Shabetai of Kozienice and his Commentary on the *Ethics of the Fathers*' [R. yisra'el ben shabetai mikoznits ufeirushav lemasekhet avot], in Rachel Elior, Israel Bartal, and Chone Shmeruk (eds), *Righteous and Virtuous People: Studies in Polish Hasidism* [Tsadikim ve'anshei ma'aseh: mehkarim behasidut polin] (Jerusalem, 1994), 127–65.

——Boaz Huss, and Haim Kreisel (eds), *Shefa tal: Studies in Jewish Thought and Culture Presented to Bracha Sack* [Shefa tal: iyunim bemahshevet yisrael ubetarbut yehudit mugashim leverakhah zak] (Jerusalem, 2004).

GRINBAUM, AARON, 'The Interpretation of Dreams, History and Sources' [Pitron halomot, korot, umekorot], *Areshet*, 4 (1966), 180–201.

GRONEMANN, SAMI, *Memoirs of a Yekke* [Zikhronot shel yeke] (Tel Aviv, 1946).

GUTTMAN, NAHUM, *In the Land of Lubengulu the Zulu King, Father of the Metabulu Nation, in the Mountains of Bulavaya* [Be'erets lubengulu melekh zulu, avi am hametabulu asher beharei bulavayah] (Tel Aviv, 1940).

HABERMAN, ABRAHAM MEIR, 'Abraham Ya'ari, the Author and Bibliographer' [Avraham ya'ari, hasofer vehabibliograf], in id., *Men of Letters and Men of Action* [Anshei sefer ve'anshei ma'aseh] (Jerusalem, 1974), 64–9.

——'An Error that Led to Errors' [Ta'ut shegarerah ta'uyot], *Kiryat sefer*, 48 (1973), 528.

——*History of Jewish Literature* [Toledot sifrut yisra'el], 7 vols (Tel Aviv, 1956), supplement to the original Hebrew edn of Zinberg, *History of Jewish Literature*.

——*Jewish Women as Printers, Typesetters, Publishers, and Promoters of Authors* [Nashim ivriyot betor madpisot, mesadrot, motsiyot la'or, utomekhot bemehabrim] (Berlin, 1933).

——*Title Pages of Hebrew Books* [Sha'arei sefarim ivrim] (Safed, 1969).

——'Unintentional and Intentional Typographical Errors' [Ta'uyot defus beshogeg uvemezid], *Molad*, 14 (1956–7), 366–9; also published as 'Errors in Manuscripts and Unintentional and Intentional Typographical Errors' [Ta'uyot bekitvei yad veta'uyot defus beshogeg uvemezid], *Hed hadefus*, 11 (Mar. 1957), 59–60.

——*The Yiddish Version of Mashal hakadmoni* [Der yidishe oysgabet fun mashal hakadmoni] (Vilna, 1939).

HACKER, JOSEPH, 'Intellectual Activity among the Jews of the Ottoman Empire in the Sixteenth and Seventeenth Centuries' [Hape'ilut ha'intelektualit bekerev yehudei ha'imperiyah ha'otomanit bame'ot hashesh-esreh vehasheva-esreh], *Tarbiz*, 53 (1984), 576–80.

——'Printers of Constantinople in the Sixteenth Century' [Defusei kushta bame'ah hashesh-esreh], *Areshet*, 5 (1972), 457–93.

HALAMISH, MOSHE, *Kabbalah in Prayer, Halakhah, and Custom* [Hakabalah bate-filah, bahalakhah, uvaminhag] (Jerusalem, 2000).

HALKIN, SIMON, *Conventions and Crises in our Literature: Twelve Conversations on Modern Hebrew Literature* [Muskamot umashberim besifrutenu: yod-beit siḥot al hasifrut ha'ivrit haḥadashah] (Jerusalem, 1980).

—— *Currents and Forms in Modern Hebrew Literature* [Zeramim vetsurot basifrut ha'ivrit haḥadashah] (Jerusalem, 1980).

—— *Modern Hebrew Literature* (New York, 1950).

HALPERN, ISRAEL, 'The Approbations of the Council of the Four Lands' [Haskamot va'ad arba aratsot], *Kiryat sefer*, 11 (1934–5), 105–11, 252–64.

—— 'The Council of the Four Lands in Poland and the Hebrew Book' [Va'ad arba aratsot bepolin vehasefer ha'ivri], *Kiryat sefer*, 9 (1932–3), 366–78.

—— 'More on the Councils of Poland and Lithuania and their Relation to the Book' [Od al va'adei polin velita beyaḥasam el hasefer], *Kiryat sefer*, 12 (1935–6), 250–3.

HARKABI, TSIDKIYAHU, 'What We Have Not Seen Is Not Proof' [Lo ra'inu einah re'ayah], *Kiryat sefer*, 19 (1942–3), 279.

HARRIS, WILLIAM V., *Ancient Literacy* (Cambridge, Mass., 1989).

HAVER, ISAAC, *Magen vetsinah* [Shield and Buckler] (Benei Berak, 1985).

—— *Pitḥei she'arim* [The Openings of Gates] (Warsaw, 1888).

HAVER, JOSEPH, *Nefesh naki* [Pure Soul] (Warsaw, 1853).

HAZARD, PAUL, *Books, Children, and Men*, 3rd edn (Boston, 1947).

—— *The European Mind, 1680–1715* (Cleveland and New York, 1969).

HEINE, HEINRICH, *And They Will Not Say Kaddish: On Jews, Judaism, and Freedom* [Vekadish hem lo yagidu: al yehudim, yahadut, veḥerut], ed. Y. Aloni and S. Tenai (Tel Aviv, 1994).

—— *Historisch-Kritische Gesamtausgabe der Werke*, ed. M. Windfuhr, 16 vols (Hamburg, 1975–97).

HELLER, MARVIN J., *Printing the Talmud: A History of the Individual Treatises Printed from 1700 to 1750* (Leiden, 1999).

HIDA *see* AZULAI, HAYIM JOSEPH DAVID

HIRSCH, SAMSON RAPHAEL, *Nineteen Letters on Judaism* (New York, 1969).

HOROWITZ, PINHAS ELIJAH, *Sefer haberit hashalem* [The Book of the Covenant] (Jerusalem, 1990).

HUBKA, THOMAS, 'The Synagogue of Gwóździec: The Gate of Heaven. The Influence of the Zohar on Art and Architecture' [Beit hakeneset begvuzdziets: sha'ar hashamayim. Hashpa'at sefer hazohar al ha'omanut veha'adrikhalut], in H. Pedaya (ed.), *The Myth in Judaism* [Hamitos bayahadut], Eshel Be'er Sheva 4 (Beersheva, 1996), 263–316.

HUNDERT, GERSHON DAVID, 'The Library of the Study Hall in Volozhin 1762: Some Notes on the Basis of a Newly Discovered Manuscript', *Jewish History*, 14/2 (2000), 225–44.

HUNT, LYNNE, *The Family Romance of the French Revolution* (Berkeley and Los Angeles, 1992).

HUSS, BOAZ, '*Sefer Ha-Zohar* as a Canonical, Sacred, and Holy Text: Changing Perspectives of the Book of Splendor Between the Thirteenth and Eighteenth Centuries', *Journal of Jewish Thought and Philosophy*, 7 (1998), 257–307.

IDEL, MOSHE, *Hasidism: Between Ecstasy and Magic* (New York, 1995).

—— *Mystical Experience in Abraham Abulafiah* (New York, 1988), 4–5.

—— 'One from a Town, Two from a Clan: The Diffusion of Lurianic Kabbalah and Sabbateanism, a Re-Examination', *Jewish History*, 7/2 (1993), 79–104.

In the Tents of the Book [Be'ohalei sefer] (Jerusalem, 1967).

JACOB BEN YIRMIYAHU IBN NAIM, *Mishkenot ya'akov* [The Dwellings of Jacob] (Salonika, 1731).

JAGEL, ABRAHAM, *Gai ḥizayon* [A Valley of Vision], *see* RUDERMAN, DAVID

Jewish Encyclopedia [Ha'entsiklopediyah ha'ivrit], 37 vols (Ramat Gan, 1949–95).

JOHNS, ADRIAN, *The Nature of the Book: Print and Knowledge in the Making* (Chicago and London, 1998).

KAHANA, ISAAC ZEEV, 'Printing in the Halakhah' [Hadefus bahalakhah], *Sinai*, 16 (1945), 49–61, 139–59.

KANDELSHEIN, ESTHER, 'Printed Publications in the Hebrew Alphabet in Erets Yisrael, 1577–1923' [Hadefus ha'ivri be-erets yisra'el 1577–1923: hebetim bibliografiyim, tarbutiyim vesotsiyo'ekonomiyim] (doctoral dissertation, Bar-Ilan University, 2004).

KARBALIO, ISAAC, *Sefer hazikhronot veḥayei yitsḥak* [The Book of Remembrance and the Life of Isaac] (Leghorn, 1761).

KARNIEL, TSEVI, *The Hebrew Feuilleton* [Hafiliton ha'ivri] (Tel Aviv, 1982).

KATZ, BEN-TSIYON, 'Y. L. Katzenelson: The Man and his Work' [Y. l. katzenelson: ha'ish ufo'alo], in Y. L. Katzenelson [Buki ben Yogli], *What My Eyes Have Seen and My Ears Have Heard: Memoirs of My Life* [Mimah shera'u einai veshame'u oznai: zikhronot miyemei ḥayai] (Jerusalem, 1947).

KATZ, JACOB, 'The Jewish Character of Israeli Society' [Ofiyah hayehudi shel haḥevrah hayisra'elit], in id., *Jewish Nationalism: Essays and Studies* [Le'umiyut yehudit: masot umeḥkarim] (Jerusalem, 1983), 85–108.

—— *Out of the Ghetto: The Social Background of Jewish Emancipation 1770–1870* (Cambridge, Mass., 1973; 2nd edn New York, 1978).

—— *Tradition and Crisis: Jewish Society at the End of the Middle Ages*, trans. B. D. Cooperman (New York, 1993).

KATZ, M., 'The Logic of Typographical Errors (from a Proof-Reader's Notebook)' [Hahigayon shebeshegiyot defus (mipinkaso shel magiha)], *Hed hadefus*, 3–4 (Sept. 1949), 20–1.

KATZ, TUVIAH, *Ma'aseh tuviyah* [The Story of Tuviah] (Venice, 1706).

Katzenellenbogen, Pinhas, *Yesh manhilin* [There Are Bequeathers], ed. Yizhak Feld (Jerusalem, 1986).

Kauffmann, David, *Die Familie Gomperz* (Frankfurt am Main, 1907).

Khalaz, Judah, *Sefer hamusar* [The Book of Ethics] (Constantinople, 1537).

Kipling, Rudyard, *Just So Stories*, trans. A Regelson as *Ken hayah* [So It Was] (Tel Aviv, 1935).

Kishon, Ephraim, 'The Memory of a Righteous Man is a Blessing' [Zekher tsadik liverakhah], in id., *Everything Depends* [Hakol talui] (Tel Aviv, 1970), 134–8.

Klausner, Israel, *Vilna, the Jerusalem of Lithuania: The First Generations, 1495–1881* [Vilna, yerushalayim delita: dorot rishonim 1495–1881] (Tel Aviv, 1989).

Klausner, Joseph, *The History of Modern Hebrew Literature* [Historiyah shel hasifrut ha'ivrit hahadashah], 1st edn, 6 vols (Jerusalem, 1939–50); 2nd edn, 6 vols (1952–59), 3rd edn, 2 vols (Jerusalem, 1960).

——(ed.), *Otsar hayahadut in Hebrew: Its Nature, Purpose, and Essence. A Sample Issue* [Otsar hayahadut bileshon ivrit: mahuto, materato, utekhunato. Hoveret ledugmah] (Warsaw, 1906).

Kohen, Isaac Joseph, '*The Ethics of the Fathers*, Commentaries on it and Translations of it in the Mirror of the Generations' [Masekhet avot, perusheiha vetirgumeiha ba'aspaklariyat hadorot], *Kiryat sefer*, 40 (1965), 104–17, 277–85.

Kohn, Pinhas, *Dik's Unknown Writings in Yiddish and Hebrew* [Diks umbekante hiburim in yiddish un hebraish], *Yivo bleter*, 1 (1931), 325–34.

——'Midwives as the Authors of Books a Hundred Years ago in Vilna' [Meyaledot kemehabrot sefarim lifnei me'ah shanah bevilna], *Kiryat sefer*, 14 (1937–8), 118–21.

——'On the Romm Printing House of Vilna' [Al beit hadefus shel rom bevilna], *Kiryat sefer*, 10 (1932–4), 244–50.

——'Towards a History of the Romm Printing House in Vilna' [Lekorot beit hadefus shel rom bevilna], *Kiryat sefer*, 12 (1935–6), 109–15.

Kovner, Abraham Uri, *The Collected Writing of Uri Kovner* [Kol kitvei uri kovner], ed. Y. Zmorah (Tel Aviv, 1947).

Krammnick, I., 'Children's Literature and Bourgeois Ideology: Observations on Culture and Industrial Capitalism in the Later Eighteenth Century', in H. C. Payne (ed.), *Studies in Eighteenth Century Culture*, 12 (1983), 11–43.

Krasney, Arielah, *The Jester* [Habadhan] (Jerusalem, 1998).

Kressel, Getzel, 'The Beginning of Haskalah in German Jewry' [Reshit hahaskalah beyahadut germaniyah], *Moznayim*, 12 (1961), 135–7.

——*Encyclopedia of Modern Hebrew Literature* [Leksikon hasifrut ha'ivrit badorot ha'aharonim], 2 vols (Bat Yam, 1965).

——'For the Sake of Precision' [Lema'an hadiyuk], *Moznayim*, ns 23/46 (1966), 428.

——*Mysteries of Books and Authors* [Sitrei sefer vesofer] (Tel Aviv, 1971).

KRESSEL, GETZEL,'Our Bibliographical Press' [Itonutenu habibliografit], in id., *Mysteries of Books and Authors*, 60–4.

——'Two Who Passed Away' [Shenayim shehalkhu], *Moznayim*, 24/47 (1967), 64–5.

Kuntres: teḥinah, teshuvah, tefilah, utsedakah [Pamphlet: Supplication, Repentance, Prayer, and Charity] (Laszczów, 1816).

KURZWEIL, BARUCH, *In the Struggle for the Values of Judaism* [Bema'avak al erkhei hayahadut] (Jerusalem and Tel Aviv, 1970).

——*Is Our New Literature a Continuation or a Revolution?* [Sifrutenu haḥadashah hemshekh o mahapekhah?] (Tel Aviv, 1965).

LACHOWER, FISCHEL, *History of Modern Hebrew Literature* [Toledot hasifrut ha'ivrit haḥadashah], 2 vols, 10th edn (Tel Aviv, 1957) (1st published in 3 vols, Tel Aviv, 1928–32).

LEBENSOHN, ADAM HACOHEN, 'Comments and Clarifications' [He'arot uve'urim], *Hakarmel*, 1/28 (6 Shevat 5621 [1861]), 224.

LEIB BEN OZER, *Sipur ma'asei shabetai tsvi* [The Story of the Deeds of Shabetai Tsevi], ed. Zalman Shazar (Jerusalem, 1978).

LEIMAN, SID Z., 'The Adventure of the Maharal of Prague in London: R. Yudl Rosenberg and the Golem of Prague', *Tradition*, 36/1 (Spring 2002), 26–58.

LESHCHINSKY, JACOB, 'Autonomism and the Letters on the Old and New Judaism' [Ha'otonimizm vehamikhtavim al hayahadut hayeshanah vehaḥadashah], in S. Rawidowicz (ed.), *The Book of Simon Dubnow* [Sefer shimon dubnov] (Waltham, Mass., 1954), 177–80.

LEVI BEN SHELOMO, *Ateret shelomo* [The Crown of Solomon] (Zolkiew, 1739).

LEVNER, ISRAEL, and Y. STEINBERG, *Chrestomathy* [Ḥaristomatiyah], readings for children (Warsaw, 1913).

LIBERMAN, HAYIM, 'Another Book Printed in Laszczów' [Od sefer midefus lasz-czow], *Kiryat sefer*, 16 (1939–40), 140.

——'Bibliographical Notes' [Bibliografishe bamerkungen], *Yivo bleter*, 11 (1937), 92–4; repr. in id., *Rachel's Tent* [Ohel raḥel], 3 vols (New York, 1981), ii. 199–200.

——'A Note on the Article "R. Eliezer Pavir and his Literary Work"' [He'arah lema'amar R. eli'ezer pavir umifalo hasifruti], *Kiryat sefer*, 36 (1961), 272; repr. in id., *Rachel's Tent*, i. 476.

——'On the Bibliography of I. M. Dik' [Tsu der bibliografie fun i. m. dik], *Yivo bleter*, 14 (1939), 171–4; repr. in id., *Rachel's Tent*, ii. 324–30.

——'On the History of Hebrew Printing in Laszczów' [Letoledot hadefus ha'ivri belaszczow], *Kiryat sefer*, 14 (1937–8), 553–4; repr. in id., *Rachel's Tent*, i. 208–10.

——'On the Printing House of the Widow and the Brothers Romm from Vilna' [Al defus ha'almanah veha'aḥim rom mivilna], *Kiryat sefer*, 34 (1959), 527–8; repr. in id., *Rachel's Tent*, i. 217–18.

——'On Translations of *Igeret ba'alei ḥayim* into Yiddish' [Latirgumim shel 'Igeret ba'alei ḥayim' leyudit], *Kiryat sefer*, 14 (1937–8), 272; repr. in id., *Rachel's Tent*, i 461.

——Rachel's Tent [Ohel raḥel], 3 vols (New York, 1981).

LICHTENSTEIN, HILLEL, Avkat rokhel [The Pedlar's Powder] (Brooklyn, 1970).

LISSAK, MOSHE (ed.), The History of the Jewish Community in Erets Yisrael since 1882, [Toledot hayishuv hayehudi be'erets yisra'el me'az ha'aliyah harishonah], 3 vols (Jerusalem, 1989-2002).

LOEWENSTEIN, LEOPOLD, Index Approbationum (Frankfurt am Main, 1923).

LOMBROSO, ISAAC, Zera yitsḥak [The Seed of Isaac] (Tunis, 1768).

LUZ, EHUD, The Meeting of Parallels [Makbilim nifgashim] (Tel Aviv, 1985).

LYONS, MARTIN, 'New Readers in the Nineteenth Century: Women, Children, Workers', in G. Cavallo and Roger Chartier (eds), A History of Reading in the West (Amherst, Mass., 1999), 313–44.

Ma'aseh Book, trans. and annotated Moses Gaster, 2nd edn (Philadelphia, 1981).

MCKITTERICK, ROSAMUND (ed.), The Uses of Literacy (Cambridge, 1992).

MCLUHAN, MARSHALL, The Gutenberg Galaxy: The Making of Typographic Man (Toronto, 1962).

MAHLER, RAPHAEL, Hasidism and Haskalah [Haḥasidut vehahaskalah] (Merhaviah, 1961).

——A History of Modern Jewry 1700–1815 (London, 1971).

MAIMON, SOLOMON, The Life of Solomon Maimon [Ḥayei shelomo maimon], introd. Fischel Lachower (Ramat Gan and Jerusalem, 1953).

MALAKHI, ELIEZER RAPHAEL, 'Dubnow in Hebrew Literature', in Simon Rawidowicz (ed.), The Book of Simon Dubnow [Sefer shimon dubnov] (Waltham, Mass., 1954), 225–39.

MANGUEL, ALBERTO, A History of Reading (New York, 1996).

MARKER, GARY, Publishing, Printing and the Origins of Intellectual Life in Russia 1700–1800 (Princeton, NJ, 1985).

MARTIN, HENRI JEAN, The History and Power of Writing (Chicago, 1994).

MARX, ALEXANDER, 'Moritz Steinschneider', in Essays in Jewish Biography (Philadelphia, 1947), 112–84.

MATRAS, HAGIT, 'Books of Remedies and Cures in Hebrew' [Sifrei segulot verefuot be'ivrit] (doctoral dissertation, Hebrew University of Jerusalem, 1997).

MAZOR, JACOB, 'The Badkhn in Contemporary Hasidic Society: Social, Historical, and Musical Observations', in Polin, 16: Focusing on Jewish Popular Culture and Its Afterlife (Oxford, 2003), 279–96.

——'The Jester and Hasidic Society: Historical, Social, and Musical Aspects' [Habadḥan baḥevrah haḥasidit: hebetim historiyim ḥevratiyim umusikaliyim], Dukhan, 15 (2000), 41–80.

Merkavah shelemah [The Entire Chariot] (Jerusalem, 1972).

MEVORAKH, BARUKH, 'A. Shohat, With the Change of Epochs: The Beginning of the Haskalah in German Jewry' [A. shoḥat, im ḥilufei tekufot: reshit hahaskalah beyahadut germaniyah] (book review), Kiryat sefer, 37 (1962), 150–5.

MEYER, MICHAEL A., *The Origin of the Modern Jew: Jewish Identity and European Culture in Germany 1749–1824*, 3rd edn (Detroit, 1979).

MICHMAN, JOZEPH, *David Franco Mendes: A Hebrew Poet* (Amsterdam, 1951).

MINTZ, ALAN, *Banished from their Father's Table: Loss of Faith and Hebrew Autobiographies* (Bloomington, Ind., 1989).

MIRON, DAN, *Between Vision and Truth: Harbingers of the Hebrew and Yiddish Novel* [Bein ḥazon le'emet: nitsanei haroman ha'ivri vehayidi] (Jerusalem, 1979).

——'On the Perplexing Background of Hebrew Literature at the Start of the Twentieth Century' [Lereka hamevukhah basifrut ha'ivrit bereshit hame'ah ha'esrim], in B. Shahewitch and M. Peri (eds), *Jubilee Volume in Honour of Simon Halkin* [Sefer hayovel leshimon halkin] (Jerusalem, 1975), 419–87.

—— *When Loners Come Together* [Bodedim bemo'edam] (Tel Aviv, 1987).

MONDSHINE, YEHOSHUA, *Shivḥei habesht: A Manuscript* [Shivḥei habesht: ketav yad] (Jerusalem, 1982).

MORGENSTERN, ARYEH, *Messianism and the Settlement of Erets Israel* [Meshiḥiyut veyishuv erets yisra'el] (Jerusalem, 1985).

NADLER, ALAN LAWRENCE, 'The War on Modernity of R. Hayyim Eleazar Shapira of Mucachevo', *Modern Judaism*, 14 (1994), 233–64.

NATHANSOHN, JOSEPH SAUL, *Sho'el umeshiv* [The Asker and the Respondent] (Brooklyn, 1954).

NIGAL, GEDALIYAH, 'Hasidic Elements in one of Agnon's Works' [Yesodot hasidiyim be'aḥat miyetsirot agnon], *Ḥadshot bar-ilan*, 30 (Mar. 1979), 14–17; repr. in Y. Friedlander (ed.), *Vehayah he'akov lemishor: Essays on a Novel by S. J. Agnon* [Al 'Vehayah he'akov lemishor': masot al novelah leshai agnon] (Tel Aviv, 1993), 165–76, and in Nigal, *Studies in Hasidism: A Collection of Articles* [Meḥkarim beḥasidut: osef ma'amarim] (Jerusalem, 1999), 335–46.

—— *Magic, Mysticism, and Hasidism* [Magyah, mistikah, veḥasidut] (Tel Aviv, 1992).

——'S. Y. Agnon and his Hasidic Sources' [Shai agnon umekorotav haḥasidiyim], in id., *East and West Studies* [Meḥkarei ma'arav umizraḥ] (Jerusalem, 2001), 251–5.

OFEK, URIEL, *Children's Literature in Hebrew: The Beginning* [Sifrut hayeladim ha'ivrit: hahatḥalah] (Tel Aviv, 1979).

—— *Children's Literature in Hebrew: 1900–1948*, 2 vols [Sifrut hayeladim ha'ivrit 1900–1948] (Tel Aviv, 1988).

—— *Give Them Books* [Tenu lahem sefarim] (Tel Aviv, 1978).

——'*Tushiyah* for the Children of Israel: Hebrew Publishers as Promoters of Children's Literature' [Tushiyah leyaldei yisra'el: molim ivriyim kemetafei sifrut yeladim], *Moznayim*, 45/6 (1978), 421–8.

OLIPHANT, LAWRENCE, *Russian Shores of the Black Sea, in the Autumn of 1852 with a Voyage Down the Volga, and a Tour through the Country of the Don Cossacks*, 4th edn (Edinburgh and London, 1854).

ONG, WALTER J., *Orality and Literacy: The Technologizing of the Word*, 4th edn (Bristol, 1987).

Oz, Amos, *A Tale of Love and Darkness* [Sipur al ahavah veḥoshekh] (Jerusalem, 2003).

Papirna, Abraham Jacob, *Collected Writings* [Kol haketavim] (Tel Aviv, 1952).

Parush, Iris, 'The Culture of Criticism and the Criticism of Culture: An Examination of A. Y. Papirna's *An Old Bottle Full of New Wine*' [Tarbut habikoret uvikoret hatarbut: iyunim besifro shel a. y. papirna, kankan ḥadash male yashan], *Meḥkarei yerushalayim besifrut ivrit*, 14 (1993), 197–239.

——*Literary Canon and National Ideology: The Literary Criticism of Frishman in Comparison to the Literary Criticism of Klausner and Brenner* [Kanon sifruti ve'ideologiyah le'umit: bikoret hasifrut shel frishman behashva'ah lebikoret hasifrut shel klozner ubrener] (Jerusalem, 1992).

——*Reading Women: The Benefit of Marginality in Nineteenth-Century Eastern European Jewish Society* [Nashim kore'ot: yitronah shel shuliyut baḥevrah hayehudit bemizraḥ eiropah bame'ah hatesha-esreh] (Tel Aviv, 2001).

——and Brakhah Fischler, 'Considerations of Language, Literature, and Society in the Controversy on Purism' [Shikulei lashon, sifrut veḥevrah bavikuaḥ al hataharanut], *Meḥkari yerushalayim besifrut ivrit*, 15 (1995), 107–35.

——— '"Hybrid" or "Unity": between "Written Scripture" and "Spoken Scripture" in the Work of Mendele Mokher Seforim' ['Kilayim' o 'aḥdut': bein mikra shekatuv lemikra shene'emar beyetsirato shel mendele mo's], *Meḥkarim belashon*, 7 (1996), 253–82.

Pedersen, Johanes, *The Arabic Book* (Princeton, NJ, 1984), 131–42.

Pelli, Moshe, *The Gate of Haskalah: Annotated Index to Hame'asef, the First Hebrew Periodical 1784–1811* [Sha'ar hahaskalah: mafte'aḥ mu'ar lehame'asef, ketav ha'et ha'ivri harishon 5544–5571] (Jerusalem, 2001).

——*The Generation of the Gatherers at the Dawn of the Haskalah* [Dor hame'asfim beshaḥar hahaskalah] (Tel Aviv, 2001).

——*Genres and Issues in the Literature of the Hebrew Enlightenment: The Maskilic Genre and its Apparatus* [Sugot vesugiyot besifrut hahaskalah ha'ivrit: hazhenre hamaskili ve'avizareihu] (Tel Aviv, 1999).

——'Hame'asef Project: The Contribution of the Haskalah Journal—Appreciations and Conclusions' [Proyekt hame'asef: terumato shel ketav ha'et hamaskili—ha'arakhot vesikumim], lecture at the World Congress of Jewish Studies (Jerusalem, 1997).

Perl, Joseph, *Al mahut kat haḥasidim* [On the Essence of the Sect of Hasidim], ed. A. Rubinstein (Jerusalem, 1977).

——*Megaleh temirin* [Revealer of Hidden Things] (Prague, 1838).

Pines, M., *The History of Yiddish Literature* [Korot sifrut yidish] (Ramat Gan, 1981).

Popkin, Jeremy D., *Revolutionary News: The Press in France 1789–1799* (Durham, NC, 1990).

——*The Right-Wing Press in France, 1792–1800* (Chapel Hill, NC, 1980).

PRILUTSKI, NOAH, 'Bibliographical Notes' [Bibliologishe notitsn], *Yivo bleter*, 1 (1931), 419–22.

——'The Unknown Old Yiddish Poet Yente bat Yitzhak' [Di umbekante altyidishe dikhterin yente bat yitzhak], *Yivo bleter*, 13 (1938), 36–52.

——'The Yiddish Consonant' [Der yidisher konsonantizm] (Warsaw, 1917).

RABINOVITS, MIKHAL, 'The Role of Initials in the Hebrew Language and in Understanding Literary Sources' [Ḥelkam shel rashei hatevot balashon ha'ivrit uvehavanat mekorot sifrutiyim], *Leshonenu*, 17 (1951), 90–4.

RABINOVITS, NATHAN NETA, *On the Printing of the Talmud: The History of the Printing of the Talmud* [Ma'amar al hadpasat hatalmud: toledot hadpasat hatalmud] (Jerusalem, 1952).

RAPPEL, DOV, 'Bibliography of Jewish Letter Collections' [Bibliografiyah shel igronot yehudiyim], *Sinai*, 57/113 (1994), 53–79, 134–62.

——'The Bookstore as an Educational Institution for the Jewish Maskil' [Ḥanut hasefarim kemosad ḥinukhi lamaskil hayehudi], in id. (ed.), *Studies in Bible and Education Presented to Professor Moshe Arend* [Meḥkarim bemikra uveḥinukh mugashim leprofesor moshe arend] (Jerusalem, 1996), 336–44.

——*The Dispute about Pilpul* [Havikuaḥ al hapilpul] (Jerusalem and Tel Aviv, 1979).

——'On the Literature of Letter Collections' [Al sifrut ha'igronot], *Meḥkarei yerushalayim besifrut ivrit*, 13 (1952), 119–35.

RAVITZKY, AVIEZER, *Zionism and Jewish Religious Radicalism* [Hakets hameguleh umedinat hayehudim: meshiḥiyut, tsiyonut, veradikalism dati beyisra'el] (Tel Aviv, 1993).

RAVNITZKY, JOSHUA CHONE, *A Generation and its Authors: Notes and Memories of the Authors of My Generation* [Dor vesoferav: reshimot vedivrei zikhronot al soferei dori], 2 vols (Tel Aviv, 1938).

RAV TSA'IR *see* TCHERNOWITZ, HAYIM

RAZ-KRAKOTZKIN, AMNON, 'The Censor, the Editor, and the Text: Catholic Censorship and Hebrew Literature in the Sixteenth Century' [Hatsenzor, haorekh, vehatekst: hatsenzurah hakatolit vehasifrut ha'ivrit bame'ah hasheshesreh] (Jerusalem, 2005).

REED, TERENCE JAMES, *The Classical Centre: Goethe and Weimar 1772–1832* (London, 1980).

REINER, ELHANAN, 'The Adventure in Bibliography' [Haharpatkah shebebibliografiyah], *Ha'arets, Sefarim* supplement (30 Mar. 1994), 9.

——'Capital, Social Class, and the Study of Torah: The *Kloiz* in Jewish Society in Eastern Europe in the Seventeenth and Eighteenth Centuries' [Hon, ma'amad hevrati, vetalmud torah: hakloiz baḥevrah hayehudit bemizraḥ eiropah bame'ot ha-17 reha-18], *Zion*, 58 (1993), 287–328.

——'Changes in the Yeshivas of Poland and Germany during the Sixteenth and Seventeenth Centuries and the Dispute about *Pilpul*' [Temurot beyeshivot polin ve'ashkenaz bame'ot ha-16 veha-17 vehavikuaḥ al hapilpul], in Israel

Bartal, Chava Turniansky, and Ezra Mendelssohn (eds), *The Jubilee Book of Chone Shmeruk* [Sefer hayoval lekhone shmeruk] (Jerusalem, 1993), 9–81.

REYNOLDS, LEIGHTON DURHAM, and NIGEL GUY WILSON, *Scribes and Scholars: A Guide to the Transmission of Greek and Latin Literature*, 2nd edn (Oxford, 1986).

RICHARZ, MONIKA, *Der Eintritt in die akademischen Berufe. Jüdische Studenten und Akademiker in Deutschland 1678–1848* (Tübingen, 1974).

RIEGLER, MICHAEL, 'The Colophon of Medieval Hebrew Manuscripts as a Historical Source' [Hakolofon bekitvei hayad ha'ivriyim miyemei habeinayim kemakor histori] (doctoral dissertation, Hebrew University of Jerusalem, 1995).

—— 'Were the Yeshivas in Spain a Centre for the Copying of Books?' [Ha'im hayu hayeshivot besefarad merkaz leha'atakat sefarim?], *Shenaton hamishpat ha'ivri*, 18–19 (1992–4), 411–26.

RINGELBLUM, EMANUEL, 'Johann Anton Krieger: Printer of Jewish Books in Nowy Dwor' [Johann Anton Krieger: der neihofer druker fun hebreishe seforim], *Yivo bleter*, 7 (1934), 88–109.

RIVKIND, ISAAC, 'History of Hebrew Printing in Poland' [Letoledot hadefus ha'ivri bepolin], *Kiryat sefer*, 11 (1934–5), 94–104, 384–95.

RODKINSON, MICHAEL LEVI [MICHAEL FRUMKIN], *The Stories of Michael Levi Rodkinson* [Sipurei michael levi rodkinson], ed. Gedaliyah Nigal (Jerusalem, 1989).

ROSENBLOOM, N. H., 'The First Hebrew Encyclopedia, its Author, and its Progeny' [Ha'entsiklopediyah ha'ivrit harishonah, mehabrah vehishtalshelutah], *Proceedings of the American Academy for Jewish Research*, 55 (1988), 15–65.

ROSENTHAL, JUDAH LEON, *The History of the Marbei Haskalah Society among the Jews in the Land of Russia from the Year of its Founding (1863) to 1886* [Toledot hevrat marbei haskalah beyisra'el be'erets rusiyah mishenat hitvasdutah 5624 ad shenat 5646] (St Petersburg, 1886).

ROSKIES, D., 'Aizik Meyer Dik and the Rise of Yiddish Popular Literature' (doctoral dissertation, Brandeis University, 1975)

—— *A Bridge of Longing: The Lost Art of Yiddish Storytelling*, 3rd edn (Cambridge, Mass., 1996).

ROSMAN, MOSHE, *Founder of Hasidism: A Quest for the Historical Ba'al Shem Tov* (Berkeley, Calif., 1966).

—— 'On the History of a Historical Source: *Shivhei habesht* and its Editing' [Letoledotav shel makor histori: sefer shivhei habesht ve'arikhato], *Zion*, 58 (1993), 180–3.

ROTH, CECIL, 'List of Books from the Commercial House of Rabbi Menasseh ben Israel' [Reshimat sefarim mibeit misharo shel r. menasheh ben yisra'el], *Areshet*, 2 (1960), 413–14.

—— 'On the Catalogue Published by Abraham Ya'ari', *Kiryat sefer*, 24 (1947–8), 85–6.

ROZENBERG, JUDAH YUDL, *Hagolem miprag uma'asim niflaim aherim* [The Golem of Prague and Other Marvellous Stories], ed. E. Yassif (Jerusalem, 1991).

—— *Sefer niflaot hazohar* [The Wonders of the Zohar] (Montreal, 1927).

ROZHNI, JOSEPH, 'The Epistle on the Elevation of the Soul by Rabbi Israel Ba'al Shem Tov: Sources and Comments' [Igeret 'aliyat neshamah' lerabi yisra'el ba'al shem tov: mekorot vehe'arot] (Master's thesis, Hebrew University of Jerusalem, 1998).

RUDERMAN, DAVID, *A Valley of Vision: The Heavenly Journey of Abraham ben Hananiah Yagel* (Philadelphia, 1990).

SADAN, DOV, *Touchstones* [Avnei bedek] (Tel Aviv, 1965).

SALMON, JOSEPH, 'Ahad Ha'am and Benei Moshe: A False Experience?' [Ahad ha'am uvenei mosheh: nisayon shelo hitsliyah?], in Zeev Gries, Haim Kreisel, and Boaz Huss (eds), *Abundance of Dew* [Shefa tal], *Studies in Jewish Thought and Culture Presented to Beracha Sack* (Jerusalem, 2004), 291–301.

SAMUEL BEN ABRAHAM ZARFATI, *Nimukei shmuel* [The Reasoning of Samuel] (Amsterdam, 1718).

SANDLER, PERETZ, *The Explanation of the Torah by Moses Mendelssohn and his Party: Its Formation and Influence* [Habe'ur latorah shel moshe mendelsohn vesiyato: hithavuto vehashpa'ato], 2nd edn (Jerusalem, 1984).

SATANOW, ISAAC, *Sefer hamidot* [The Book of Virtues] (Berlin, 1784).

SCHÄFER, PETER, *Synopses of Heikhalot Literature* [Sinopses lesifrut haheikhalot] (Tübingen, 1981).

SCHAPIRA, ISRAEL, *Commentators on Rashi on the Pentateuch* [Parshanei rashi al hatorah] (New York, 1940).

SCHATZ-UFFENHEIMER, RIVKA, *Hasidism as Mysticism: Quietistic Elements in Eighteenth-Century Hasidic Thought* (Princeton, NJ, 1968).

SCHIDORSKY, D., *Library and Book in the Land of Israel in the Late Ottoman Period* [Sifriyah vesefer be'erets yisra'el beshilhei hatekufah ha'otomanit] (Jerusalem, 1990).

SCHIRMAN, H., *The History of Hebrew Poetry in Christian Spain and Southern France*, revised and completed E. Fleischer (Jerusalem, 1997).

SCHOLEM, GERSHOM, 'And the Mystery Remains Intact' [Vehata'alumah be'einah omedet], *Behinot*, 8 (1957), 79–95; repr. in id., *Researches in Shabateanism*, 250–87.

—— *Ascend to Scholem* [Alu leshalom] (Jerusalem, 1937).

—— *Bibliographica Kabbalistica* (Leipzig, 1927).

—— *From Berlin to Jerusalem: Memoirs of my Youth* (New York, 1981).

—— *Kabbalah* (Jerusalem, 1974).

—— 'On the Problem of the Book of the System of the Divinity and its Commentators' [Leba'ayot sefer ma'arekhet ha'elohut umefarshav], *Kiryat sefer*, 21 (1944 5), 293 5.

—— 'The People of the Book' [Am hasefer], in id., *Another Thing: Chapters on*

Heritage and Renaissance [Od davar: pirkei morashah vetehiyah], ed. A. Schapira (Tel Aviv, 1990), 153–61.

——'R. Eliyahu Hacohen Haitamari and Shabateanism' [R. eliyahu hakohen haitamari vehashabta'ut], in *The Jubilee Book of Alexander Marx* [Sefer hayovel le'aleksander marks], Hebrew section (New York, 1950), 451–70.

—— *Researches in Shabateanism* [Mehkarei shabeta'ut] (Tel Aviv, 1992).

—— Response to Ya'ari on 'And the Mystery Remains Intact', *Behinot*, 9 (1955), 80–4; repr. in id., *Researches in Shabateanism*, 250–87.

—— *Shabetai tsevi* (Heb.), 2nd edn, 2 vols (Tel Aviv, 1973); English edn: *Sabbatai Sevi, The Mystical Messiah, 1626–1676* (Princeton, NJ, 1975).

——'Some Reflections on Wissenschaft des Judentums' [Mitokh hirhurim al hokhmat yisra'el], in id., *Devarim bego*, ed. A. Shapira (Tel Aviv, 1976), 385–403.

—— *Studies and Texts Concerning the History of Shabateanism and its Metamorphoses* [Mehkarim umekorot letoledot hashabeta'ut vegilguleiha] (Jerusalem, 1974).

—— *Walter Benjamin: The Story of a Friendship* (Philadelphia, 1981).

SCHORSCH, ISMAR, *From Text to Context: The Turn to History in Modern Judaism* (Hanover, 1994).

SCHOTTENLOHER, KARL, *Books and the Western World: A Cultural History* (Jefferson, NC, 1989).

SCHWARZBAUM, HAIM, *Studies in Jewish and World Folklore* (Berlin, 1968).

SHAKED, GERSHON, *Books and their Audience: Four Chapters in Reception Theory* [Yetsirot venim'aneihem: arba'ah perakim betorat hahitkablut] (Tel Aviv, 1987).

—— *Modern Hebrew Literature 1880–1970* [Hasifrut ha'ivrit hahadashah 1880–1970], 5 vols (Jerusalem and Tel Aviv, 1988).

SHALHAV, SHULAMIT, 'Ben-Avigdor and "Penny Books": The Publishing and Commercial Move' [Ben-avigdor vesifrei agorah': hamahalakh hamoli vehamishari], *Sadan*, 4(2000), 281–300.

——'From Intentions to Deeds: A First Chapter in the History of Modern Secular Hebrew Publishing' [Mikavanot lema'asim: perek rishon letoledot hamolut ha'ivrit hahilonit] (Master's thesis, Tel Aviv University, 1994).

SHAPIRA, HAYIM ELEAZAR, *Divrei torah* [Words of Torah] (Jerusalem, 1980).

—— *Minhat elazar* [The Offering of Eleazar] (Mucachevo and Pressburg, 1902–30).

—— *Sha'ar yisakhar* [The Gate of Yissakhar] (Mucachevo, 1938).

SHAPIRA, HAYIM NAHMAN, *The History of Modern Hebrew Literature* [Toledot hasifrut ha'ivrit hahadashah] (Tel Aviv, 1967).

SHARPE, KEVIN M., *Reading Revolutions: The Politics of Reading in Early Modern England* (New Haven and London, 2000).

SHARVIT, SIMON, 'The Custom of Reading *The Ethics of the Fathers* on Shabbat and the History of the *Baraitot* That Were Appended To It' [Minhag hakeriyah shel avot beshabat vetoledot habaraitot shenispehu lah be'ikvotav], *Bar Ilan*, 13 (1976), 169–78.

SHATZKY, JACOB, *A Cultural History of the Enlightenment in Lithuania: From Ancient Times to Hibat Zion* [Kultur geshikhte fun der haskalah in lita: fun alteste tseitn biz ḥibat tsion] (Buenos Aires, 1950).

——*History of the Jews of Warsaw* [Geshikhte fun yidn in warshe], 3 vols (New York, 1947–53).

——'On the History of Jewish Printing Shops in Poland: A Bibliographical Note' [Tsu der geshikhte fun di yiddishe drukerien in polin (bibliografishe notitz)], *Yivo bleter*, 6 (1934), 178–82.

——'The Yiddish Editions of the Play *War on Peace*, by Eliezer Pavir, "The Book of the Greatness of Joseph, A Bibliographical Sketch"' [Di yiddishe oisgabes fun der drame *Milḥamah beshalom* le'eli'ezer pavir, 'Sefer gedulat yosef, a bibliografisher etude'], in id. (ed.), *Arkhive fer der geshikhte fun yiddishen teater un drame* (Vilna, 1930), 151–8.

SHAVIT, ZOHAR, 'The Function of Yiddish Literature in the Development of Children's Literature in Hebrew' [Hafunktsiyah shel sifrut yidish bahitpatḥut shel sifrut hayeladim ha'ivrit], *Hasifrut*, NS 10/3–4 (Summer 1986), 148–53.

——*Poetics of Children's Literature* (Athens, Ga. and London, 1986); Hebrew edn, revised and enlarged, with B. Even-Zohar, *Childhood Story: Introduction to the Poetics of Children's Literature* [Ma'aseh yaldut: mavo lepo'etikah shel sifrut yeladim] (Tel Aviv, 1996).

——'The Rise and Fall of the Literary Centres in Europe and America and the Establishment of the Centre in the Land of Israel' [Aliyatam venefilatam shel hamerkazim hasifrutiyim be'eiropah uve'amerikah vehakamat hamerkaz be'erets yisra'el], *Iyunim betekumat yisra'el*, 4 (1994), 423–39; abridged version published in ead. (ed.), *The History of the Jewish Community in Erets Israel since 1882*, pt. 1: *The Construction of Hebrew Culture in Erets Israel* [Toledot hayishuv hayehudi be'erets yisra'el me'az ha'aliyah harishonah: beniyatah shel tarbut ivrit] (Jerusalem, 1999), 43–56.

——and HANS HEINO EWERS (eds), *Deutsch-Jüdische Kinder und Jugendliteratur von der Haskala bis 1945* (Stuttgart, 1996).

SHEFI, NA'AMAH, *German in Hebrew: Translations from German in the Hebrew Yishuv 1882–1948* [Germanit be'ivrit: tirgumim migermanit bayishuv ha'ivri 1882–1948] (Jerusalem, 1998).

SHEM TOV GAON, *Kuntres harav shem tov gaon* [The Booklet of R. Shem Tov Gaon], as transmitted by Solomon ben Adret in *Likutim mirav ḥai gaon* [A Compilation of Rav Hai Gaon's Writings] (Warsaw, 1798).

SHMERLER, ELIYAHU TSEVI, *Toledot rabad* [The History of Rabad] (Lemberg, 1890).

SHMERUK, CHONE, 'The Eastern European Versions of the *Tsena urena* (1706–1850)' [Di mizraḥ eiropishe nusḥaot fun der Tsena urena (1786–1850)], in Lucy S. Dawidowicz et al. (eds), *For Max Weinrich on His Seventieth Birthday Studies in Jewish Languages, Literature, and Society* [Max Weinrich tsi zein zibentsiksten geboirn tog] (London, 1964), 195–211; repr. in Hebrew in Shmeruk, *Yiddish Literature in Poland*, 147–64.

——'The First Jewish Woman Author in Poland: Rivkah Bat Meir Tiktiner and her Works' [Hasoferet hayehudit harishonah bepolin: rivkah bat me'ir tiktiner vehibureiha], *Gal-ed*, 4–5 (1979), 13–23; repr. in id., *Yiddish Literature in Poland*, 56–69, and in M. Wunder (ed.), *The Crown of Rebecca: Four Books of Women's Prayers and 'Meneket rivkah'* [Ateret rivkah: arba'ah sifrei tehinot nashim vesefer 'meneket rivkah'] (Jerusalem, 1992), 148–60.

——*Illustrations of Yiddish Literature in the Sixteenth to Seventeenth Centuries* [Ha'iyurim lesifrut yidish bame'ot hashesh-esre sheva-esreh] (Jerusalem, 1986).

——*Yiddish Literature: Chapters in its History* [Sifrut yidish: perakim letoledoteiha] (Tel Aviv, 1978).

——*Yiddish Literature in Poland* [Sifrut yidish bepolin] (Jerusalem, 1981).

——(ed.), *Biblical Plays in Yiddish, 1697–1750* [Mahazot mikra'iyim beyidish, 1697–1750] (Jerusalem, 1979).

——(ed.), *Correspondence between S. J. Abramovits, H. N. Bialik, and Y. C. Ravnitzky, 1905–1908* [Halifat mikhtavim bein s. y. abramovits levein h. n. bialik ve y. c. ravnitsky beshanim 1905–1908] (Jerusalem, 1976).

——and ISRAEL BARTAL, 'The Trials of Moses: The First Geographical Book in Yiddish and a Description of the Land of Israel by Moses the son of Abraham the Proselyte' [Tela'ot moshe: sefer hage'ografiyah harishon beyidish vetiyur erets yisra'el shel moshe bar avraham hager], *Cathedra*, 40 (1986), 121–37.

——and CHAVA TURNIANSKY (eds), *Yiddish Literature in the Nineteenth Century: An Anthology of Yiddish Literary Research and Criticism in the Soviet Union* [Di yiddishe literatur in neintseten yorhundert: zamlung fun yiddisher literatur—forshung un kritik in ratn—farband] (Jerusalem, 1993).

SHOHET, AZRIEL, *The Institution of the Official Rabbinate* [Mosad harabanut mita'am] (Haifa, 1986).

——*With the Change of Epochs: The Beginning of Haskalah in German Jewry* [Im hilufei tekufot: reshit hahaskalah beyahadut germaniyah] (Jerusalem, 1961).

SHOHETMAN, BARUKH, 'Review of Jacob Shatzky', *Kiryat sefer*, 28 (1952–3), 353–4.

SHPIELMAN, JACOB MEIR, *Tal orot* [Dew of Lights], 4 vols (Lvov, 1876–85).

SHULVASS, MOSES AVIGDOR, *From East to West: The Westward Migration of Jews from Eastern Europe During the Seventeenth and Eighteenth Centuries* (Detroit, 1971).

SLATKINE, MENAHEM MENDEL, *The Beginnings of Bibliography in Hebrew Literature* [Reshit habibliografiyah basifrut ha'ivrit] (Tel Aviv, 1958).

——*From the Memoirs of a Lithuanian Rabbi 5,548 Years from the Creation: Selected Chapters* [Misefer hazikhronot shel rav litai 5548 tukin laberiyah: perakim nivharim] (Paris, 1949).

——*Titles of Hebrew Books According to their Type, Nature, and Objectives* [Shemot hasefarim ha'ivriyim lefi sugeihem hashonim, tekhunatam veye'udam], 2 vols (Neuchâtel and Tel Aviv, 1950–4).

SLONIMSKY, HAYIM ZELIG [HAZAS], Letters, published by H. R. Rabinovitz in
    Areshet, 4 (1966), 447–60.
SLOUSCHZ, NAHUM, *A History of the New Hebrew Literature* [Korot hasifrut
    ha'ivrit haḥadashah], 3 vols (Warsaw, 1906).
SLUTSKY, JUDAH, *The Jewish Russian Press in the Nineteenth Century* [Ha'itonut
    hayehudit-rusit bame'ah hatesha-esreh] (Jerusalem, 1971).
—— 'Migration as a Factor in the History of the Jews in Eastern Europe until 1881'
    [Hahagirah kegorem betoledot hayehudim bemizraḥ eiropah ad 1881], in *The
    Wanderings and Migrations of Israel among the Nations* [Nedudei amim vehagirah
    betoledot yisra'el veha'amim], proceedings of the Fifteenth Conference of the
    Israel Historical Society (Jerusalem, 1993), 67–79.
SOKOLOW, NAHUM, *Men* [Ishim] (Jerusalem, 1958).
SOLOVEITCHIK, HAYIM, *Responsa as a Historical Source* [She'elot uteshuvot
    kemakor histori] (Jerusalem, 1991).
—— 'Rupture and Reconstruction: The Contemporary Orthodoxy', *Tradition*, 28/4
    (1994), 64–130.
SPEKTOR, MORDECAI, *Der Hoiz Friend*, 5 vols (Warsaw, 1894–6).
SPUFFORD, MARGARET, *Small Books and Pleasant Histories: Popular Fiction and its
    Readership in Seventeenth-Century England* (Cambridge, 1981).
STAMPFER, SHAUL, 'Knowledge of Reading and Writing among the Jews of
    Eastern Europe in the Modern Period: Context, Sources, and Consequences'
    [Yedi'at kero ukhtov etsel yehudei mizraḥ eiropah batekufah haḥadashah: hek-
    sher, mekorot, vehashlakhot], in S. Almog et al. (eds), *Changing Patterns in
    Modern Jewish History: Collected Essays in Honour of Shmuel Ettinger* [Temurot
    bahistoriyah hayehudit haḥadashah: kovets likhvod shmuel etinger] (Jerusalem,
    1988), 459–83.
—— 'Rabbi Hayim of Volozhin and his Approbations' [Rabi hayim mivolozhin
    vehaskamotav], *Alei sefer*, 4 (1977), 165–7.
STANISLAWSKI, M., *For Whom Do I Toil? Judah Leib Gordon and the Crisis of
    Russian Jewry* (New York, 1988).
—— *Tsar Nicholas I and the Jews: The Transformation of Jewish Society in Russia,
    1825–1855* (Philadelphia, 1983).
STEINBERG, SIEGFRIED HENRY, *Five Hundred Years of Printing*, rev. J. Trevitt
    (London, 1996).
STEINSCHNEIDER, MORITZ, *Jewish Literature* [Sifrut yisra'el] trans. into Hebrew
    by Zvi Malter, with new additions and corrections by the author (Warsaw, 1897).
—— *Lectures on Hebrew Manuscripts* [Hartsaot al kitvei yad ivriyim] (Jerusalem,
    1965).
STRAYER, JOSEPH REESE, 'Review of L. White Jr., *Medieval Religion and
    Technology*', *Technology and Culture*, 21 (1980), 82–5.
SUSSMANN, JACOB, 'Manuscripts and Textual Traditions of the Mishnah' [Kitvei
    yad umasorot nusaḥ shel hamishnah], in *Proceedings of the Seventh World*

Congress of Jewish Studies [Divrei hakongres ha'olami hashevi'i lemada'ei haya-hadut] (Jerusalem, 1981), 215–50.

TANUGI, JUDAH, *Erets yehudah* [The Land of Judah] (Leghorn, 1797).

TA-SHMA, ISRAEL, *The Revealed Within the Hidden: Towards the Study of the Remnants of Halakhah in the Book of the Zohar* [Hanigleh shebanistar: leheker shikei hahalakhah besefer hazohar] (Tel Aviv, 2001).

——'Tosefot gornish', *Sinai*, 68 (1971), 153–61.

TAYLOR, ANNE, *Laurence Oliphant, 1829–1888* (Oxford, 1982).

TCHERNOWITZ, HAYIM [RAV TSA'IR], *Complete Works: A Collection of Memoirs, Portraits, and Evaluations* [Kol kitvei rav tsa'ir: masekhet zikhronot, partsufim, veha'arakhot], 2 vols, vol. ii: *The Sages of Odessa* [Hakhmei odesa] (New York, 1945).

——*History of the Halakhah* [Toledot hahalakhah], 4 vols (New York, 1934–40).

——*The History of Halakhic Decision-Makers* [Toledot haposekim], 3 vols (New York, 1946–7).

——'On the History of the *Shulhan arukh* and its Diffusion' [Letoledot hashulhan arukh vehitpashtuto], *Hashiloah*, 4 (1898), 303–10, 394–404, 515–7; 5 (1899), 127–36, 430–40; 6 (1900), 128–36, 233–40, 319–28, 517–30.

TISHBY, ISAIAH, 'The Conception of Haskalah and its Estimation in the Writings of Tsevi Hermann Schapira' [Tefisat hahaskalah veha'arakhatah bikhetavim shel tsevi herman shapira], in E. Fleischer (ed.), *Studies in Hebrew Literature Presented to Simon Halkin* [Mehkarei sifrut mugashim leshimon halkin] (Jerusalem, 1973), 263–80; repr. in Tishby, *Studies in Kabbalah and its Offshoots*, ii. 565–82.

——*Studies in Kabbalah and its Offshoots* [Hikrei kabalah usheluhoteiha], 3 vols (Jerusalem, 1993).

——'Tsevi Hermann Schapira as a Haskalah Writer, the Author of *Masekhet hasidim* (*Masekhet shirayim*)' [Tsevi herman shapira kesofer haskalah, ba'al 'masekhet hasidim' ('masekhet shirayim')], *Molad*, NS 4/26 (1972), 556–74, 696–712; repr. in id., *Studies in Kabbalah and its Offshoots*, ii. 524–64.

TOLEDANO, JACOB MOSES, *Canopy* [Apirion] (Jerusalem, 1905).

TRITHEMIUS, JOHANNES, *In Praise of Scribes / De Laude Scriptorum*, ed. and introd. Klaus Arnold, trans. Roland Behrendt (Lawrence, Ka., 1974).

TSAMARIYON, TSEMAH, *Hame'asef: The First Modern Periodical in Hebrew* [Hame'asef: ketav ha'et hamoderni harishon be'ivrit] (Tel Aviv, 1988).

TURNER, VICTOR, 'Passage, Margins, and Poverty: Religious Symbols of Communitas', in id., *Drama, Fields, and Metaphors: Symbolic Action in Human Society*, 5th edn (Ithaca and London, 1987), 231–70.

TURNIANSKY, CHAVA, 'The Grace After Meals and Sabbath Hymns in Yiddish' [Habentsherel vehazemirot beyidish], *Alei sefer*, 10 (1982), 51–92.

——'The History of the Yiddish Translation of the Pentateuch and its Compilers' [Letoledot hateitsh-humesh mit hiber], in *Literary Reflections: Lectures*

Delivered at an Evening in Honour of Dov Sadan on his Eighty-Fifth Birthday
[Iyunim besifrut: devarim shene'emru ba'erev likhvod dov sadan bimelot lo she-
monim veḥamesh shanah] (Jerusalem, 1988).

TURNIANSKY, CHAVA, 'A Maskilic Version of *Tsena urena*: An Unknown
Manuscript of Herz Homberg' [Nusaḥ maskili shel 'tsena urena': ketav yad bilti
yadua shel herts homberg], *Hasifrut*, 2 (1969–70), 835–41.

——'*Mikra mefurash* by Eleazar Zussman Rudelsum: An Exceptional Book for the
Study of the Pentateuch in Yiddish' [Mikra mefarash le'elazar zusman rudelsum: sefer yotse dofen lelimud haḥumash beyidish], in S. Japhet (ed.), *Scripture
and its Commentators (A Memorial to Sarah Kamin)* [Hamikra umefarshav (sefer
zikaron lesarah kamin)] (Jerusalem, 1994), 497–517.

——'The *Tsena urena* of Herz Homberg' [Hatsena urena shel herts homberg]
(doctoral dissertation, Hebrew University of Jerusalem, 1967).

UNGERFELD, MOSES, 'Between Letteris and Smolenskin' [Bein leteris lesmolen-
skin], *Moznayim*, NS 23/46 (1966), 250.

URBACH, EPHRAIM E., 'Jacob Bernais, his Judaism, and his Influence on Jewish
Studies' [Ya'akov berna'is, yahaduto vehashpa'ato al mada'ei hayahdut], in id.,
Researches in Jewish Studies [Meḥkarim bemada'ei hayahadut], 2 vols (Jerusalem,
1998), ii. 833–50; 1st published in *Tarbiz*, 51 (1982), 107–24.

VAN GENNEP, ARNOLD, *The Rites of Passage* (Chicago, 1960).

VELAY-VALLANTIN, CATHERINE, 'Tales as a Mirror: Perrault in the Bibliothèque
Bleue', in Roger Chartier (ed.), *The Culture of Print: Power and the Uses of Print
in Early Modern Europe* (Princeton, NJ, 1989), 92–135.

VENTURA, ELIYAHU BEN ABRAHAM, *Kokhba deshavit* [The Comet] (Salonika,
1799).

VINOGRAD, YESHAYAHU, *The Treasure of the Hebrew Book* [Otsar hasefer ha'ivri],
2 vols (Jerusalem, 1995).

WALSHAM, ALEXANDRA, '"Domme Preachers"? Post-Reformation English
Catholicism and the Culture of Print', *Past and Present*, 168 (Aug. 2000), 72–123.

WAQUET, FRANÇOISE, 'Qu'est-ce que la république des lettres? Essai de séman-
tique historique', *Bibliothèque de l'École des Chartes*, 147 (1989), 473–501.

WEBER, MAX, *The Protestant Ethic and the Spirit of Capitalism* (London, 1930).

WEILL, GEORGES, *Le Journal: Origines, évolution et rôle de la presse périodique* (Paris,
1934).

WEINER, SAMUEL, *The Congregation of Moses* [Kehilat mosheh] (Petrograd,
1893–1918).

WEISSLER, CHAVA, 'The Traditional Piety of Ashkenazi Women', in A. Green
(ed.), *Jewish Spirituality*, 2 vols (New York, 1987), ii. 247–75.

——*Voices of the Matriarchs: Listening to the Prayers of Early Modern Jewish Women*
(Boston, 1998).

WERSES, SHMUEL, *Awaken My People! Haskalah Literature in Modern Times*
[Hakitsah ami! Sifrut hahaskalah be'idan hamodernizatsiyah] (Jerusalem, 2001).

—— 'A Bibliographer of our Literature' [Bibliograf shel sifrutenu], in *In the Tents of the Book* [Be'ohalei sefer] (Jerusalem, 1967), 8–10.

—— 'Erter's "Transmigration of the Soul" in the Yiddish Version of Isaac Meir Dik' [Gilgul nefesh shel erter, begilgulo leyidish shel yitshak meir dik], *Huliyot*, 2 (Summer 1994), 29–49; repr. in id., *From Language to Language: Compositions and their Metamorphosis in our Literature* [Milashon el lashon: yetsirot vegilguleihen besifrutenu] (Jerusalem, 1996), 211–31.

—— 'The Expulsion from Spain and Portugal in Yiddish Literature' [Gerush sefarad veportugal besifrut yidish], *Pe'amim*, 69 (1997), 115–59.

—— 'From Changes of Language to Changes of Meaning: The Play *The Kingdom of Saul* in Yiddish Translation' [Mihilufei lashon lehilufei mashma'ut: hamahazeh malkhut sha'ul betirgumo leyidish], *Huliyot*, 6 (Autumn 2000), 55–78.

—— 'The Jewish Maskil as a Young Man' [Hamaskil hayehudi ke'ish tsa'ir], in id., *Awaken My People!*, 88–101.

—— 'Mendele in the Mirror of Hebrew Criticism' [Mendele bere'i habikoret ha'ivrit], in id., *The Critique of Criticism* [Bikoret habikoret] (Tel Aviv, 1982), 34–62.

—— 'A Monument for Yiddish Literature: Scholars in the Soviet Union' [A denkmal far yidisher literatur: forshers in ratn ferband], *Di Goldene Keit*, 137 (1993), 205–16.

—— 'On Scholarship in Haskalah Literature Today' [Al mehkar sifrut hahaskalah beyameinu], *Yedi'on ha'igud ha'olami lemada'ei hayahadut*, 25 (1985), 19–37; 16 (1986), 21–47; 17 (1987), 41–6; repr. and expanded in id., *Trends in and Forms of Haskalah Literature* [Megamot vetsurot besifrut hahaskalah], 356–412.

—— 'On Isaac Satanow and his Work, *The Proverbs of Asaf*' [Al yitshak satanov vehiburo 'mishlei asaf'], *Tarbiz*, 32 (1963), 370–92; repr. with corrections and additions in id., *Trends in and Forms of Haskalah Literature*, 163–86.

—— 'The Paths of Autobiography in the Haskalah Period' [Darkhei ha'oto-biografiyah bitekufat hahaskalah], *Gilyonot*, 17 (1945), 175–83; repr. in id., *Trends in and Forms of Haskalah Literature*, 249–60.

—— 'The Right Hand Pushes Away, the Left Brings Close: On the Relationship between Haskalah Writers and the Yiddish Language' [Yad yamin dohah, yad smol mekarevet: leyahasam shel soferei hahaskalah leleshon yidish], *Huliyot*, 5 (1999), 9–49; repr. in id., *Awaken My People!*, 238–80.

—— 'The Satirical Method of Joseph Perl' [Shitat hasatirah shel yosef perl], in id., *The Story and its Foundation* [Sipur veshorsho: iyunim behitpathut haprozah ha'ivrit] (Ramat Gan, 1971), 45–9.

—— 'Tensions between Languages in and around the Maskilic Periodical *Hame'asef*' [Hametahim habein-leshoniyim bikhtav ha'et hamaskili hame'asef usevivav], *Dapim lemehkar besifrut*, 11 (1998), 29–69; repr. in id., *Awaken My People!*, 193–237.

—— *Trends in and Forms of Haskalah Literature* [Megamot vetsurot besifrut hahaskalah] (Jerusalem, 1990).

WERSES, SHMUEL 'The Voice of Women in the Yiddish Weekly *Kol mevasser*' [Kol ha'ishah beshevu'on beyidish *Kol mevasser*], *Ḥuliyot*, 4 (Summer 1997), 53–82; repr. in id., *Awaken, My People!*, 321–50.

WETZLER, ISAAC, *The Libes Briv of Isaac Wetzler*, ed. and trans. M. M. Faierstein (Atlanta, Ga., 1996).

WHITE, LYNN, JR., *Medieval Religion and Technology* (Berkeley, Calif., 1987).

WIENER, MAX, *The Jewish Religion in the Period of the Emancipation* [Hadat hayehudit bitekufat ha'emantsipatsiyah] (Jerusalem, 1974).

WITTMANN, REINHARD, 'Was There a Reading Revolution at the End of the Eighteenth Century?', in G. Cavallo and Roger Chartier (eds), *A History of Reading in the West* (Amherst, Mass., 1999), 284–312.

WODZINSKI, MARCIN, 'Jakob Tugenhold and the Maskilik Defense of Hasidism', *Gal-ed*, 18 (2002), 13–42.

WUNDER, MEIR, *Encyclopedia of the Sages of Galicia* [Entsikopediyah leḥakhmei galitsiyah] (Jerusalem, 1989).

YA'ARI, ABRAHAM, *Belles Lettres in Hebrew (Original and in Translation) from Rabbi Moses Hayim Luzzatto to the Present (1729–1926): A List of Books Found in the Library* [Hasifrut hayafah be'ivrit (hamekorit vehameturgemet) mi'r. moshe hayim lutsato ad hayom hazeh (1729–1926); reshimat hasefarim hanimtsa'im beveit hasefarim] (Jerusalem, 1927).

——'Bibliographical Gleanings 1: On the History of Hebrew Printing in Novy Dvor [Sarmusel]' [Likutim bibliografiyim 1: letoledot hadefus ha'ivri benovy dvor], *Kiryat sefer*, 10 (1933–4), 371–2.

——'Bibliographical Gleanings 3: *The Prince and the Monk* in Yiddish' [Likutim bibliografiyim 3: sefer ben hamelekh vehanazir beyudit], *Kiryat sefer*, 10 (1933–4), 376–8.

——'Bibliographical Gleanings 8: For a Bibliography of Isaac Meir Dik' [Likutim bibliografiyim 8: lebibliografiyah shel isaac meir dik], *Kiryat sefer*, 11 (1934–5), 515–20.

——'Bibliographical Gleanings 10: Three Translations of *Shivḥei habesht* into Yiddish' [Likutim bibliografiyim 10: sheloshah tirgumim shel shivḥei habesht leyudit], *Kiryat sefer*, 12 (1935–6), 129–31.

——'Bibliographical Gleanings 11: The Hebrew Printing House in Laszczów' [Likutim bibliografiyim 11: hadefus ha'ivri belaszczov], *Kiryat sefer*, 12 (1935–6), 238–47.

——'Bibliographical Gleanings 12: Spelling Rules for the Yiddish Language from the Year 1819' [Likutim bibliografiyim 12: kelalei ketiv lelashon yudit mishnat 5579], *Kiryat sefer*, 12 (1935–6), 248–9.

——'Bibliographical Gleanings 13: Publications of the Play *The Greatness of David and the Kingdom of Saul*' [Likutim bibliografiyim 13: hotsaot hamaḥazeh gedulat david umelukhat shaul], *Kiryat sefer*, 12 (1935–6), 384–8.

——'Bibliographical Gleanings 18: Three Translations of *Igeret ba'alei ḥayim* into

Yiddish' [Likutim bibliografiyim 18: sheloshah tirgumim shel igeret ba'alei ḥayim leyudit], *Kiryat sefer*, 13 (1936–7), 394–8.

——'Bibliographical Gleanings 19: An Unknown Yiddish Translation of *Ḥovot hale-vavot*' [Likutim bibliografiyim 19: tirgum yidi bilti yadua shel ḥovot halevavot], *Kiryat sefer*, 13 (1936–7), 398–410.

——'Bibliographical Gleanings 36: The Printing Shop of the Rebbetzen Yehudit Rosanis in Lvov' [Likutim bibliografiyim 36: defusah shel harabanit yehudit rosanis belevov], *Kiryat sefer*, 17 (1940), 95–108.

——'Bibliographical Gleanings 42: Hebrew Printing in Minkovtsy' [Likutim biblio-grafiyim 42: hadefus ha'ivri beminkovits], *Kiryat sefer*, 19 (1942–3), 267–76.

——'Bibliographical Gleanings 52: Jewish Printing in Berdichev' [Likutim biblio-grafiyim 52: hadefus ha'ivri beberdichev], *Kiryat sefer*, 21 (1944–5), 100–1.

——'The Books by Isaac Meir Dik that are in Jerusalem' [Sifrei yitsḥak meir dik she-biyerushalayim], *Kiryat sefer*, 32 (1957), 76–92, 211–29.

——'Books of Jesters' [Sifrei badḥanim], *Kiryat sefer*, 35 (1960), 109–26.

——*Emblems of the Hebrew Printers* [Diglei hamadpisim ha'ivriyim] (Jerusalem, 1944).

——'From a Folk Tale to an Artistic Story: A Parallel to "And the crooked shall be made straight"' [Misipur amami lesipur omanuti: hakabalah le 'vehayah he'akov lemishor'], *Davar*, 13/40, sabbath and holiday supplement 29 Av (July 1938), unpaginated; repr. in Y. Friedlander (ed.), *Vehayah he'akov lemishor: Essays on a Novel by S. J. Agnon* [Al 'vehayah he'akuv kemishor': masot al novelah leshai agnon] (Tel Aviv, 1993), 21–7.

——'The Hebrew Press in Moghilev' [Hadefus ha'ivri bemogilev], *Kiryat sefer*, 23 (1946–7), 312–13.

——*Hebrew Printing in Constantinople* [Hadefus ha'ivri bekushta] (Jerusalem, 1967).

——'Hebrew Printing in Shklov' [Hadefus ha'ivri beshklov], *Kiryat sefer*, 22 (1945–6), 49–72, 135–60.

——*In the Tents of the Book* [Be'ohalei sefer] (Jerusalem, 1939).

——*Jewish Printing in the Lands of the East* [Hadefus hayehudi be'artsot hamizraḥ] (Jerusalem, 1937).

——'The Metamorphosis of a Yiddish Poem about the Ten Commandments' [Gilgulo shel shir beyidish al aseret hadibrot], *Kiryat sefer*, 41 (1966), 397–410.

——*Mystery of a Book* [Ta'alumat sefer] (Jerusalem, 1954).

——'A Note on Heilperin's *The Council of the Four Lands in Poland and the Hebrew Book* [Va'ad arba aratsot vehasefer ha'ivri], *Kiryat sefer*, 9 (1932–3), 393–4.

——'Note on the List of Wunderbar' [He'arah al reshimat wunderbar], *Kiryat sefer*, 22 (1945–6), 84.

——'The Original Catalogue of the Printing House of Menasseh ben Israel in Amsterdam' [Katalog mekori mibeit defuso shel menasheh ben yisra'el be' amsterdam], *Kiryat sefer*, 21 (1944–5), 192–201.

YA'ARI, ABRAHAM, 'R. Eliezer Pavir and his Literary Work' [R. eli'ezer pavir umifalo hasifruti], *Kiryat sefer*, 35 (1960), 499–520.

—— 'Response to Roth', *Kiryat sefer*, 24 (1947–8), 86–8.

—— 'Response to Scholem's "And the Mystery Remains Intact"', *Behinot*, 9 (1955),
71–80.

—— 'Review of Friedberg, *History of Hebrew Printing in Poland*', *Kiryat sefer*,
9 (1932–3), 432–9.

—— 'A Story to Prove the Plethora of Hebrew Elements in the Yiddish Language'
[Sipur ma'aseh lehokhiah ribui hayesodot ha'ivriyim bileshon idish], *Kiryat
sefer*, 40 (1965), 286–92.

—— *Studies of the Book* [Mehkarei sefer] (Jerusalem, 1958).

—— 'Supplements to the Bibliography of Printing in Poland–Russia' [Tosafot labib-
liografiyah shel defusei polin–rusiyah], *Kiryat sefer*, 21 (1944–5), 298.

—— 'Supplements to the Bibliography of Printing Houses in Poland–Russia 3'
[Tosefet lebibliografiyah shel defusei polin–rusiyah 3], *Kiryat sefer*, 21 (1944–5),
298–301.

—— 'Supplements to Books of Jesters' [Miluim lesifrei badhanim], *Kiryat sefer*, 36
(1961), 264–72.

—— 'Supplements to Earlier Chapters [of the Bibliographical Gleanings]' [Miluim
leferakim kodmim], *Kiryat sefer*, 13 (1936–7), 533–8.

—— 'Supplements to the Emblems of Hebrew Printers' [Miluim lediglei hamadpisim ha'ivriyim], *Kiryat sefer*, 31 (1956), 501–6.

—— 'Two Basic Editions of *Shivhei habesht*' [Shetei mahadorot yesod shel shivhei
habesht], *Kiryat sefer*, 39 (1964), 249–72, 394–407, 552–62.

YALON, HANOKH, 'Chapters from *The Gatherer from all the Camps* by Rabbi
Solomon Almoli' [Perakim min 'hame'asaf lekol hamahanot' le r. shlomo
almoli], *Areshet*, 2 (1960), 96–108.

—— 'Tsipor (tsiper) hanefesh', *Sinai*, 14 (1944), 264–5; repr. in id., *Chapters of Speech*
[Pirkei lashon] (Jerusalem, 1971).

YASSIF, ELI, *The Hebrew Folk Tale: Its History, Genres, and Significance* [Sipur ha'am
ha'ivri: toledotav, sugav, umashma'uto] (Jerusalem, 1994).

YATES, FRANCES, 'Print Culture: The Renaissance', in ead., *Ideas and Ideals in the
North European Renaissance: Collected Essays*, 3 vols (London, 1982–4), iii. 185–92.

YUDLOV, ISAAC, 'On the Interpretation of Dreams by Rabbi Hai Gaon' [Al pitron
halomot lerav hai gaon], *Alei sefer*, 6–7 (1979), 107–20.

—— *Printers' Emblems* (Heb.) (Jerusalem, 2002).

ZALKIN, MORDECAI, *Daybreak: Haskalah and Judaism in the Russian Empire in the
Nineteenth Century* [Ba'alot hashahar: hahaskalah vehayahadut ba'imperiyah
harusit bame'ah hatesha-esreh] (Jerusalem, 2000).

ZARFATI, VIDAL, *Hasagot al perush haram* [Critiques on the Commentary of
Haram [R. Elijah Mizrahi]], printed in Samuel ben Abraham Zarfati, *Nimukei
shemuel* [The Reasonings of Samuel] (Amsterdam, 1718).

ZEIDAH, JACOB, 'Birds That Grow on Trees: The Echoes of Superstition' [Ofot hagedelim be'ilanot: hedei emunah tefelah], *Korot*, 1/7–8 (1956), 275.

ZFATMAN-BILER, SARAH, '*Ma'aseh Bukh*: Outlines for a Picture of a Genre in Old Yiddish Literature, with the Discovery of *Ma'aseh Bukh* MS Jerusalem Heb. 8°5245' [Ma'aseh bukh: kavim lidemuto shel genre besifrut yidish hayeshanah: im giluyo shel ma'aseh bukh k'y yerushalayim heb. 8°5245], *Hasifrut*, 28 (Apr. 1979), 126–52.

—— 'Narrative in Yiddish from its Origin to *Shivḥei habesht* (1504–1814)' [Hasiporet beyidish mireshitah ad *Shivḥei habesht* (1504– 1814)], 2 vols (doctoral dissertation, Hebrew University of Jerusalem, 1983).

——*Narrative in Yiddish: From its Origin to Shivḥei habesht (1504–1814): Annotated Bibliography* [Hasiporet beyidish: mireshitah ad *shivḥei habesht* (1504–1814), bibliografiyah mu'eret] (Jerusalem, 1985).

ZIMMELS, TSEVI JACOB, 'Birds that Grow on Trees' [Ofot hagedelim be'ilan], in *An Offering of First Fruits in Honour of Rav Arieh Swartz* [Minḥat bikurim likhvod harav ariyeh shwarts] (Vienna, 1921), 1–9.

ZINBERG, ISRAEL, *A History of Jewish Literature*, ed. and trans. from the first Hebrew translation of the original Yiddish text by Bernard Martin, 12 vols (Cincinatti and New York, 1974).

—— *The History of Jewish Literature* [Toledot sifrut yisra'el], trans. Shlomo Zalman Ariel, David Kena'ani, and Baruch Qaru; revisions and supplements Abraham Meir Aberman and Mendel Piekarz (revised and expanded Hebrew translation of the original Yiddish text), 7 vols (Tel Aviv, 1953).

ZIPPERSTEIN, STEVEN J., *Elusive Prophet: Ahad Ha'am and the Origin of Zionism* (Berkeley, Calif., 1993).

ZITRON, SAMUEL LEIB, *Behind the Screen* [Me'aḥorei hapargod], 2 vols (Vilna, 1924); Yiddish edn: *Apostates: Types and Silhouettes from Our Near Past* [*Meshumadim: tipn un siluetn funm naenten avar*] (Warsaw, 1930).

——'The People and Literature' [Ha'am vehasifrut], *Hashiloaḥ*, 6 (1899–1900), 'miscellaneous' section.

ZUCKERMAN, ABRAHAM, and KALMAN SHAPIRA, Inventory in the front pages of *Hashaḥar*, 8/5 (1877).

ZUNZ, LEOPOLD, 'Something about Rabbinical Literature' [Mashehu al hasifrut harabanit], in P. Mendes-Flohr (ed.), *Wissenschaft des Judentums: Historical and Philosophical Aspects* [Ḥokhmat yisra'el: hebetim historiyim ufilosofiyim] (Jerusalem, 1980), 81–100.

Index of Books and Periodicals

Index of Places

Index of People

Index of Subjects

Printed and bound by CPI Group (UK) Ltd, Croydon, CR0 4YY

13/04/2025

14656581-0007